BRAND BREAKOUT

HOW EMERGING MARKET BRANDS WILL GO GLOBAL

NIRMALYA KUMAR

JAN-BENEDICT E.M. STEENKAMP

palgrave
macmillan

First published 2013 by
PALGRAVE MACMILLAN

Palgrave Macmillan in the UK is an imprint of Macmillan Publishers Limited, registered in England, company number 785998, of Houndmills, Basingstoke, Hampshire RG21 6XS.

Palgrave Macmillan in the US is a division of St Martin's Press LLC, 175 Fifth Avenue, New York, NY 10010.

Palgrave Macmillan is the global academic imprint of the above companies and has companies and representatives throughout the world.

Palgrave® and Macmillan® are registered trademarks in the United States, the United Kingdom, Europe and other countries.

ISBN: 978–1–137–27661–2

This book is printed on paper suitable for recycling and made from fully managed and sustained forest sources. Logging, pulping and manufacturing processes are expected to conform to the environmental regulations of the country of origin.

A catalogue record for this book is available from the British Library.

A catalog record for this book is available from the Library of Congress.

Typeset by Aardvark Editorial Limited, Metfield, Suffolk

"*Brand Breakout* is a must-read, not only for those who run local companies and brands expanding internationally, but for all of us who compete against them in their own territories, and are compelled to win with global brands and strategies against a variety of very local realities."

Juan Alanis, General Manager
The Estée Lauder Companies Inc., Mexico

"As two of the most well-known marketing scholars on emerging markets in the world, Nirmalya Kumar and Jan-Benedict Steenkamp provide a definitive guideline for emerging market brands here. The eight routes proposed in this book lay out a comprehensive roadmap for those aspiring companies and countries to effectively enter global markets, and will have a far-reaching impact in the years to come. It also provides great insights on the transition of the economic development mode of China. A novel and thought-provoking masterpiece!"

Yubo Chen, Professor & Deputy Chair
of Marketing, Tsinghua University

"Outstanding book. It is fascinating and undoubtedly a must-read piece for managers in both Western and emerging market companies. It was eye-opening to see how Chinese and other emerging market firms are changing from a clear focus on manufacturing and supply chain efficiencies to building brand equities and allocating enough resources behind them. This is our new competition. It seems they now realize that the real value of their companies is in their brands. And it is not until they fully comprehend this that the expansion of these brand equities can really take place; Corona from Mexico is a good example."

Henry Gomez, Vice-President Business
Development for Latin America, Pepsico

"Emerging market firms are still better at manufacturing than branding. *Brand Breakout* provides CEOs with a timely and systematic roadmap of recommendations to change this."

John Quelch, Professor, Harvard Business School & Former Dean of CEIBS (China Europe International Business School)

"An encouraging and integral reading about how emerging markets companies could rapidly expand the value of their offering. It recognizes how crucial it becomes to unlock value through 'the art' of brand building with tangible and relevant principles. Certainly, leveraging the full potential of the cross-cultural diaspora strategy will be fundamental for brands determined to thrive in global markets. An extraordinary book with priceless insights that every marketing manager should treasure."

Leandro Berrone, Marketing VP Cuauhtémoc Moctezuma, Part of the Heineken Company

To MK – emerging market conception, hopefully on the way
to becoming a global brand
NK

To my father – without whom I would never have been
where I am now –
and to Valarie – whose love ensures I am happy where I am
JBS

Also by the Authors

Nirmalya Kumar and Jan-Benedict E. M. Steenkamp,
Private Label Strategy: How to Meet the Store Brand Challenge
(Boston: Harvard Business School Press, 2007)

CONTENTS

LIST OF FIGURES

LIST OF TABLES

PREFACE

We are fortunate to have lived through a remarkable transformation. One of us grew up in Calcutta, a city that was the byword for human and economic misery, located in a country that was almost as segregated from the world economy as its neighbor, China. The other, born in Amsterdam, had to study *Asian Drama*, a book about the dismal future of a continent mired in a downward spiral of population growth and poverty. Shortly after publication, its author, Gunnar Myrdal, was awarded the 1974 Nobel Prize for Economics. Asian nations as well as those from Africa and South America were routinely referred to as underdeveloped countries, or the more derogatory "Third World." The term "emerging markets" was unknown. Developed countries accounted for more than 80 percent of world GDP and world trade. And any global brands like Coca-Cola and Mercedes that existed were exclusively from the West.

Fast-forward 50 years. The global economic reality under which multinational corporations now operate has changed beyond the wildest dreams of even the most optimistic "Third World" policy-maker of the 1960s. The 1979 opening of China to the world economy initiated a process that has led to an accelerated convergence between nations today. In the intervening years, more and more of the world has become integrated with the global economy. As examples, consider the collapse of the Soviet Union, the 1991 economic reforms of India, the fall of the apartheid regime of South Africa, and the unfolding opening-up of Myanmar.

What were previously underdeveloped countries are now not only emerging markets, but the central focus of multinational corporations in their quest for growth.

Our own careers mirror the changing focus of multinational corporations and their executives. We met over 20 years ago in the United States. Since then, we have collaborated on many different research, teaching, and consulting projects related to global strategy, marketing, and branding. This book originated, as have many of our projects, during a casual conversation over a bottle of Bordeaux. It began with a question: why don't we observe global brands from emerging markets? This predictably led to an argument on why this is so, with each of us trying to develop a stronger rationale for what currently exists (or "best practice" in that all observed global brands are from the developed nations). But, as always, we did not stop there. We began imagining "next practice" or what is to come. Several hypotheses were generated on how emerging market brands could go global. The outcome of that debate, with years of research intervening, is this book.

The book was a journey of discovery for us. Our research led us to voraciously read books, cases, and articles about emerging market brands. We made, individually as well as a team, numerous trips to emerging markets in order to interview executives who aspired to build global brands. We observed companies and factories from Brazil to India, to South Africa, and of course China. We had research associates and collaborators in the Americas, Europe, and Asia to help us gather data, where and when we were unable to be there. We learnt about companies we had never heard of and observed green shoots of global brands where there had once been ignorance on our part.

As was true for us, we realize that, for the moment, it is difficult for many Western consumers to spontaneously recall a consumer brand by an emerging market company. Let us conduct a simple test: Have you heard of Haier? What products does it sell? And, finally, do you know what the brand stands for? If the answer to any of these questions is "No," then this book is for you. After all, with $25 billion in revenues, Haier is one of the few brands that can lay claim to being a global consumer brand from an emerging economy. Going ahead, in the spirit of next practice, we are convinced that we will witness the rise of global brands from emerging markets. Many will try, some will fail, and a fortunate few will succeed. Since fortune favors the prepared mind, we develop eight different routes that emerging market brands can take to global success.

It would be a folly, though, to assume that the book is intended for, or useful to, only the executives and owners of emerging market companies. Previously, Western managers have been blindsided for first underestimating the Japanese brands (e.g., Toyota, Sony, and Canon), and subsequently the Korean brands (e.g., Hyundai, LG, and Samsung), who swept aside supposedly invulnerable incumbents like Philips, General Motors, Ford, and RCA. They surely do not want to be blindsided a third time.

ACKNOWLEDGMENTS

Our first and deepest gratitude is to all the managers who took time from their busy schedules to teach us about their firms, brands, and strategies. Therefore, we start by thanking those who shared their unique experience:

Ambarella Shanghai Co. – Vivian Yang; Adidas China – Richard Hu; ASD – Amanda Chen, Carol, Lisa Du; Bright Food Group – Jun Jie Ge; China Huiyuan Juice Group – Zhen Tan; China Unicom – Hengyuan He; Chunlan – Bin Feng, Raymond Huang; Combi Group – Agrius Oleme; Costa Crociere Shanghai – Michael Shen; Dell China – Danny Ntui; Dabur – Sunil Duggal; Dragon Sourcing – Veronique Balla; Emirates Airlines – Maurice Flanagan; Galanz – Bruce Chang, Daisy Gao; GongDong Midea Holding Co – Marc Upton, Leon Hu; Guangzhou Pearl River Piano Group – June Wang; Haier – James Leiss; Hongye – Yuexin Wei; HTC – Matthew Costello; Huawei – Hagen Fendler, Sandra Qian Xiao; Jaguar Land Rover – John Edwards; Lenovo – Chris Tang, Farmer Fang, Helen Zhang, Johnson Jia, Lisa Liang, Mark McNeilly; Levi Strauss China – Aaron Boey, Xiaojing He; Mahindra & Mahindra – Anand Mahindra; Pran Foods – Ahsan Khan Chowdhury; Shanghai Jahwa United (Herborist) – Zhuo (Joe) Wang, Aaron Ke; Shanghai Tang – Eric Tang; South China Tire and Rubber Co. – Xiang Dong Fu, Jian Ping Feng, Melissa Ruan, Wei Hua Huang; Tata Motors – Ravi Kant; Xinxing Pipes Group – Charles Ekoko; ZTE – Maggie Cui, Jackie Jiang, Tony Tang, James Zheng.

Our trips to China to interview many of the executives named above would not have been possible without the incredible generosity of our hosts Ping Zhao and Yubo Chen at Tsinghua University (Beijing), Jiaxun (Justin) He at East China Normal University (Shanghai), and Lianxiong Jiang at Sun-Yat Sen University (Guangzhou). They went out of their way not only to organize our interviews with the top executives of leading Chinese firms, but also to ensure that we did not get lost in the process. We are extremely indebted to them for the countless hours they spent trying to explain China, its companies, and their strategies to us.

Special thanks to our colleagues Simona Botti (London Business School), Steven M. Burgess (Nelson Mandela Metropolitan University, South Africa), Bill Fisher (IMD), Yun He (Sun Yat-Sen Business School), Angela Liu (Tsinghua University), Miguel Angel Lopez Lomeli (ITESM, Mexico), Phanish Puranam (INSEAD Singapore), and Naufel Vilcassim (London Business School) for sharing their perspective on brands and emerging markets with us.

We gratefully acknowledge the insightful comments we received on earlier drafts from Marnik Dekimpe, Anne Gro Gulla, Carlos Silva Lopes, Kathrine Mo, and especially Kirsten Sandberg.

We were fortunate to be supported by a great team in the course of our research. A special thanks to Ada Wu, David Ernsthausen, Donna Everett, Elizabeth Hajicek, Inga Katharina (Lili) Radziejewski, Jena Vickery, Jiang Fan, Klien Deng, Runqi Xie, Sunita Sidhu, Suseela Yesudian, and Yuanyuan Cai. Erin Mitchell did an outstanding job designing the many figures and tables for the book.

The research costs for this book were borne by the Centre for Marketing and the Aditya Birla India Centre at London Business School and by the Massey Chair at the Kenan-Flagler Business School. We thank Kumar Mangalam Birla and Knox Massey for their generosity in supporting our efforts.

INTRODUCTION

In the last two decades, the world has witnessed the most dramatic shift in its economic center of gravity since 1500 AD. About 500 years ago, the center of economic activity started to shift decisively to the West – first Western Europe, and then the North Atlantic, which has dominated since. What are now called emerging markets began the challenge to this status quo from December 1978, when the Chinese, under the leadership of Deng Xiaoping, started a program of economic reforms (改革开放). It took some time before the other major markets joined in. Between 1989 and 1994, India initiated its economic reform, Brazil launched its Plano Real, South Africa replaced its internationally and economically isolated apartheid rule with democratic government, Mexico signed the North America Free Trade Agreement, and the Soviet Union collapsed. Vast countries and their populations opened to the global economy.

These developments quickly had an impact. In 1990, the emerging markets together accounted for 20 percent of global output, versus 80 percent for the developed world. By 2010, the share of emerging markets had doubled to 40 percent, and this share will likely surpass that of developed countries before the end of this decade. Such a shift in relative economic weight is unprecedented in 10,000 years of human history.

Emerging markets are now driving a large proportion of global economy and trade. They account for more than 75 percent of mobile phone subscriptions, 75 percent of steel consumption, more than 50

1

percent of motor vehicle sales, almost 50 percent of all retail sales, and 25 percent of financial assets worldwide.[1] They also account for more than 50 percent of the gross domestic product (GDP) in purchasing parity terms, 75 percent of the foreign exchange reserves, 50 percent of inward foreign direct investments, and more than 30 percent of the stock market capitalization. They lag only in public sector debt (less than 20 percent) – and they can do without that!

CHINA AS THE LEADING EMERGING MARKET

From Asia to Latin America and Africa, economies are growing briskly, and none so more than that of China. China's GDP is as large as that of the next four largest emerging economies combined (Brazil, India, Russia, and Mexico). China has overtaken Japan to become the world's second-largest economy and is widely expected to surpass that of the United States before this decade ends.

China has become the world's factory; it makes many of our best-loved products, from Apple iPhones to most of what one can buy at a Disney store. The "Made in China" label is ubiquitous in the West. Distressed to find so many Chinese made products among her family's 2004 Christmas gifts, an American reporter decided to boycott Chinese goods for a year. Within a few months, her four-year-old son launched a countercampaign by declaring, "When we can buy China things again, let's never stop."[2] The reporter concluded, "After a year without China I can tell you this: You can still live without it, but it's getting trickier and costlier by the day. And a decade from now I may not be brave enough to try it again."[2]

"Made in China" has been driving economic growth over the past three decades at a rate unparalleled in human history. Between 1979 and 2012, China's average annual GDP growth rate was almost 10 percent.[3] Yet if you ask a person on the street in the West to "name a Chinese brand," you will draw a blank. Even though Western consumers are surrounded by Chinese products, these consumers have no awareness of Chinese brands.

A study of consumers in France, Germany, and the United Kingdom revealed low spontaneous recall of any Chinese brand.[4] Chinese companies are painfully aware of this. They feel that their country's image handicaps them and presents an obstacle to selling their branded products to Western consumers. In a J. Walter Thompson study of US and UK consumers, Chinese companies ranked near the bottom in consumer perceptions of quality, ethical behavior, and environmental consciousness.[5] And the Interbrand 2012 list of the hundred "best global brands" did not include a single brand from mainland China.[6]

The absence of brands from China in the consciousness of Western consumers begs the question, "Can the Chinese develop consumer brands that will become popular in the Western world?" One side argues that the poor perception of China with Western consumers and the lack of brand-building skills in Chinese companies doom any such aspirations. This side points to failures such as the Chinese sportswear brand Li-Ning's hitherto futile attempt to crack the US market.

On the other side, we advocate "brand breakout." We agree with Saatchi's observation that "we don't see any reason why Chinese brands cannot have the same impact in the US, as US brands have had in China."[7] We believe that, in the coming decade, Chinese brands will become increasingly global and ubiquitous in the Western world. We base these beliefs on two fundamental observations, as described below.

CHINA IS BUILDING WORLD-CLASS CAPABILITIES

As the factory of the world, China has invested in developing world-class manufacturing and engineering capabilities, albeit for foreign brands. It has laid a vast foundation to produce global-quality goods exceptional for an emerging market, past or present. But China's low-cost competitive advantage is eroding. The financial crisis in the West has deterred China from passing higher costs to customers, and fewer orders are coming from Europe. The demographic changes in the Chinese population coupled with increasing labor shortages have led to a quintupling of wages in the last decade and diminishing margins of late. Emboldened workers demand better working conditions. Midea, a home appliances manufacturer, has had to build extensive and costly housing and recreational facilities in order to induce workers to come back after their annual leave. For these reasons, former CEO of General Electric Jack Welch recently argued, "China can no longer rely on exports and low-cost production for economic growth and must innovate by building global brands."[8] The headline screamed, "China Must Create '10,000 Apples,' Welch Says."[9] Turning their products into globally recognized consumer brands has become the "holy grail" for Chinese firms.[10]

And why not? *Historically, there is no precedent of a country evolving into a developed economy without having some global brands emerge from it.* Consider Japan. When we were teenagers in the early 1970s, "Made in Japan" equated to shoddy quality and poor workmanship. One of the authors recalls that he asked his father why that person in the neighborhood was driving "that Japanese car." His father answered: "I don't know. I guess he is poor." How perceptions have changed! And they have changed because the quality of Japanese products improved dramatically as Japanese manufacturers increased their skills and capabilities. Companies like Sony and Toyota transformed themselves as well as Japan's image. As Japan moved up the quality chain, South Korea took over low-end manufacturing and has since developed leading global consumer brands such as Hyundai, LG, Kia, and Samsung. Sooner or later, China as well as other emerging markets will need to launch brands to the Western world, what we refer to as "brand breakout."

CHINA'S POLITICAL AND ECONOMIC WEAKNESS WAS AN ANOMALY

The relative economic decline of China after 1800 AD is an historical anomaly. Recall that when Rome built its breathtaking empire, China was already 1,500 years old, and the contemporary Han dynasty was Rome's only plausible global rival. The Roman Empire fell two centuries after the Han Empire did and never rose again, despite the efforts of many (e.g., Charlemagne, Charles V, and Napoleon). With the Tang dynasty (618–907), China came back more glorious than ever, and 11th-century Song China produced more iron than Britain did in the 18th century.

Three centuries ago, "Made in China" had a quality and prestige connotation. Consider porcelain, a unique product resulting from a process invented by Chinese craftsmen, passed down from master to apprentice. In the 16th and 17th centuries, Portuguese and Dutch traders introduced Europe to the stunning Ming dynasty (1368–1644) porcelain pieces now showcased in many major Western museums. European royals and other wealthy individuals coveted these imports.

European potters attempted to produce porcelain in Florence, but with little success.[11] It took more than a century of experimentation before European craftsmen could make quality porcelain. In 1710, a French Jesuit priest carefully documented the secrets of Chinese manufacturing processes, and Saxon Court Chancellery proclaimed the establishment of the famous Meissen porcelain factory in Germany. Our point is that China has a history of innovation and had established itself as a consumer "brand" in Western countries. Tableware, as a result, is still referred to as "china" or even "fine china" by the British and the Americans.

WHY DO WE SEE SO FEW CHINESE CONSUMER BRANDS IN THE WEST?

Fortune magazine annually ranks the world's largest 500 companies by sales revenue. The 2012 list included 73 Chinese firms, not including the six from Taiwan, up from 61 in 2011, and 12 in 2001. Only the US, with 132 companies, has more appearances on this list. Yet, as mentioned earlier, no Chinese brands appear on the 2012 list of the top 100 global brands, and few Western consumers can spontaneously recall a Chinese brand. What explains this dichotomy?

How a developing country's corporations interact with the world economy follows a development trajectory. Initially, the natural resources endowment or the differential wage rates are the primary sources of the country's competitive advantage. As a result, the first companies going global tend to be supplying either natural resources or manufacturing products to the specifications of branded firms from the developed world. For example, Brazil leads in coffee exports, Ivory Coast leads in cocoa, Pakistan leads in soccer balls, and China in shoes, but consumers cannot recall a single brand from those countries in those sectors. Exporters from emerging markets are in the world of business-to-business (B2B) marketing – companies selling to other companies and brands.

Selling branded products to the developed world would require building a brand name with consumers, a prohibitively expensive process for an emerging market firm. Access to these consumers requires a sophisticated distribution system, a trusted network of retailers to stock a relatively unknown brand, and an aggressive marketing campaign to sell consumer products from an unknown company based in a country not known for quality. *Fortune 500* companies from the "BRIC" countries (Brazil, Russia, India, and China) are therefore mostly natural resource firms (e.g., Gazprom and Petrobras), some B2B marketing companies (e.g., Baosteel and Reliance Industries), and a sprinkling of primarily domestically focused branded players (e.g., China Mobile and State Bank of India). To develop global brands for Western consumers, Chinese firms must confront perceptions of China with Western consumers, acquire new capabilities, and transform existing business models.

CONFRONTING WESTERN PERCEPTION OF "MADE IN CHINA"
Fairly or not, Western consumers associate Chinese products primarily with "low price." An August 2011 survey in the US

found that 12 percent of buyers refused to consider buying any kind of Chinese product. Most were unwilling to buy higher priced products, and only 4 percent were willing to consider buying a Chinese automobile.[12] This resistance is usually the first issue that Chinese managers raised with us when discussing their global aspirations: How can we dispel associations of "cheap" and "poor quality" with our country?[13] For example, Gu Jun Jie, Vice President of Bright Foods, observed:

> Although China has a large GDP, we do not have a brand like Coca-Cola, Pepsi, or Carrefour. As entrepreneurs, we must solve this if we wish to transform China from a strong country to a powerful one. Brands are very important and we always wonder if we can have a brand like Nestlé from China.[14]

Branding is not merely about differentiating products; it is about striking emotional chords with consumers. It is about cultivating identity, attachment, and trust to inspire customer loyalty. Chinese brands score low on attributes such as "sophisticated," "desirable," "innovative," "friendly," and "trustworthy." Brands from Brazil, India, Mexico, Russia, and Vietnam – all countries with large populations and vibrant economies – score similarly on these attributes.

However, China faces an additional hurdle, related to the broader political environment within which Chinese firms operate. So far, none of the world's leading global brands has come from countries with political systems starkly different from that of the US or from state-owned enterprises.[15] In other words, Chinese brands must overcome the West's negative associations with "communism."

ACQUIRING NEW CAPABILITIES

As China's economic liberalization is only three decades old, large Chinese companies are still relatively young, often no more than 20 years old, at least in their new market-driven phase of development. Most of the firms listed on the Shanghai or Shenzhen stock exchange have such complex control and ownership structures that even the most astute institutional investor cannot easily disentangle the privately held from the government controlled. In either case, the hand of government looms large.[16] Typically, the state set up these firms to extract natural resources or to serve domestic production and consumption of energy, banking, insurance, telecommunications, and so on. They thrive because of monopolistic competition and preferential access to capital, resources, and the large growing domestic market, rather than because of organizational mastery of brand-building or innovation.

Then there are the thousands of exporters who have converted China into the world's factory. Their growth derives primarily from large investments in manufacturing capabilities coupled with a tiny sales capability. These Chinese exporters usually have no need for marketing or branding. Firms from around the world and their local brokers constantly scour emerging markets for cheaper and larger supply sources. While the ability of these Chinese firms to produce sophisticated technological products is awe-inspiring, "when it comes to understanding the concept of branding, they seem to struggle with the notion."[17]

Even large branded companies that compete for the Chinese domestic market suffer from a significant hurdle to launching global consumer brands: the rampant intellectual property violations stifle returns to innovation and branding. Only 10 percent of the 16,000 brands registered in China are estimated to be profitable, due to the lack of intellectual property rights enforcement.[18] Why should firms invest in branding and innovation if existing and potential competitors can easily rip it off?

Furthermore, these domestic branded players benefit from inexpensive land, lax intellectual property protection, and other privileges specific to China. For example, most Chinese manufacturers of mobile phone handsets would be subject to significant licensing fees if they sold their products outside China.[19] As a result, domestic branded firms diversify into other businesses within China, putting their brand on many different products. For example, Huoli 28 sells detergent and mineral water under same name, while the Yuetu brand extends from cigarettes to female sanitary protection.[20] But, by standing for everything, these brands end up owning nothing in the minds of consumers.

TRANSFORMING THE BUSINESS MODEL

The many success stories of Chinese firms and entrepreneurs are of those who have aggressively pursued excellence in manufacturing and product engineering. Given constant price pressure, the leaders of these companies manage with an engineering and financial mindset that relentlessly emphasizes productivity and efficiency. Low cost is their *raison d'être*.

The resulting business model of successful entrepreneurial Chinese firms is characterized by low, steady returns. Managers deploy capital only when similar investments have yielded financial returns. That is why Chinese companies invest confidently in manufacturing technologies but hesitate to plunge capital into global consumer branding. They lack experience working with consumers in developed markets and using foreign media to build brands. Chinese entrepreneurs and executives prefer manufacturing, engineering, and finance – the hard stuff – over all the emotional branding stuff that seems fluffy, if not irrelevant to them.

In contrast, it is precisely large investments in such intangibles that drive the business models of global consumer brands like Coca-Cola and Nike. Financial returns to such brand investments are difficult to quantify, especially in the short run. If one could financially demonstrate that brand investments pay off, and there were more Chinese entrepreneurial success stories beyond Lenovo and Haier, then 500 Chinese firms would jump at the global branding opportunity.[21]

Finally, building a truly iconic brand such as Toyota, Sony, or Samsung usually takes decades. Chinese financial models are biased against such a long-term horizon for large investments allied with high uncertainty. The risk–return ratio is not consistent with their risk preferences. And they are too impatient. Instead of developing an indigenous Chinese brand, many of them would argue that buying and revitalizing a distressed Western brand like Weetabix or Volvo is a more financially sound strategy.

CAN THE NEXT SAMSUNG COME FROM CHINA?

In 1989, Herman Lo founded Hu Fong Industrial Company to design, manufacture, and market plastic baby toys. Headquartered in Hong Kong, Fu Hong won contracts to manufacture baby care items for global brands such as Gerber and Disney.[22] The molder saw that its products marketed under foreign global brands were selling in the Chinese market for five times the amount that these Western brands were paying Fu Hong to manufacture them. Yet these global companies were constantly applying pressure on Fu Hong to lower prices. To avoid margin compression, founder and chairman Lo decided to launch his own branded business, known as Qin Qin Wo ("kiss me") in China, and as Kidsme outside Asia.

In 2012, two years after the launch, Lo expects his branded business to surpass his private contract manufacturing business. The first branded product marketed overseas was a polypropylene and silicone teether with a worldwide patent. To cultivate a marketing and branding mindset, the firm hired 1,500 university graduates and put them through 12 months of training, before finally selecting a core staff of 20. Reflecting on the experience of building a brand, the founder Lo observed, "I have to say thanks to my customers. They gave us too much pressure ... I had to think of another way to survive."[22] Competing in foreign markets forced Fu Hong to innovate, thus helping it move away from its image as a producer of cheap products, even in the Chinese market.

Many Chinese firms have started the same transformation that Japan and South Korea went through. Soon we will be buying

Chinese-branded products just as we are buying "Made in China" Western-branded products today. In our conversations with the managers and owners of the leading Chinese companies, we have been struck by their global ambition. For many, building their own brand into a global brand, and one accepted by consumers in the developed economies, is a matter of national pride. In June 2011, 11 influential Chinese entrepreneurs formed an alliance called the International Best Brand.[23] They expect to enlist 500 leading privately owned Chinese companies to help promote Chinese brands on the global market.

The return of many young Chinese to the mainland is accelerating the push to brands. These Chinese, often the children of entrepreneurs, have obtained their MBAs from leading international schools and bring a keen understanding of branding as well as a desire to see Chinese brands on the global stage. Branding philosophy and skills are slowly infusing Chinese firms. Haier's marketing deal with the (US) National Basketball Association shows that Chinese firms embrace the need to invest in building brands and connecting with Western consumers. Chinese brands such as Lenovo have signed endorsements deals with Hollywood movies. In *Transformers 3*, a spiky-haired robot named Brains with bulging fluorescent blue eyes transforms itself from a Lenovo ThinkPad Edge computer.[24] Lenovo's chief marketing officer stated, "We want to be the first big consumer brand to come out of China."[25] The result is that a story filed by a reporter attending the largest annual exhibition of the consumer electronics industry held in Las Vegas was entitled "How Long Until China Produces the Next Samsung?" The opening paragraph began with "The biggest trend of the 2013 Consumer Electronic Show ... is the rise of the Chinese brands – Hisense, Haier, Huawei, ZTE, TCL and countless others – many of which have pumped up their presence at this year's CES with Lance Armstrong-level enhancements."[26]

The automotive sector also demonstrates how Chinese firms are systematically grappling with the challenges of building global brands. No longer satisfied by either meeting domestic demand or producing components for foreign brands, the leading automakers have begun the process of transitioning to global brands. For example, JAC Motors (officially Jianghuai Automobile Co., Ltd.) has taken a small but significant market share position in Brazil. In 1989, China exported just six cars, but in 2012 it exported close to one million cars, even if not to the US as yet.[27]

But exporting to other emerging markets differs from selling to demanding European and US consumers. This entails creating quality products that meet Western specifications and are appealing to foreign tastes. One Chinese automaker deployed a team of scientists, including anthropologists and psychologists, to identify the best features of the most innovative countries in the world. They sought to understand what consumers had come to expect in products from those countries. The automaker embodied the team's findings in a facility some 200 miles from Beijing.[17] Within this facility, researchers devoted rooms to the sensory experiences of each country. For example, the "Nordic room" was misty and smelled of freshly cut grass, while the "German room" had a conservative feel with deep resonance and demonstrated how Germans perceive mechanical movement. "Looking at a sliding door, it opens slowly, then speeds up, before slowing down to a perfect stop. In contrast, the Chinese door would swish open quickly and stop with an abrupt bang."[17]

Other European assaults are in the works. Geely Motors, the new owner of Volvo, plans to sell a mid-range sedan in the UK, while Chery Automobile plans to use its newly acquired Fiat plant in Sicily as its base for Europe. In 2012, Great Wall Motor set up a production plant in Bulgaria to help sell its base Voleex C10 model, the Steed 5 pick-up, and the Hover H5 4×4. The Chinese automakers realize that they must succeed in Western markets not only to generate sales overseas, but also to grow their domestic market, where foreign competition is intense.

Sergio Marchionne, CEO of Fiat and Chrysler, admonished global car-makers to take China's ambitions seriously: "Even assuming China were to export only 10 per cent of what it produces" – which some analysts forecast will be 30 million vehicles in 2015 and 40 million by 2020 – "the risk we face in our home markets is enormous."[28] Beyond the automotive sector, one may argue that the Chinese brands, such as Galanz, Haier, Hisense, Huawei, Lenovo, Pearl River Piano, Shanghai Tang, Tsingtao, and ZTE, are already global brands, even if they are not top-of-mind for Western consumers.

WHAT ABOUT OTHER EMERGING MARKETS?

Given the size and growth of its economy, China will dominate brand breakout from emerging markets to the West. It is a global game-changing country, both economically and politically. Yet most of our arguments are valid for other emerging markets, and our examples serve managers in those countries too. They share weak national images, poor marketing capabilities, low cost as the sole competitive advantage, and limited business models, but with aspirations to launch successful global brands as a matter of national pride.

The desire to have global brands from emerging markets is the commonality that interests us in this book. For example, Vietnam is the world's second largest coffee exporter after Brazil. However, 90 percent of the beans are exported in the raw form. Vietnam's "Coffee King" Dang Le Nguyen Vu, whose privately held company Trung Nguyen is the country's largest processor of coffee beans and exports to 60 countries, observed: "These beans carry no brands. That needs to be changed ... Our ambition is to become a global brand."[29] Trung Nguyen also runs the largest chain of coffee houses and has ambitions to take on Nestlé and Starbucks. But he is candid in admitting that "we are like a grasshopper fighting against a giant elephant." In terms of technology and marketing, these global brands are way ahead of his firm's competencies.[29]

Despite the common ambitions of emerging giants, emerging markets are not homogeneous; they differ from each other and especially from China on many dimensions, but most critical to brand breakout are demographics, access to state capital and clout, and openness of the economy. Regarding demographics, the smaller the domestic population, particularly the size of the middle class, the more difficult the process of achieving global scale within the domestic market before attacking foreign shores. China has the greatest advantage here, with India a close second.

Chinese firms also benefit from greater government support and easier access to low-cost capital. While the leaders of other emerging markets, including Brazil, India, Malaysia, and Russia, explicitly or implicitly foster national champions, their governments lack the resources to support them as China does. That said, many of these countries have longer histories of relatively open markets, free enterprise, and entrepreneurship. As a result, their firms have greater experience competing domestically against other local and global brands. For instance, few doubt the branding capabilities of Indian firms, however untested they are in global markets.

Finally, excellence can sprout in otherwise mediocre environments, so even the most undeveloped market has one or two potential global brands worth studying. Hence, we incorporate their stories where appropriate throughout. Table I.1 outlines a sample of emerging market brands that are going global, that have already demonstrated some success with Western consumers, and that we have included in our book. As a result, we document insights and experiences from all regions of the world, covering a diverse set of industries, services, and products, from aerospace and cars, to food, drinks, and cosmetics.

Table I.1 **Eight routes to global brands**

Route	Some examples
The Asian Tortoise route: Migrating to higher quality and brand premium	• Haier (China) • Pearl River Piano (China) • Wanli (China)
The business to consumer route: Leveraging B2B strength in B2C markets	• ASD (China) • Galanz (China) • Huawei (China) • Mahindra (India) • ZTE (China)
The diaspora route: Following emigrants into the world	• Corona (Mexico) • Dabur (India) • Jollibee (Philippines) • Maybank Islamic (Malaysia) • Mandarin Oriental (China) • Pran (Bangladesh)
The brand acquisition route: Buying global brands from Western multinationals	• Bimbo (Mexico) • Geely (China) • Lenovo (China) • Tata Motors (India) • TCL (China)
The positive campaign route: Overcoming negative country of origin associations	• Chang Beer (Thailand) • Ospop (China) • Roewe (China) • Shanghai Vive (China) • Sheji/Sorgere (China)
The cultural resource route: Positioning on positive cultural myths	• Havaianas (Brazil) • Herborist (China) • Shanghai Tang (China) • Shang Xia (China)
The natural resources route: Branding commodities in four steps	• Café de Colombia (Colombia) • Concha y Toro (Chile) • Forevermark (South Africa) • Habanos (Cuba) • Natura (Brazil) • Premier Cosmetics (Israel)
The national champion route: Leveraging strong support from the state	• China Mobile (China) • Comac (China) • Embraer (Brazil) • Emirates Airlines (Dubai) • Proton (Malaysia)

Note: B2C, business to consumer; B2B, business to business.

EIGHT PATHWAYS: HOW BRANDS FROM EMERGING MARKETS WILL BREAK OUT

In Table I.1, we develop eight different pathways that emerging market brands can pursue to break out into global markets and connect with consumers worldwide. For each pathway, we outline how to follow it effectively and what to avoid. We use examples to bring each pathway to life. As with the launch of Western brands, failure is always a possibility, and none of the examples used is perfect. We do not claim that these organizations are adopters of best practices in all business areas; rather, they exemplify branding through a particular pathway. The pathways themselves and their underlying strategic brand-building principles are solid.

THE ASIAN TORTOISE ROUTE

Japanese companies (e.g., Toyota, Honda, Sony, and Panasonic) pioneered this path, South Korean companies (e.g., Samsung, Hyundai, and LG) followed, and now a host of Chinese companies (e.g., Hisense, Pearl River Piano, and perhaps the most famous, Haier) have embarked on this "mother of all routes." The basic principles are (1) to establish a beachhead in a Western country by selling a decent product for a very low price to a niche market, and then (2) in an upward spiral of interlocking steps, to increase quality and to price the new version slightly higher, thereby attacking the segment immediately above, and so on, until the brand achieves dominant market presence across the entire price/quality range.

THE BUSINESS TO CONSUMER ROUTE

Many leading B2B firms come from emerging markets. Some of these firms see themselves evolving into a consumer brand, perhaps in an adjacent product category or in a higher value-added business. For example, Huawei is the world's largest mobile network equipment company ahead of long-established players such as

Ericsson, Nokia Networks, Siemens, Alcatel-Lucent, and Motorola. Not content with this, Huawei entered the handset market and now ranks among the top 10 handset-makers in the world with an ambition to be among the top three brands by 2015. Galanz in microwave ovens is also following this route, as in the past two decades it has gone from being a contract manufacturer to a branded player.

THE DIASPORA ROUTE

The principle here is to tap into the unprecedented cross-border flows of people living outside their country of origin. Many migrants retain some brand preferences and consumption patterns. India's Reliance BIG cinemas, Malaysia's Maybank Islamic, and Pran of Bangladesh have successfully expanded internationally through the diaspora. Jollibee Foods (the Philippines), Pollo Campero (Guatemala), ICICI (India), and Dabur (India) have used the diaspora as a beachhead to take their brands mainstream in Western countries. Finally, Mandarin Oriental hotels (China) and Corona beer (Mexico) have used the reverse diaspora, where Westerners visit emerging markets, consume local goods, and seek the same experience on their return to their home country.

THE BRAND ACQUISITION ROUTE

The principle here is to expand rapidly and aggressively into Western markets by serially acquiring critical assets from mature Western multinationals in those territories. Such acquisitions not only secure brands and channel access, but also pre-empt similar moves by competitors. The acquiring firm must decide whether to retain each acquisition as a separate brand in its portfolio or to merge its homegrown brand and its acquisition into a single brand. Lenovo pursued the brand migration strategy after acquiring IBM's personal computer business. Companies that opted for brand retention include Geely's takeover of Volvo and Tata Motors' takeover of Jaguar Land Rover. However, acquisitions are never easy, and TCL's experience highlights some of the post-acquisition challenges.

THE POSITIVE CAMPAIGN ROUTE

The principle here is to overcome negative associations with the country of origin. Emerging market brands such Stella Luna, Ospop, and Kayserburg (Pearl River Piano) have used various marketing strategies to alter consumer perceptions, such as obscuring the country of origin, offering extra guarantees, or branding components. Companies and governments can also join forces and launch national ("Incredible India") or regional ("The Future Made by Taiwan") branding campaigns.

THE CULTURAL RESOURCES ROUTE

In a particular product category, one country may elicit unique positive associations from Western consumers (e.g., silk from China, yoga from India, or beach culture from Brazil). The principle here is to position the emerging market brand on these specific attributes, thereby turning its country of origin into an advantage, as Shanghai Tang and Herborist from China and Brazil's Havaianas have done.

THE NATURAL RESOURCES ROUTE

Natural resources are usually sold as commodities. The concept of a "natural resource brand" is a textbook example of an oxymoron. But that is the underlying principle here, to brand a natural resource in a sequence of four interlocking steps as these companies have done: Premier (Israel), Forevermark (South Africa), Natura (Brazil), Habano (Cuba), Concha y Toro (Chile), Pure Ceylon Cinnamon and Pure Ceylon Tea (Sri Lanka), and Café de Colombia.

THE NATIONAL CHAMPION ROUTE

Last but not least, the emerging market company can call on the power of the state. The principle here is to secure substantial help from the state, either directly (e.g., subsidies) or indirectly (e.g., preferential treatment, barriers to entry for competitors). These resources and protection are utilized to win domestically and then to expand subsequently into international markets.

Sometimes after an initial gestation period, the state leaves these firms to market forces or privatization (e.g., Embraer) although the brands still align closely to state interests (e.g., Emirates). Although it is customary among Western policy-makers and business people to be highly critical of state capitalism, we take a more nuanced view. Under specific conditions fostering national champions will lead to global branding success in consumer markets.

WHO SHOULD READ THIS BOOK?

This book shows how brands from emerging market companies will become increasingly familiar to Western consumers over the next decade. Rather than document current "best practice," that is document what currently exists in companies, we focus on "next practice," that is, the core skills and knowledge that companies in both developed and developing economies should be cultivating. Brand-building usually takes time, sometimes generations. However, the pace is accelerating, as the examples from Japan and South Korea show. Ultimately, we believe that some of these emerging market brands will become household names in the West sooner than some may believe.

While Chinese companies feature prominently, we also elaborate on the many innovative practices that have been pioneered by firms from other emerging markets such as India, Brazil, South Africa, and Mexico. Some of our showcase companies are as yet not large by global standards. But they are still able to compete successfully against Western giants. Both Chinese and other emerging market firms attempting to develop global brands can learn much from each other. We agree that these emerging brands will face many challenges and must overcome the handicap of their country's image. And, as with all ambitious strategies, some will fail. Nevertheless, the principles underlying the eight routes to global brands will remain.

Managers of emerging market companies should find this book useful in taking their brands global. But it would be a fatal mistake if managers of Western firms believed that this book was not for them. A golden rule in strategic management is that understanding your competitors is a crucial prerequisite for being able to develop effective counterstrategies. In the past, companies ranging from RCA and American Motors to Philips Electronics, Thomson, and Peugeot were caught napping while Japanese and Korean brands entered the global marketplace. Where are these companies now? They are either bankrupt or relegated to a minor position in markets they once dominated. Now, there is less room for complacency and surprise than ever before. Moreover, in the networked 21st century, competition and collaboration often go hand in hand. We urge Western managers to plot both counter- and cooperative strategies, to forge successful alliances, mergers, and acquisitions, and by no means to underestimate these emerging market companies attempting brand breakout.

ONE

THE ASIAN
TORTOISE ROUTE

MIGRATING TO HIGHER QUALITY
AND BRAND PREMIUM

What do Toyota and Samsung have in common? They are the only two Asian companies that appear on both the Interbrand list and the Millward Brown list of the most valuable global brands (Table 1.1). To rank on the Interbrand 100, a brand must have a *global sales footprint*. Toyota and Samsung do, along with eight other Asian brands from the automotive and electronics industries of Japan and South Korea. To make the Millward Brown list, a brand need not be global, just have *financial clout*. Again, Toyota and Samsung are not the only Asian brands on this list: many domestic Chinese brands have clout, thanks to their monopolistic position in a large domestic market.

Toyota and Samsung are quintessential Asian Tortoises: they crawled into the low end of a developed market and crept steadily upward to the top drawer. Japanese companies (e.g., Toyota, Honda, Nissan, and Panasonic) pioneered this path to global brands, followed by Korean firms (e.g., Samsung, Hyundai, and

Table 1.1 **Leading Asian brands, 2012**

Interbrand rank	Brand	Country of origin	Sector	Brand value ($m)
9	Samsung	South Korea	Electronics	32,893
10	Toyota	Japan	Automotive	30,280
21	Honda	Japan	Automotive	17,280
30	Canon	Japan	Electronics	12,029
40	Sony	Japan	Electronics	9,111
53	Hyundai	South Korea	Automotive	7,473
56	Nintendo	Japan	Electronics	7,082
65	Panasonic	Japan	Electronics	5,765
73	Nissan	Japan	Automotive	4,969
87	Kia	South Korea	Automotive	4,089
Millward Brown rank	**Brand**	**Country of origin**	**Sector**	**Brand value ($m)**
10	China Mobile	China	Telecom	47,041
13	ICBC	China	Financial services	41,518
24	China Construction Bank	China	Financial services	24,517
25	Baidu	China	Internet services	24,326
28	Toyota	Japan	Automotive	21,779
37	Tencent/QQ	China	Internet services	17,992
38	Agricultural Bank of China	China	Financial services	17,867
47	NTT DoCoMo	Japan	Telecom	15,981
53	China Life	China	Financial services	14,587
55	Samsung	South Korea	Electronics	14,164

Note: Throughout the book, unless noted otherwise, $ refers to US dollars.
Source: Adapted from Interbrand (2012), Millward Brown Optimor (2012).

LG), and now Chinese companies (e.g., Haier, Hisense, Pearl River Piano, and South China Tire & Rubber Company) are pursuing what we consider the mother of all routes. The basic principle is to enter a developed market with a decent product, sold initially at the lowest entry price possible. This cheap product provides access to price-sensitive consumers. Subsequently, the aspiring global brand increases quality and price, attacks the next lowest segment, and so on up the market, until it achieves a dominant position. Finally, it assails the premium segment, usually with a high-end product and premium brand, such as Lexus of Toyota or Acura of Honda.

This chapter walks managers step by step down this path for emerging market companies.

RISE OF THE JAPANESE AUTOMOTIVE GLOBAL BRANDS

Today, Toyota, Nissan, Honda, Suzuki, Mazda, Mitsubishi, Subaru, and Isuzu are all global brands and among the 30 largest vehicle-makers in the world. In 1980, when Japan overtook the United States to become the leading car manufacturing country in the world, it surprised many. In 1953, the country produced fewer than 10,000 cars. By the late 1950s, Japan began exporting a few hundred cars a year. Annual exports exceeded 10,000 cars for the first time in 1961. How Japan built a leading automobile industry populated with global brands is the stuff of legend and provides inspiration for emerging market companies.

JAPAN'S POSTWAR INDUSTRIAL STRATEGY

After World War II, Japan needed to build its industrial base and economy. With the Japanese predisposition for *monozukuri* ("thing-making"), the government committed itself to the development of an export-oriented manufacturing base.[1] In 1950, Japan's per capita income was lower than that of Colombia, Greece, Peru, and South Africa. Japan's labor force was cheap as well as plentiful because large numbers of surplus agricultural workers continued to migrate in the postwar years to modern industry. This moderated wage increases in a relatively populous country. Relying on cheap labor, entrepreneurs started small neighborhood factories making textiles, toys, tools, and electronics. As population growth slowed, and the nation became increasingly industrialized in the mid-1960s, wages rose significantly, but salary increases kept within the range of productivity gains.[2]

The Japanese government prepared domestic manufacturing industries for the world stage by providing substantial capital investment, assisting in the acquisition of foreign technologies, and protecting the domestic market from imports while allowing fierce rivalry between domestic firms to hone their competitive skills. In those days, other countries seldom criticized Japan's protectionism since, for example, its car market was globally inconsequential. In 1953, imports accounted for nearly 60 percent of total auto registrations in Japan; they dipped to 1 percent by 1960 and did not reach 2 percent until 1988.[3]

Under the guidance of the Ministry of International Trade and Industry, the Japanese auto-industry began to weed out small companies through mergers that led to the global powerhouses of today.[4] The various government and quasi-government entities continue to retain strong ties with the automakers.[5]

In early stages of development, the Japanese reverse-engineered and copied many of the American and European products. As a latecomer to modernization, Japan avoided some of the trial and error necessary to develop industrial processes. By the 1970s and 80s, Japan had improved its industrial base through technology licensing and patent purchases. Initially, it was imitation, and subsequently improving foreign inventions.

In the 1980s, industry stepped up its own research and development, and many Japanese firms made names for their creativity and process innovations (e.g., lean manufacturing and continuous improvement) as well as collaborative management–labor approaches. As these companies developed more of their own intellectual property, they pressed the Japanese government for laws to protect their patents and copyrights.[6]

THE ASIAN TORTOISE STRATEGY OF
JAPANESE AUTOMOBILE COMPANIES

Twelve years after World War II, the automaker Fuji (now Subaru) exhibited its Prince Skyline Deluxe at the Paris Salon; it was the first Japanese car to appear in a European show. In the same year (1957), Toyota exported its Toyopet Crown Deluxe, the first Japanese car ever shipped to the US. In 1958, Nissan marketed its Datsun 1000 in the US; in 1966, Mazda introduced its 1000 coupé and 1600/1800 series simultaneously to Europe and the US. In 1968, Honda entered European markets with its N360.

Westerners ridiculed all the early Japanese models as cheap imitations with underpowered engines and poor reliability. Some of them were classic marketing mistakes, such as Datsun naming its first American car the "Bluebird," as in the "bluebird of happiness." In a market dominated by Ford Thunderbirds, the Bluebird failed miserably.[6]

Despite the poor reputation of Japanese cars, these low-priced small cars appealed to income-constrained consumers in a US market dominated by large and more expensive gas guzzlers. Japanese automakers realized that, to succeed, they needed to design specific models for the rising middle-class American consumer. Despite initially imitating and reinterpreting existing American designs, Bryan Thompson, a designer for Nissan and Volvo, recalled that, in the 1960s, Japanese designers sought "to find their aesthetic ... much as Chinese automakers are doing today."[7]

In 1965, Toyota introduced its first Americanized model, when it launched the Corona at under $2,000. Corona offered automatic transmission and air-conditioning as options, unusual in imported small cars at that time. Nissan attacked a different segment with an affordable sports car. Nissan had already produced the successful series of Fairlady roadsters to compete against the popular English sports cars. But Nissan product planners envisioned a new line of cars, stylish, innovative, fast, and relatively inexpensive, by sharing parts with other vehicles. The Datsun Fairlady exemplifies how the Japanese car-makers adapted and improved. When it came out in the 1960s, it was allegedly difficult to start and stop as well as underpowered compared with the MGB and other competitors. In a few years, Datsun improved its Fairlady into a reasonable machine that ranked third among all foreign cars in the US by 1970.[8]

Toyota led the quality improvement movement in manufacturing that shifted the global automotive leadership from Detroit to Japan. The many manufacturing and supply chain innovations earned Japanese brands top spots for quality and reliability in the annual evaluations published by *Consumer Reports*, the magazine of the US Consumer Union. Toyota emerged as a world-class thought leader in designing and managing productions systems, popularizing such concepts as "quality is free," "continuous improvement," "just-in-time inventory," "learning organization," "zero-inventory," and "quality circles."

Toyota sales in the US, which amounted to only 6,400 vehicles in 1965, reached 71,000 by 1968 and nearly doubled each year, until by 1971 they were selling over 300,000 vehicles per year. The 1973 oil shock increased the popularity of Japanese cars because of their relatively superior fuel economy. By the early 1970s, Japan was exporting more than a million cars a year to other countries. In 1986, Toyota America passed the milestone of selling one million vehicles in a single year.

As Japanese cars became increasingly popular with American consumers, US manufacturers predictably cried foul. In the late 1970s and 80s, US politicians railed against "unfair competition," the "manipulated" low value of the yen against the US dollar, and the "protected-from imports" Japanese market. In 1981, Japan agreed voluntarily to restrain its exports to the US to 1.68 million automobiles annually. This quota forced Japanese autofirms to set up production facilities in the US and change the product mix of exports to higher priced, premium models. Toyota, Honda, and Nissan all launched new luxury models. Today, Toyota alone sells over one million vehicles (almost 30 percent of its global sales) annually in the US.

PIONEERED BY JAPANESE, FOLLOWED BY SOUTH KOREA

The Asian Tortoise strategy of the Japanese automotive companies was subsequently copied by the South Korean electronics and automobile manufacturers. Of these, Samsung is perhaps the most spectacular success. However, Hyundai, Kia, and LG have also done remarkably well at transforming themselves into global brands. Table 1.2 identifies the general building blocks of the Asian Tortoise strategy.

Samsung is one of the world's leading companies and global brands. Its 2011 worldwide sales were $143 billion, with profits of almost $12 billion. At the start of the 21st century, company representatives stated that Samsung's primary goal was to catch up with its Japanese rivals, especially Sony. Currently, it leads in consumer electronics, competing with Apple for the title of World's Top Seller of Smartphones. Along the way, it has surpassed its Japanese rival, both in sales and brand value (see Table 1.1).

Samsung began as a domestic producer. Through joint ventures, alliances, and technology licensing agreements over the years, it developed the capabilities to start exporting electronic products. Initially, it sold its branded products at a discount to its American and Japanese competitors to price-sensitive buyers in overseas markets (the "build to cost" phase of Table 1.2). It added sales volume by obtaining relatively large orders as a private ("white") label manufacturer for other foreign companies (the "build to volume" stage of Table 1.2).

To develop innovative new products, Samsung invested in upgrading its market research and product development capabili-

Table 1.2 **The tortoise strategy to build global brands**

	Alliances	Functional focus	Strategic advantage	Technology profile	Valued customer	Value proposition
Build to cost	Suppliers, labor	Manufacturing and supply chain	Low-cost location and inputs	Laggard, reverse-engineering	Overlooked segments	Cheapest price
Build to volume	Large customers and markets	Sales and distribution	Protected home market	Fast follower	Price-conscious buyers	Acceptable quality at low price
Build to quality	R&D/technology agreements	R&D	Rapid quality leaps	Lead selectively	Smart buyers, mass market	Irresistible rational value
Build to brand	Marketing alliances	Design and branding	Mass advertising, premium brands	Reinvent industry	All segments	Logic and magic – add emotional value

Note: R&D, Research and development.

ties, raising the R&D budget, conducting extensive consumer research, and setting up manufacturing and distribution operations in major export markets of Australia, Germany, the United Kingdom, and the US. These initiatives and its alliances with leading technology firms helped Samsung enter the television and mobile phone categories (the "build to quality" stage of Table 1.2).

Samsung's global brand development initiative evolved from the Seoul 1988 Olympics. In the late 1990s, the firm committed a billion dollars to make Samsung a global brand, and deleted other brands such as Wiseview, Tantus, and Yepp from its brand portfolio. These investments paid off handsomely. Samsung now regularly shows up on global lists of most innovative companies, most valuable brands, and most respected companies. Not bad for a firm that originally exported dried fish and vegetables to China!

KEY SUCCESS FACTORS FOR THE ASIAN TORTOISE STRATEGY

To benefit aspiring tortoises from other emerging markets, we have distilled the key success factors (often referred to as KSFs) of the Asian Tortoise strategy and organized them at the country, company, and category level. We believe that these KSFs – some of which are beyond the control of industry leaders or even government officials – must be in place before a company can build a global brand using this pathway. Corporate and brand strategists can use the following lists to assess whether they can follow the Asian Tortoises' lead.

COUNTRY-LEVEL FACTORS
- A relatively large population to provide the cheap labor.
- Weak protection for labor to avoid union militancy and wage escalation.
- No natural resource bounty to distort the economy and incentives.
- Commitment to an export-oriented manufacturing sector.

- A protected home market to allow experimentation by domestic firms.
- Multiple domestic rivals within an industry to spur competitiveness.
- A long-term oriented culture.

The noticeable absence of these factors in today's emerging markets other than China, and perhaps Vietnam, helps us understand why we see primarily Chinese firms following this route. Brazil, Russia, much of the Middle East, and parts of Africa (e.g., Nigeria and Angola) suffer from an abundance of natural resources, which distorts rewards, overvalues the currency, and all too often incubates cronyism and corruption.

These factors also explain why China, with its "state-sponsored" private firms and Confucian culture, will more likely take this route than will impatient Indian companies. Tortoises are patient, and none of them completed their journey in less than two decades. As Confucius himself said, "It does not matter how slowly you go, so long as you do not stop." Conversely, in our experience, Indian business seeks quick returns; India's business culture aligns more closely with the West's short-term view.[9] In addition, while India lacks natural resources, it also lacks a commitment to export-oriented manufacturing and has relatively strong labor protection. In sum, India's country characteristics do not favor the tortoise.

The country-level factors also explain why Malaysia failed to build a world-class auto-industry. Its national champion, Proton, had a monopoly in a protected market – and monopolies have little incentive to experiment and improve. Similarly, most national airline carriers fail: to win the title of national champion, you must actually have national competition. Remarkably, China encourages competition among even state-owned or state-sponsored domestic players. Rivalry forces companies to hone their capabilities and to tighten operations, whereas monopolists grow complacent and flabby.

CORPORATE-LEVEL FACTORS

Asian Tortoises require these organizational characteristics to complete their path:

- The pursuit of world-class manufacturing processes and innovation.
- Humility to learn from leading foreign firms and reverse-engineer their products.
- Alliances with global leaders to acquire and absorb technology.
- Prioritization of the developed country markets.
- A focus on a single brand, usually also the name of the firm, to leverage marketing investment.

The pursuit of world-class manufacturing excellence, innovation, and scale typically requires large capital investments. Think of the humongous state-of-the-art factories that mushroomed in China. Without access to cheap capital, the Asian Tortoise strategy is less viable. High interest rates and tight capital markets discourage Indian and Brazilian firms from throwing substantial capital at opportunities with uncertain returns. Only through enhancements in manufacturing processes and a sustained investment in R&D can companies obtain the quality improvements so necessary to meet global consumer expectations.

Consider China's Pearl River Piano Group, the largest piano manufacturer in the world. Fifty years ago, it made only four pianos a month. Today, it accounts for 18 percent of the American market and 15 percent of that in Europe. Its Asian Tortoise strategy? Make the cheapest pianos first, then the most pianos, then the best piano, and finally the most desired brand of pianos – a succession by no means complete. Yet an examination of the company's history demonstrates that corporate-level factors were mostly put in place.

In 1994, Pearl River Piano formed a joint venture with Japan's Yamaha in Guangzhou, China, learned what it could from

Yamaha, and then dissolved the relationship. The results were probably not what Yamaha expected. Wikipedia observes: "After learning and emulating Yamaha's production processes, the Pearl River Piano Group ousted Yamaha's ownership of the factory along with the backing of the Chinese government."[10]

To improve the quality, operations, and brand perception, Pearl River Piano also engaged many of the world's top designers and technicians such as Charles Corey (director of Wurlitzer Piano) and David Campbell (technical director of Steinway) for as much as RMB 20,000 a day, at a time when an annual salary of RMB 10,000 was above average in China.[11] Lothar Thomma, a Swiss national and master piano designer who had worked for leading German manufacturers, was responsible for designing many of the more premium Pearl River pianos, and they carry his signature.

Pearl River Piano first targeted the US, the largest piano market outside China. The company determined that Americans would be more willing than Europeans to try unfamiliar but good value brands. In 2000, a Pearl River piano cost a third of a brand new Yamaha piano ($9,000) and less than a second-hand piano. This lower price attracted enough people to try the Pearl River products; by 2003, Pearl River Piano had a US market share of 13 percent.[11]

In 2005, Pearl River Piano partnered with the world's top piano brand, Steinway & Sons. Steinway designed several new Essex pianos, the firms developed them jointly, and Pearl River manufactured them in their Guangzhou factory. Pearl River Piano became Steinway's first Chinese original equipment manufacturer partner, and President Tong Zhicheng "hoped to learn more from time-honored Steinway & Sons with over 150 year-old history."[12]

Pearl River Piano now produces over 100,000 pianos annually; its main factory (over three million square feet) employs about 5,000 workers. Says one dealer, "We'll be the first to say that these pianos are not as good as Yamaha, but they're so close most people can't tell the difference. Why pay thousands more for a Yamaha? You owe it to yourself to at least take a look at these very good quality yet very economical pianos."[13]

Pearl River Piano also acquired one of Europe's top 10 piano brands, Ritmüller, including its trademarks, technical blueprints and parameters, and other intellectual property rights. This allows Pearl River to offer a choice to those consumers who are shy of purchasing a "Chinese" piano, even if they are all made in China.

CATEGORY-LEVEL FACTORS

Take another look at the Interbrand list of Asian global brands in Table 1.1: all the tortoises operate in the electronics and automotive sectors. Why? What is unique about these products compared to categories such a consumer packaged goods and cosmetics where no tortoise ever made it? Consider these characteristics:

- There is a large price-sensitive segment so that the barely acceptable product at the cheapest price will find a target segment of unserved customers.
- Objective quality is important, and can be assessed, as this allows price and quality to be judged relatively independently of each other.
- Product (development and new products) quality determines brand reputation rather than vice versa.
- Substantial economies of scale exist.

In Figure 1.1, we array product categories on an axis from product quality-driven categories (where objective product quality primarily drives brand perceptions) to brand-driven categories (where brand reputation primarily drives product quality perceptions).[14] In electronics, the firm with the best products also tends to have the most popular brand. It is an industry where new products come fast and furious, and brand perceptions are typically driven by the innovativeness of the firm's most recent products. Therefore, no firm stays on top for long. Sony topped the lists with its Walkman and Playstation; then Nokia with its mobile phones; and recently Research in Motion with its BlackBerry. Now, Apple has the coolest and most innovative products and, not surprisingly, is also considered among the world's most valuable brands.

Figure 1.1 **Product–brand spectrum**

In contrast, cosmetics is a product category where quality is ephemeral. Who can objectively judge whether one perfume smells better than another? And pretty much all antiaging creams, despite their claims, cannot stop the skin from aging. In this category, cosmetic companies develop the brand promise and positioning first, then the product packaging, and finally the product itself. It is a pure marketing game. Customers and experts cannot judge product quality independently of price, and promising a cheaper product does not attract substantial sales.

Between the two extremes lie other product categories:

- automobiles and tires, where products are important but image plays an important secondary role;
- consumer packaged products such as detergents, where both product quality and brand image matter equally to the consumer decision-making process;
- apparel, where brand image dominates product quality, although not to the same extent as for cosmetics.

Electronics and automobiles are also product categories where economies of scale matter a great deal. Consequently, the emerging market firm can scale up production to high volume, necessary to finance the next step, "build to quality." Besides, electronics and automobiles are relatively big ticket items and more durable products. This makes consumers more price and quality conscious. It allows low-cost emerging market firms to enter the developed market with the low-price strategy, and use the profits generated to launch better and better products. The rapid product life-cycles and successive new product releases are newsworthy. As a result, major newspapers, magazines, and websites generate reviews and comparisons for consumers to evaluate the new products of different brands against each other. Releasing ever better quality products builds brand clout and company reputation. Even a relatively unknown brand can generate sales by offering a good product without spending substantial advertising dollars. The bottom line – these categories are vulnerable to the Asian Tortoise strategy.

The Asian Tortoise journey of the South China Tire & Rubber Company that sells the Wanli and Sunny brands in the international markets is an example here. This is a firm that sold around a million tires and generated RMB 290 million in sales in 1997. In 2011, it sold more than 11 million tires and had sales of RMB 3.8 billion. In the US, Wanli targets consumers who purchased a second-hand car or own an older car and now need replacement tires. A Wanli tire typically has a price index of 60–70 in contrast to a Michelin or Goodyear that sells at 100. Through steady improvements in quality and brand perception over the years, this price gap has narrowed from what was 80 percent previously. In our meetings at their factory, they stated that central to their goals for the next five years is to further reduce this price gap.

HAIER AND HIGHER WITH THE ASIAN TORTOISE STRATEGY

Haier Chairman Zhang Ruimin proclaimed, "If a country has no global brand, then it cannot stand on the top. Haier is willing to be the pioneer." Although many consumers in the US and Europe are still apt to ask "Haier who?," Haier is one the most exciting global consumer brands to emerge from China. Outside China, Haier has prevailed not only in developing markets, but also in the highly contested, sophisticated markets for white goods of the US and Europe. Indeed, in a relatively short period of time, Haier has become the global leader in home appliances, with 7.8 percent global market share.[15] Household names such as LG (4.9 percent), Whirlpool (4.5 percent), Samsung (3.4 percent), Electrolux (2.9 percent), General Electric (2.9 percent), Panasonic (2.8 percent), Siemens (2.5 percent), and Bosch (2.3 percent) are followers in this mega-category of washing machines, air-conditioners, refrigerators, freezers, and other such products. In 2012, Haier generated profits of around $1 billion on sales exceeding $25 billion. Overseas sales accounted for 25 percent.[16]

ORIGINS AND TURNAROUND OF HAIER

Originally a manufacturing collective started in the 1920s, Haier was established as the Qingdao General Refrigerator Factory in 1958 with a mandate to supply refrigerators to the domestic market. Until Zhang took charge of the factory in 1984, Haier, like many of its peers, had struggled with quality control. Zhang was an avid reader of Western and Japanese business practices and management techniques. He realized that the factory's lax quality control was endangering its survival.

In 1985, a customer brought a faulty refrigerator back to the factory and showed it to Zhang. Zhang and the customer searched for a replacement among Haier's entire inventory of 400 refrigerators. In the process, Zhang discovered 76 dud refrigerators – a 20 percent failure rate. To emphasize the importance of product, Zhang asked workers to line up the duds on the factory floor. He then distributed sledgehammers and ordered them to destroy the refrigerators. The workers hesitated; the cost of a refrigerator was about two years of wages. Seeing their distress, Zhang ordered,

"Destroy them! If we pass these 76 refrigerators for sale, we'll be continuing a mistake that has all but bankrupted our company." They smashed the refrigerators to pieces – and enshrined one of the hammers at company headquarters as a reminder. Employees got the message, and Haier got free publicity.[17]

To improve quality, Haier struck a technology licensing agreement with Liebherr of Germany. Zhang explained, "First we observe and digest. Then we imitate. In the end, we understand it well enough to design it independently."[18] This smart learning approach led to a substantial technological upgrade of Haier.

Through a series of acquisitions, Haier entered adjacent product categories. In each case, it overtook established leaders, such as Chunlan Group in air-conditioners and Little Swan in washing machines. It also became the leader in the freezer market.[19] By 2000, the success of Haier's core business in white goods had solidified its position as one of China's leading brands. It currently has a market share of 30 percent. Its campaign "Try your best and strive to be number one" made a strong impact on a Chinese public hungry for better quality products. Our field research in Beijing, Shanghai, Chengdu, and Xiamen shows that Haier passes the litmus test of a strong brand in terms of spontaneous associations that consumers have with the brand:

In my mind Haier stands for good quality. I don't need to worry about it. (Shanghai)

It's the leading brand in household appliances. We can definitely trust Haier. (Chengdu)

Haier has thorough product lines. (Beijing)

It's the pride of China. (Shanghai)

Haier stands for safety and quality. (Shanghai)

Haier is the most promising brand to succeed in international-ization (among all the Chinese brands), and I hope it can leverage the advantage of "made-in-China." (Xiamen)

A brand with such strong associations at home is well placed to go international – and go, Haier did.

INTERNATIONALIZATION STRATEGY

Haier's internationalization started in 1995 via several joint ventures with local white goods producers in Indonesia, the Phil-ippines, and (the former) Yugoslavia. Then it boldly entered the US and Europe before it had established itself in other emerging markets. Instead of the "easy way first" approach, Haier did the opposite, taking the "hard way first" approach.[20] Only by entering the fiercely competitive and large developed markets could Haier test and refine its key competencies to create a truly "world famous brand."[21]

Zhang observed that, in the US and Europe, Haier was facing mature brand names that had been trusted for generations – Maytag, Whirlpool, GE, Bosch, Siemens, Electrolux. He explained:

The most difficult thing is to get consumers to acknowledge the value of the [Haier] brand ... these brand names have been in existence for many decades. But it's only been a few years since Haier first moved into these overseas markets. So this is a major challenge we must overcome.[22]

To win market share in the competitive American market, Haier's strategy was to launch innovative, value-priced products for niche consumer markets and then move up the value chain. Specifically, Haier introduced a value-priced line of compact fridges, popular in American college dorm rooms. Competitively priced at just over $100, this line was available through Wal-Mart and eight of the 10 largest retailers in the US. Haier then launched affordable wine coolers, refrigerated beer keg dispensers, window-mounted air-conditioners, and eventually a sophisticated line of flat screen televisions.

Established industry leaders would not easily relinquish their share of well-heeled consumers in the upscale appliance and electronics categories, especially not to a Chinese low-end white goods company. Haier had to build both satisfactory products and brand equity to appeal to image-conscious consumers who wanted value, but who also associated Chinese brands with lower quality.

Haier's exports to the US had grown enormously – its mini refrigerator had a 40 percent market share. Haier saw the US as a lead market: where the US would go, so might other countries. In 1999, Haier founded Haier America and built a $40 million plant in Camden, South Carolina. In 2002, Haier paid $14.5 million for the landmark Greenwich Savings Bank building in Midtown Manhattan to serve as headquarters for the Western hemisphere. To accelerate growth in the US, Haier considered acquisitions, but its bids for Maytag and GE's Kentucky-based appliance unit went nowhere.

Across the Atlantic, Haier launched Haier-branded products in Germany and established a joint venture with electronics giant Philips in the Netherlands. Managing these joint ventures and off-shore manufacturing facilities helped Haier to prepare for expansion. It created Haier Europe and acquired the Meneghetti SpA refrigerator factory in Italy. By early 2000, most major European retail chains sold Haier-made goods, although sales of the Haier brand lagged far behind sales of the brands that Haier supplied as an original equipment manufacturer.

Meantime, between 2001 and 2005, Haier entered joint ventures and established local production facilities in Asia, the Middle East, and Africa. By 2008, Haier had surpassed rival Whirlpool as the world's top refrigerator producer in terms of sales, and by 2011 Haier was ranked the number one appliance brand in the world. It is active in 165 countries around the world.

LOCALLY DESIGNED, LOCALLY MADE, LOCALLY SOLD

Haier established the "locally designed, locally made, locally sold" marketing system in both the US and European markets. This "three-in-one" system enabled Haier to acquire the latest market information and understand changes in local consumer demands before its competitors did. As a result, Haier could produce suitable products for local markets, provide consumers with better service, manufacture locally, and rapidly respond to the market demand. Consistent with its "three-in-one" system, Haier localized its promotions. Its US advertising slogan was "What The World Comes Home To," while in Europe it was "Haier and Higher."[23]

In the US market, Haier set up its design center in Los Angeles, its manufacturing base in South Carolina, and its marketing headquarters in New York. In Europe, Haier established design centers in Lyon (France) and Amsterdam (the Netherlands), and manufacturing in Italy. It established regional marketing headquarters in Milan and more sales centers in Spain, the UK, the Netherlands, and Italy.[23]

Key to Haier's success in winning market share was the ability to differentiate the brand with innovative products and with niche products in much larger product categories. Examples included Haier's "No-Tail" TV using wireless technology for both power and video transmission; fridges with a compartment in the middle that could be set to refrigerate or freeze; and a dishwasher with food particle sensors to determine when plates were clean. In the US, Haier unveiled a line of ecofriendly, tech-rich appliances priced at $600 to $1,500, a departure from Haier's value-priced offerings at $200 to $300.

Although it took Haier executives a year to get the initial sales appointment with Wal-Mart, other chains soon followed once the giant retailer started carrying Haier products. By 2009, Haier had gained distribution in nine of 10 of the nation's largest retailers as well as in over 7,000 regional stores. In Europe, Haier had penetrated mainstream distribution channels: Kesa, Carrefour, Expert,

Media Markt, and Darty (the largest electronics retailer in France) among others.[24]

On the supply side, Haier leveraged its flexible and less costly Chinese manufacturing capacity to produce a wide range of goods in smaller production runs, customized to meet any retailer's or retail customer's specific needs. For example, when Home Depot asked Haier to equip its refrigerators with locks for cubicle and dorm room security, Haier immediately developed a new model with locks.[25] A Target customer once suggested that Haier replace text descriptions with easy-to-read icons on its air-conditioning units. Haier did.[25]

GLOBAL BRAND STRATEGY

Haier dubbed its global brand strategy "Go Out, Go Into, Go Up." "Go out" means global presence so that people recognize the brand. "Go into" means local acceptance to become mainstream. "Go up" means movement into higher value-added products. Haier has realized "Go out" and is now focusing on "Go into" and "Go up."

Traditionally, Haier had sold its products under a single brand name, focusing on moving "Haier" from a cheap brand into a mainstream brand. Now, Haier has adopted the dual-brand strategy. Haier invited world's top designers to develop nonconventional high-end refrigerators in French, Italian, and American styles. The result was "Casarte," positioned as an imported product made in the US. In 2006, Haier introduced Casarte into the US. Like Toyota's Lexus, Haier positions Casarte at the high end, with Haier serving the mass market.[26] In Europe, other brands dominated the low-price/low-technology segment, so Haier Europe tweaked its "Go up" strategy to target the segment between the high-end and low-end brands. René Aubertin, Chairman of Haier Europe, explained, "We hope to attract customers with the help of excellent design and unique elements, and of course also with prices more attractive than other high-end products."[27] In Nuremberg, Haier built an R&D division to develop products targeted at European consumers. According to Aubertin, "Our goal is to, in the next three to five years, decrease the proportion of low-end products in total revenue from the current level of 20–25 percent to 5–10 percent."[27]

Without the huge marketing budgets of the US titans to install salespeople in America's retail chains or to buy prime-time TV spots and glossy spreads in national magazines, Haier had to spend its money smarter. Initially, it leveraged packaging, social media, and trade advertising. For example, instead of the black and white boxes of other air-conditioning products, Haier products were packaged in bright reds and yellows. It also provided instructions on matching the cooling power to the size of the room and calculated the energy savings of its product against US energy consumption standards. In effect, each package sold itself.[23]

Since 2006, Haier's main US consumer brand-building has consisted of "the official HDTV of the NBA." The company has sponsored an all-star competition, "Haier Shooting Stars," featuring top players shooting hoops. At the grass-roots level, Haier has reached out to consumers directly. For instance, for the past two years, Haier has decked out a tractor trailer truck with a full product line assortment – fridges, laundry, and TVs. The truck has traveled to big US cities to showcase Haier's broad product range at festivals such as the "Taste of Chicago," a huge annual food event attended by Haier's key target market. There, it has staged cooking and other demonstrations from the truck.

These investments are paying off. Haier's brand awareness in many product categories has tripled or more from just five years ago. It has 10,000 patents from the 3 to 5 percent of sales it has consistently plowed back into research and development.[15] *Businessweek* has recognized it among the 50 most innovative companies in the world. Achieving such international recognition and financial growth in less than 20 years makes Haier, for the moment, one of the most successful global consumer brands to emerge from China.

LIMITS OF THE ASIAN TORTOISE STRATEGY

The Asian tortoise strategy still holds great promise. However, it has definite limits, even for Chinese companies. Consider the Chinese automotive industry. Three decades ago, China signed joint venture agreements with General Motors and Volkswagen to build a world-class industry. Yet foreign brands with a 70 percent share still dominate the domestic market.[28] Despite some success in exports, no Chinese brand has matched Toyota or even Kia. China is the world's largest automotive market, so why is there not a single global Chinese automotive brand?

There are four reasons for this. First, with membership of the World Trade Organization and liberalization of free trade, China cannot so easily protect its domestic market as robustly as before. A majority of global automakers have set up Chinese manufacturing plants, forcing Chinese automakers to compete against, while catching up with, their more established foreign rivals. As the growth in developed markets has slowed, the foreign carmakers have become even more aggressive in the growing emerging markets. Consequently, the domestic brands have recently *lost* share.

Second, the Asian Tortoise depends on a low-cost position against established foreign competitors. While Chinese wages are lower than those in other major automotive countries, today all the major players have global supply chains that can access the low Chinese wages and auto components. That means that Chinese automakers cannot offer as low a relative price for a poorer quality product as the Japanese and Korean automakers could in the 1960s and 80s when they had a low-wage advantage.

Third, unlike the privately owned Japanese and Korean firms, Chinese automotive companies are mostly state owned, with Party officials appointed to run them. Management commits to the long-term viability of the Party, not necessarily to the company.[29] Often the company heads are seeking to move to the next major assignment rather than remaining for life at the firm and turning its fortunes around.

Finally, with so many troubled Western car-makers and auto parts manufacturers for sale, the Chinese have acquired global brands with relative ease. SAIC Motor Corporation (China's marker leader) acquired the MG Rover Group, Beijing Automotive Industry Holding Company bought Saab, and Geely bought Volvo. These acquisitions may subvert the enthusiasm to develop the competitive fitness and organizational capabilities such as the Japanese and Koreans had to develop over time and at great cost.

Despite these limitations, we believe that Western automakers should not write off Chinese automotive companies, which now export more than a million cars, although mostly to other emerging markets. And the Chinese have improved quality and reliability: the 2011 J.D. Power quality ratings indicated that Chinese brands sold domestically were rated overall as having 30 percent fewer problems per 100 vehicles, compared to 2010.[30] However, they still have a long way to go, with 232 quality problems for every 100 Chinese-brand cars purchased compared to 131 defects per 100 cars for foreign brands.[31]

Since almost all the major Chinese auto firms are state owned, there is no immediate pressure to earn profits quickly. The flow of cheap loans gives managers time to transform some of them into global brands. Says Ratan Tata, Chairman of Tata group: "China has emerged as the largest car market and car producing centre of the world. Chinese brands have started to appear in world markets and in all probability these will grow into international brands in the next few years."[32]

MANAGERIAL TAKEAWAYS

The tortoise is a reptile that moves slowly but inexorably over land on its short sturdy legs. It lives in Asia, Africa, and parts of the Americas.

Its dome-shaped shell is thick and heavy to protect it for many decades from predatorial strikes. It is patient but persistent, and its survival takes time and perseverance. Haier, South China Tire & Rubber, and Pearl River Piano have demonstrated that the tortoise strategy can work for Chinese firms, as it did in South Korea and Japan, taking them through a succession of stages: "build to cost," "build to volume," "build to quality," and "build to brand." The tortoise may work in Bangladesh, Myanmar, Vietnam, and other emerging markets.

To determine whether the tortoise's path will lead their company, executives should ask themselves the following questions.

Country considerations
- Can we count on a large population to provide the cheap labor?
- Can we avoid union militancy and prolong wage escalation?
- Are we free of the trappings of natural resources, such that incentives are aligned with results?
- Is our government committed to an export-oriented manufacturing sector?
- Is our domestic market protected from outsiders so that we can experiment?
- Do we have multiple domestic rivals within our industry to spur competitiveness?
- Does our culture value long-term goals and effort?

Corporate level
- Are we humble enough to learn from leading foreign firms?
- Are we skilled enough to reverse-engineer foreign products?
- Can we form alliances with global leaders to acquire and absorb technology?
- Will we pursue world-class manufacturing processes and innovation?
- Will we prioritize important and fiercely competitive markets?
- Can we focus on a single brand?

Category level

- Are we targeting a large, price-sensitive segment?
- Does quality matter, and can it be judged independently of price?
- Do product features and new releases determine brand reputation?
- Can we gain substantial economies of scale as we grow?

If the answer is "yes" to most or all of these questions, executives should feel more confident about moving the strategy forward within their firm. Where executives have answered "no," they should ask themselves, "Can we change it to a 'yes'?" That is, is it something that we can control and address, so that we can move forward? If the answer is "no" to many of these questions, and conditions are beyond management's control, then better to study the remaining chapters in this book. Read on!

TWO

THE BUSINESS TO CONSUMER ROUTE

LEVERAGING B2B STRENGTHS IN B2C MARKETS

Global firms from emerging markets tend to compete in business markets, that is, they sell their output to overseas companies (B2B) or governments (B2G) rather than to households (B2C) in foreign countries. In business markets, a firm typically targets a limited set of organizational customers, who buy in bulk based on rational price and quality, not on brand. Branding activities are often unnecessary, and distribution is less important since large global customers have their own distribution capabilities. Even if a firm must set up a distribution network, it need reach only the relatively fewer business customers.

In contrast, global consumer products require strong brand names that mean something to foreign consumers as well as supporting distribution and service networks that can effectively serve individual households in distant lands. Starting from scratch to launch a consumer brand in developed markets using traditional marketing strategies is often prohibitively expensive for entrepreneurs and small businesses in those markets; imagine how expensive the exercise would be for many emerging market firms. Furthermore, convincing dealers and retailers in the developed world to stock an unknown brand from an unfamiliar or ill-famed country is too big a hurdle. Without brand image, a firm cannot form a distribution network or generate sales to fund advertising and branding initiatives. It is the classic "chicken and egg" problem for emerging market firms.

This chapter explores one pathway to building a global consumer brand from emerging markets, namely the leveraging of business market strengths to begin serving end users. Brands or companies such as ASD, Midea, Galanz, Huawei, HTC, Mahindra, Tata Motors, and ZTE are following this approach. While none of them is, as yet, a "top-of-mind" consumer brand in the developed world, we can draw some general lessons from their efforts to transform from B2B to B2C players.

UNDERSTANDING B2B COMPANIES

Before we look at this path to building consumer brands in B2C markets, we want to distinguish between two types of business marketing firm, namely the contract manufacturers and the global B2B players.

CONTRACT MANUFACTURERS

Millions of small and medium enterprises are exporters that exploit the natural or demographic advantages of a country such as its agricultural conditions, its energy resources, or the low labor costs of mining or manufacturing. They compete for large contracts with global retailers such as H&M and Wal-Mart or global consumer brands such as Apple and Nike that want to outsource functions not critical to their brand value. These exporting firms largely toil in the shadows, unknown to the press or the consuming public. If they do receive publicity, it is generally unflattering.

Consider the Western press coverage of the labor practices of Asian suppliers to Apple, Nike, and Wal-Mart. Such contract manufacturers export their output, not their brands, or as Figure 2.1 illustrates, only their *products* go global.

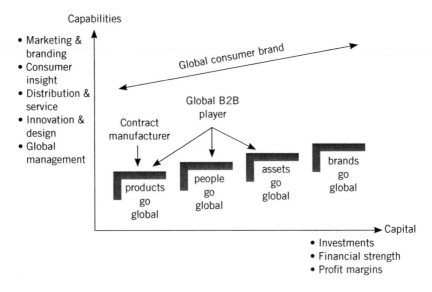

Figure 2.1 **Different global footprints**

GLOBAL B2B ENTERPRISES

Then there are the large global B2B enterprises from emerging markets that appear on the 2012 list of the largest (*Fortune* 500) companies in the world. Of the around 100 emerging market companies on this list, most of them are business marketing firms such as Gazprom, Reliance Industries, Petrobras, Sinopec Group, and Vale. Beyond selling their products globally, these firms have global capabilities as their people (e.g., subsidiaries and sales-people) and assets (plants and warehouses) exist across the world. They know how to manage in global markets. However, because of their focus on the business customers, they usually lack the consumer insights, branding expertise, and marketing capabilities that are necessary to build a global brand name with end users.

BUSINESS MODELS OF B2B COMPANIES

For both contract manufacturers and global B2B companies, the move from industrial to consumer markets requires changes in their business models. Contract manufacturers, also known as private label suppliers, white label producers, or original equipment manufacturers (OEMs),[1] must learn to market consumer products, not just make them. Galanz has done this in microwave ovens, while HTC has succeeded with smartphones. In contrast, global B2B enterprises already know how to make and market their own products; they need to select adjacent consumer categories in which they can potentially build consumer brands. For example, Tata Motors expanded from trucks to cars, while Mahindra has diversified from tractors to small utility vehicles. Similarly, the Chinese telecommunications network equipment manufacturers Huawei and ZTE are now selling branded handsets and smartphones to consumers.

To appreciate the challenges of the transitions needed to become a consumer brand, let us examine these two types of business marketer in terms of a popular marketing model called the "3Vs," where V stands for *value*.[2] The 3Vs model articulates a firm's strategy based on *valued customer* or who to serve; *value proposition* or what to offer; and *value network* or how to deliver. Table 2.1 presents the typical 3Vs model for a contract manufacturer, a global B2B firm, and a global consumer brand in order to contrast how they compete in the marketplace.

FROM CONTRACT MANUFACTURER
TO CONSUMER BRAND

Contract manufacturers tend to have a few large customers and little pricing power, since their output is undifferentiated from

Table 2.1 **Strategic analysis of the key success factors for three kinds of companies**

	Contract manufacturer	Global B2B firm	Global consumer brand
Valued customer ("Who to serve")	Very few large customers; sometimes only one	Portfolio of organizational customers; typically segmented as large, medium, and small	Millions of end users served through resellers/ e-channels; multiple segments served
Value proposition ("What to offer")	Meet customer specifications at lowest cost Ability to ramp capacity up/down	Rational quality at competitive cost Ability to demonstrate value	Rational and emotional value (logic and magic) Proposition differs by segment
Value network ("How to deliver")			
R&D	Minimal to none Product specification and design received from customer	Technical and product focus Joint development with lead customers	Consumer insight driven Perception and product focus
Operations	Few products Prefer long runs Large orders Efficiency obsessed Built to order	Between a contract manufacturer and consumer brand, depending on the industry/firm	Many products Shorter runs Quick response Quality and cost focus Build to stock
Marketing	No marketing activities No brand development	Limited marketing activities Corporate brand focus	Sophisticated marketing Well-defined brand architecture
Sales	Inbound sales Strong management of limited accounts, often by owner	Outbound sales Strong key account management to large customers Relationship marketing	Key account management to dedicated resellers Point of sales activities Trade/customer promotions
Distribution/ service	No service capabilities No distribution capabilities beyond organizing logistics	Distribution network to reach business customers Technical support to knowledgeable customers	Distribution network to reach end users Distributed service network for widespread consumers with low knowledge

that of competing producers. As a result, the customer can easily replace them. Think of the thousands of small garment manufacturers in Bangladesh, tea-growers in Sri Lanka, and soccer ball manufacturers in Pakistan, and the millions of contract manufacturers in China.

Given the price pressures, contract manufacturers concentrate on increasing efficiency, flexibility, and productivity in the manufacturing process to meet customer specifications and control cash flow. They typically lack research and development (R&D) activities. Instead, learning is focused on how to manufacture more sophisticated products. Their operations are geared to producing large quantities, once they receive orders and specifications from customers. Their customers are constantly seeking optimal supply chains. As a result, contract manufacturers need a limited sales function and no real marketing capabilities. In most cases, few employees play a marketing role, even if their job titles contain the word *marketing*. More often than not, the owner/CEO is personally responsible for managing major accounts and obtaining orders. As Table 2.1 shows, the distribution and service capability of these firms is limited to logistics, usually to deliver products to the warehouses of their customers.

Some of the contract manufacturers based in China have grown into large enterprises as China has become the world's factory. China now exports as much in a *day* as it did in a *year* in 1979. The most famous of the contract manufacturers is Taiwan-based Foxconn, also known as Hon Hai, a *Global Fortune 500* company with a $117 billion turnover in 2011 and a major supplier to brands such as Apple.[3] Since 2000, it has had a compound annual growth rate greater than 50 percent, higher than that of Apple. In fact, Apple is estimated to account for two-fifths of its revenues. Yet, as Table 2.2 demonstrates, Hon Hai works off wafer-thin gross margins of 7 percent and a net margin of 2 percent. In other words, 93 percent of its revenues relate directly to the cost of manufacturing. Clearly, this model has little room for error.

Table 2.2 **Financial models**

	Contract manufacturer	Branded contract manufacturer	Global B2B firm	Global consumer branded firms	
	Hon Hai	HTC	Huawei	Apple	Procter & Gamble
Revenue[a] ($ billions)	117	16	29	108	83
Revenue (%)	100	100	100	100	100
Cost of goods sold (%)[b]	93	72	60	59	49
Gross margin (%)[c]	7	28	40	41	51
R&D expense (%)	1	3	9	2.5	3[e]
Sales, general and administrative (SG&A) (%)	4	10	17	7.5	29
Operating margin (%)[d]	2	15	14	31	19

Notes:
[a] 2011 financial year, sourced from annual reports with the authors' calculations.
[b] Percentages have been rounded off.
[c] Gross margin = revenues − cost of goods sold.
[d] Operating margins = gross margin − R&D − SG&A.
[e] Authors' estimate.

The low margins result from intense competition at this end of the value chain, where local entrepreneurs can easily replicate the model and leverage local advantages. Therefore, local hubs begin to specialize in a particular industry as a network of expertise emerges in a geographical area. For example, 75 percent of the hand-sewn soccer balls in the 1990s were produced in Sialkot, Pakistan. In 2009, the average worker received 59 cents to sew 32 polyurethane outer panels of a soccer ball that Nike or Adidas sold for 50 dollars in the United States.[4] If the manufacturer attempts to increase prices, customers will simply switch to another local supplier. When press reports pressure these firms to increase wages and improve labor conditions, the customer usually must agree to fund such improvements, as Apple did for Foxconn in 2012.[5]

Beyond margins, the low profitability and lack of access to capital markets severely limit the ability of the contract manufacturer to make the major investments needed to compete as a global brand, especially in developed markets. In China, banks tend to loan to large state-sponsored organizations, not to small entrepreneurial enterprises. Investing in marketing and branding capabilities is unrealistic for these small and medium firms, whose gross and net margins probably look a lot worse than that of the mammoth Foxconn. Beyond marketing, they would also have to invest in R&D, distribution, and service networks. Their only real competence is low-cost manufacturing to received specifications (see Table 2.1). In general, they deploy no people, assets, or brands outside their home country (see Figure 2.1). However, some of these contract manufacturers, faced with higher costs and ambitions, dream of becoming global consumer brands. Galanz is one Chinese contract manufacturer that is attempting to make this switch.

GALANZ: FROM WORLD'S PLANT TO GLOBAL BRAND

In 1978, when the Chinese government established Special Economic Zones in China, Guizhou Eiderdown Company was founded by Qingde Liang, an administrator in Guizhou township. He proposed that the town set up an enterprise – 100 percent owned by the local government – to process duck feathers and goose down. By the early 1990s, its annual sales were around $19 million. Faced with intense price competition, Qingde decided to change tack in 1992 after observing the popularity of microwave ovens during a business trip to Japan. "Actually, we did well in selling eiderdown goods overseas, but I felt there were limits," said Qingde, "so, I considered transition."[6] Qingde made a deal with Toshiba of Japan to produce 10,000 Toshiba-branded microwave ovens.[7] At the same time, the firm changed its name to Galanz Group of Guangdong, and eventually purchased the microwave division of Toshiba. To comply with the change in government policy, it also converted to a private company by selling the stock to managers. While building its contract manufacturing business, Galanz also pursued selling microwaves under its own independent brand name in Shanghai. Starting from there, by 1995 Galanz had captured 25 percent of the domestic market. By 1998, it had half of the Chinese market.[8]

On a European trip, Galanz executives discovered that it cost manufacturers $100 to produce a microwave oven in Europe because of the different operating practices. For example, in France, a factory operated one shift, four days a week, with expensive labor, while a Galanz factory worked three shifts, seven days a week, with vastly cheaper labor. By promising to produce microwaves at half the European cost, Galanz managed to persuade European manufacturers to outsource the entire production to Galanz. As a consequence, the Europeans shipped their more advanced manufacturing equipment to Galanz. Suddenly, Galanz could not only scale up, but also manufacture more sophisticated products. Since Galanz sold its own brand only in the domestic market, the European brands did not consider it a competitor. With over 200 such partnerships, Galanz produced one million units in 1996, and 12 million in 2001. By 2008, the company was producing over 15 million microwave ovens a year, accounting for about 40 percent of the world market.

"Price Butcher" was the title given to Galanz by the media. Early on, Galanz took advantage of price wars to beat its rivals and expand the market. Over time, Galanz realized that its costs were rising and the exchange rate was moving in an unfavorable direction. A Chinese observer of the household products industry noted, "The 'Destroy-by-Price Theory' established by Galanz in the past is facing the pressure ... Therefore, Galanz needs a brand-new and complete reform from inside to outside, including management system, staff incentive, marketing mode and product R&D."[9] Said Yu Yaochang, the Executive Vice President of Galanz:

We are also working on turning the image of "Price Killer," and propose the change "from world-class manufacturer brand to world-class consumer brand." In next stage, while being a good manufacturer, we will try our best to build the brand of "Galanz."[9]

The Galanz Group invested 3 percent of its annual revenue in R&D. In 1995, it established the Research Institute of Household Electrical Appliances in China. Subsequently, it set up research centres in Chicago, Osaka, and Seoul. Its global technical R&D capability has attracted authoritative overseas experts, who specialize in the top technologies and new materials, and has furthered intellectual application research for consumer products.[10] Galanz now has 600 patents in microwave oven technology. But it was a visit to their factory and premises that left us more impressed. Among some of the innovative products developed and introduced by Galanz were the following:

- A beautiful microwave called Uovo which looked like a large space helmet. The unique design prevented water condensing on the top and then falling onto the food. The control buttons reminded one of an iPhone showing the different apps. It was developed in 2008 and is marketed in France, Germany, and the United Kingdom under the brand names of their clients. But in Eastern Europe and other emerging markets, it sells under the Galanz brand.
- A microwave that had a small TV built into the front cover to allow cooking instructions to be demonstrated while following a recipe, a 2009 innovation that was selling in South Korea.
- A small footprint multifunction microwave oven that can also grill food. In addition, it converts into a rotisserie simply by flipping the electric coil built into the top of the oven down to the back of the machine. Introduced in

2009, it became very popular in China and is now exported overseas.

- A combination toaster–oven and coffee-maker, with a top on which a kettle can be placed to boil, a 2006 innovation that is being sold all over the world and is especially successful in Latin America.

Galanz's transformation from contract manufacturer to consumer brand innovator has been slow but steady. Today, Galanz is the largest player in the world in microwave ovens, with a 40 percent global share. It produces 30 million units out of two locations in China. Global sales are about RMB 35 billion, of which 60 percent comes from international markets. Galanz sells microwaves in more than 150 countries. The Galanz brand is available in 40 countries, mostly in Eastern Europe, Africa, and Asia. In the rest of the world, they are contract manufacturers to brands such as Electrolux, GE, Miele, Whirlpool, and Zelmer as well as retailers such as Carrefour, Metro, Sears, Target, and Wal-Mart. They often license the Western brand and pay them a royalty to use it. Country-level distributors are then responsible for marketing and promotion, while Galanz does service and after-sales support.

MILLIONS OF CONTRACT MANUFACTURERS, MILLIONS OF DREAMERS

The Galanz story demonstrates that it is possible for a contract manufacturer to evolve into a branded player. All over China, we met many contract manufacturers who were curious about whether such a transformation was possible for them. The most logical approach being followed, as at Galanz, is to initially develop a brand for the domestic Chinese market. For example, Midea in the same white goods industry has worldwide sales of $22 billion and 170,000 employees. It sells its Midea brand only in China. According to BrandZ, Midea is the sixth most valuable brand in China, with a brand value of $8.3 billion. International sales are to 200 countries, but only as an OEM manufacturer. When we visited their enormous warehouse with 54 truck-loading docks, there were packaged microwaves boxes bearing famous brand names such as Akai, Bosch, Cusinart, Electrolux, Emerson, Ericsson, General Electric, Godrej, Kenwood, Panasonic, Toshiba, Whirlpool, and Zelmer.

In a second step, such contract manufacturers may sell their brand in other emerging markets. In this sense, this strategy is the opposite of the Asian Tortoise strategy in its international evolution. In the Asian Tortoise strategy, the initial international focus is on the developed world. Figure 2.2 contrasts the two strategies.

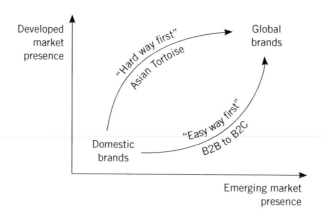

Figure 2.2 **Contrasting the Asian Tortoise and B2B routes**

Will these B2B players later migrate to selling their brands in developed markets at some stage? The story of ASD, a Chinese firm selling cookware, is instructive here. ASD began as a scrap metal business and started selling cookware in 1987 as an OEM supplier to international companies. Even in the domestic market, ASD simply sold products to the large retailers rather than trying to support the brand with marketing and advertising.

Three changes helped the company transform its business from that of an exclusive OEM supplier. First, it decided to focus on becoming a "brand" company rather than a sales company in

China. Second, it established all the management functions that were needed to run such a brand company beyond having the capability to run an efficient factory combined with a small sales staff. This also led to a research capability that resulted in innovations such as the nonsmoke wok, a whirl bottom for better spreading of heat, and ceramic coating. Third, by succeeding in the domestic and international markets, they obtained the scale to acquire top management skills and world-class processes.

As labor costs increased in China, ASD recognized the need to have highly automated plants and that this would also improve quality. They acquired the assets of an Italian cookware manufacturer, which was, like many European cookware manufacturers, going out of business. The Italian factory, which was equipped with an excellent production system, was dismantled and moved to China. In 2011, sales for the cookware division were RMB 2.1 billion or about $350 million. They have the dominant position in China with the ASD brand, and 50 percent of the company's sales are derived from the domestic market. The marketing concept behind the brand is healthy living, and it focuses on the kitchen with not only pots and pans, but also electrical appliances such as rice cookers and coffee-makers.

The other 50 percent of sales derive from international markets, with 60 percent of these coming from the US. All sales to Europe and the US are in the company's capacity as an OEM supplier. ASD has a strategic cooperation with all the five largest cookware companies in the world, and its three biggest customers are Caphalon, Cuisinart, and Le Creuset. ASD also supplies private label products to many large retailers such as Auchan, Carrefour, Metro, and Wal-Mart. The business in Asia (e.g., Thailand, Iran, Singapore, and Taiwan) and the Middle East is smaller, but it sells under the ASD brand. The company feels that it would currently be difficult to sell the ASD brand in these developed markets because these consumers think of China as being associated with poor quality and the cheapest product. As

Amanda Chen, Chairman of the Board of ASD explained to us in an interview:

> We would not be able to change their minds to switch to a Chinese brand against brands that have a long history. As a result, perhaps it is easier for us to buy a European or American brand and then market our products manufactured in China under this acquired brand.

Beyond the image issues, a decision to move from contract manufacturing to branded player places stress on the business model. It requires top management's commitment to be willing to take such a risk. For example, the Taiwanese firm HTC manufactured smartphones for branded handset companies such as Siemens as well as telecom operators such as O2, Vodafone, and T-Mobile. Around 2007, Cher Wang, HTC's chairwoman and a global citizen, decided to transform HTC into a branded player.[11] This was a board-level decision and not an easy one. Many in the company questioned the decision because HTC had an extremely profitable business model with margins of around 20 percent compared to the usual contract manufacturer margins of less than 5 percent. Many worried that HTC would be competing with its own customers and risking substantial sums on launching a consumer brand that might not take off. Furthermore, the initiative would require not only new marketing and branding capabilities, but also a culture change to reorient the firm toward end users. Shareholders worried, too: HTC's share price plummeted to half its previous levels.

To transform itself into a B2C player, HTC upgraded its R&D capability. It opened a new research center, "Magic Labs," and hired Horace Luke, creator of Microsoft's Xbox, as chief innovation officer. In 2007, HTC developed and launched touch screen smartphones sold under the HTC brand, providing telecom operators with a cheaper alternative to the newly launched iPhone. Apple initially restricted the distribution of the iPhone to a single operator in each market, so HTC could capitalize on the increased demand.

The annual reports from those years reveal the financial impact of turning into a branded player. The sales and marketing expenses jumped from 1 percent of sales in 2005 to 6 percent in 2008. The R&D expenses doubled in the same period, from 3 percent to 6 percent. HTC's smartphone has not been as successful as the iPhone, but HTC Touch and its successors provided enough revenues to allow HTC to exit the traditional contract manufacturing business in 2009.

In 2009, HTC's global brand awareness hovered around 16 percent, so HTC launched its first global brand campaign. The campaign and the success of its products have raised HTC's brand awareness to almost 60 percent.[12] In 2011, HTC became the first brand from Taiwan to make Interbrand's list of 100 Best Global Brands. HTC debuted at rank 98, and its brand was valued at $3.6 billion. However, given the vagaries of the electronics industry, as noted in the previous chapter, HTC fell out of the list the following year as Samsung became ascendant.

ASD, Galanz, and HTC all underscore the need for contract manufacturers to invest early in developing an R&D capability and over time making innovation a world-class function. Furthermore, the need to develop branding and marketing capabilities comes later after the products have been developed. The old saying "Nothing kills a bad product faster than lots of advertising" comes to mind. Furthermore, contract manufacturers must generate adequate surplus in their OEM business in order to be able invest in global R&D capability and branding initiatives. The Galanz story also reveals the short-sightedness of Western appliance manufacturers that regarded Galanz as a mere supplier of products, and not as a potential competitor.

A MOVE TO ADJACENT CONSUMER
CATEGORIES FOR GLOBAL B2B FIRMS

Unlike a contract manufacturer that concentrates on a single task in the value network – manufacturing – a global B2B company has global scale, experience operating in foreign markets, a well-developed value network, and assets deployed across the world. It has everything except a brand familiar to consumers (see Figure 2.1). Furthermore, global B2B firms do invest substantially in R&D (Tables 2.1 and 2.2) while having worldwide distribution and service networks in place. Yet few B2B companies evolve into B2C companies, unless the existing category expands into consumer markets, as computers did. That is how Microsoft and Dell became household names.

Why do B2B companies rarely transform into B2C companies? The reason is that the business model is substantially different. A successful B2B company is built around technical excellence, rational product features, large customers, and a sales culture. The successful B2C firm is built around consumer segments, understanding emotional and rational needs, brand management, marketing, and the management of diverse distribution networks. The differences are systematic and deeply embedded in every activity of the value network (see Table 2.1). For example, despite the presence of substantial R&D capabilities, B2B firms usually lack the capacity to innovate for end users because they lack a process for gaining end-user insights. Similarly, they have a global distribution and service network, but that does not reach end users directly. The result is that successful B2B companies differ from successful B2C companies in how they think, how they organize, how they operate, and even who they recruit.[13]

Not surprisingly, there are relatively few examples of firms that began as B2B firms in emerging markets and then became global consumer brands. The best examples of this transformation are Mahindra, Tata Motor, ZTE, and Huawei. We will use

Huawei's transformation from a telecom networks equipment manufacturer into a consumer smartphones marketer to demonstrate some general lessons of this pathway.

HUAWEI: BECOMING A BLOCKBUSTER GLOBAL BRAND

China's Huawei Technologies may not be an instantly recognized, top-of-mind, brand for Western consumers. For most of its history, Huawei provided products and services to telecom networks around the world. Founded in 1988, Huawei had grown into a $32 billion company with 140,000 employees by 2012. Huawei placed its products and solutions in over 140 countries and supported the communication of one-third of the world's population. To date, approximately 80 percent of the world's top 50 telecoms companies – including BT, Motorola, T-Mobile, and Cox Communications – have worked with Huawei. With revenues for the first half of 2012 of $16.1 billion, Huawei claimed to have overtaken Ericsson with sales of $15.25 billion over the same period. Huawei's adjacency strategy provides insights into winning as a global consumer brand.

Ren Zhengfei established Huawei with just RMB 24,000 (at the time about $3,400). The company started as a sales agent for a Hong Kong firm selling private branch exchange (PBX) switches, but founder Ren wanted to innovate. Almost immediately, Huawei began researching, developing, and marketing its own PBX technology. Soon after, Huawei began developing products one by one that met supply gaps in China's telecom industry at a lower cost than international suppliers.

Huawei's expansion in China was inspired by Mao Zedong's military strategy – grow in the countryside, then expand into the cities. Huawei first targeted rural areas neglected by Huawei's better connected rivals, expanded into lower-tier cities, and finally blanketed the entire country. This strategy enabled the company to achieve a commanding position in its home base in a short period of time. Along the way, Huawei has become a source of national pride. Our field research among Chinese consumers uncovered many positive associations:

> A giant in telecommunication industry. (Chengdu)

> Number one private enterprise in recent years. (Chengdu)

> They spend a huge amount of money on R&D. (Beijing)

> It stands for the telecommunication competency of China. (Beijing)

> Huawei has the biggest B2B telecommunication system. (Shanghai)

> People are working so hard inside Huawei. They have strict management and great capability. We can trust the products. (Shanghai)

Huawei's international expansion

Huawei approached the international market as it did its domestic market, attacking "soft" targets first before moving into tough markets (Figure 2.2). Well-established firms controlled the lucrative European and American markets. So Huawei focused initially on the rest of Asia, Latin America, and Africa. There were many underserved segments in these markets, mainly clients with limited resources that could not afford the products of established multinational companies. Finding these clients took six years (1995–2000). By the sixth year, Huawei had established a client base in over a dozen countries in Africa and Asia and generated an annual revenue of $300 million – peanuts compared to the high-end sales of Western competitors but enough to gain a foothold in these markets. By 2006, sales in Africa were over $2 billion.[14] Huawei expanded successfully into Eastern Europe and Southern Europe. Only then did it enter the most advanced markets of Western Europe and North America.

By 2005, Huawei had become the preferred supplier to both British Telecom and Vodafone; its international revenue exceeded domestic sales for the first time. In 2009, Huawei became the world's number two telecom-equipment provider behind Ericsson. A slew of lucrative, prestigious contracts followed, and Huawei prevailed over Ericsson and Nokia Siemens for a deal to build Norway's pioneering 4G cellphone network. The success of Huawei as a B2B player demonstrates its patience in executing a deliberate strategy. Internally, the company used the analogy "like a wolf" to describe its core culture: Huawei senses the prey quickly, is ruthless in attack, and works in packs. Huawei is not to be underestimated in its desire to build a global consumer brand.

R&D as a driver

Influenced by its founder's determination to innovate consistently, Huawei's R&D has been the strategic driver from the beginning. Key to innovation was creating links to partners and markets in the West. Huawei selected alliance partners based on their R&D capabilities, to "stand on the shoulders of giants." Huawei preferred first to learn and absorb other competitors' intelligence, and then improve upon this in higher level innovations. Furthermore, Huawei set up innovation centers within major clients such as Deutsche Telecom, China Mobile, Vodafone, and Telefonica to understand what telecom carriers need, to commoditize R&D, and to exploit economies of scale. By forming strategic alliances, Huawei gained access to technology and internalized it, leading to a more efficient and cost-effective method than solely developing the technology in-house. However, true innovation is still lacking, despite having invested around 10 percent of annual revenues in R&D over the past 18 years. Huawei acknowledges in its 2010 Annual Report:

> [so] far we have not had one single original product invention. What we achieved is advancing our capacity of improving and

integrating the function and feature of the products invented by the western companies.[15]

Huawei's approach to R&D has been "market based," one that requires a thorough understanding of client needs. To facilitate this, Huawei assigned 5 percent of its R&D staff to the marketing function, and 5 percent of its marketing staff to the R&D function. This allocation of talent enables the two groups to share knowledge and consumer insights. In addition, Huawei holds its research people responsible not only for products, as most companies do, but also for sales performance.

By 2012, Huawei had established 23 research institutes outside China. As a result, almost half (44 percent), or over 60,000, of Huawei employees were engaged in R&D activities in cities such as Munich, Paris, Milan, Moscow, Bangalore, Dallas, and Ottawa. In 2008, *Fast Company* named Huawei the fifth most Innovative Company in the world, right after global brand superstars Facebook, Amazon, Apple, and Google. The numbers provide the evidence. As of 2011, Huawei had applied for more than 50,000 patents globally and had been granted 23,522 patent licenses, of which 90 percent were invention patents. Yet, as the HTC experience shows, there is no room for complacency as success in this business is often ephemeral. Founder Ren understands this well:

> many of our employees ... think that we are a top company in the world. These employees do not know either what these competitors are really capable of doing, or the advanced technologies those competitors haven't shown yet. Huawei is indeed a very young and immature company.[16]

Huawei's consumer devices

Huawei did not plan to enter the devices market and become a consumer brand; this was serendipitous. In 2003, it won its first 3G contract from Etisalat of the United Arab Emirates. One of the terms was to include a cellphone in the package. Unable to find an appropriate handset provider, Huawei decided to manufacture its own device. In 2004, it established a device business unit. In 2006, a five-year contract made it Vodafone's only 3G phone provider in 16 countries, where Huawei 3G phone products will be sold under brand "Vodafone." Supplying a private label handset to telecom operators represented the majority of Huawei's handset business, but margins as an OEM supplier were being squeezed hard. Building a brand name mobile phone for the rapidly expanding global mass consumer market was increasingly the name of the game – and a game that Huawei wanted to play.

Huawei launched a value-priced, high-performance smartphone, marketed it as the world's most affordable smartphone, and sold it through the distribution channels of its mobile carriers. Huawei's goal was to "democratize" the mobile phone and make Huawei a household brand name around the world. Huawei designed its value-priced phones to appeal to cost-conscious buyers, predominantly young adult "social networkers" – the most lucrative market segment.[17] Available in several colors – black, yellow, blue, and purple – Huawei smartphones offered connectivity with up to eight devices (through a built-in Wi-Fi connection) for game-playing. Press releases and blog reviews highlighted additional functions such as voice dialing and navigation, apps running off the SD card, as well as 70,000 applications (running on Google's Android operating system). Seeking to raise its profile among consumers, Huawei opened several flagship stores in 2011 in China.

Huawei's main goal in developed markets was building top-of-mind brand awareness. To do this, the brand established a unique design identity on the consumer market. "If we are recognizable, as a Huawei phone, we can communicate with consumers directly and establish our brand name recognition," observed Hagen Fendler, Chief Design Director for handsets. Huawei announced its latest device at the 2012 Consumer Electronics

Show (the industry's big annual event held in Las Vegas). In 2012, thin was in. Whether it was flat panel televisions, netbooks, or smartphones, everyone was scrambling to make thinner devices. In response, Huawei unveiled a new flagship mobile phone, heralding it as the "world's slimmest smartphone." Measuring a mere 6.7 mm thick, the Ascend P1S weighs only 130 g.

The engineering also focused on the most important aspect in the design feature of the smartphone: the screen. The Ascend P1's screen went over the (front) edge of the phone, around to the back cover. The back cover was designed with special material to enhance the user's grip on the thin phone. According to Richard Yu, Chairman of Huawei Device, "The Ascend P1S demonstrates our ongoing commitment to innovating high quality devices that utilize the latest hardware and software technologies."[18]

Huawei Devices division staffed its research team in the US with employees who had previously worked for top American companies. In addition to its mobile phones, Huawei's value-priced tablet PCs sales (which began with the launch of the IDEOS S7 in the US, Australia, and Europe in 2010) were expected to build brand awareness as consumers welcomed an alternative to Apple's iPad. Huawei billed its S7 as a "next-generation" device, at less than half an inch deep with 720p HD video playback, Bluetooth, Wi-Fi, and 3G connectivity, all for under $300.

Huawei is striving to rank among the top three global brands for mobile phones by 2015, according to Huawei Device CEO, Wan Biao. Huawei is considering developing its own smartphone operating system in order to distance itself from Android. Wan Biao explains: "We're also devoting resources into coming up with a phone operating system based on our current platform in case other companies won't let us use their system one day."[19]

In 2011, Huawei consumer business contributed 22 percent to overall revenue and grew at 44 percent. Huawei expects to sell 60 million smartphones in 2012, versus the three million sold in 2010.[20] In 2012, *Bloomberg BusinessWeek* proclaimed, "The

New Smartphone Powerhouse: Huawei."[21] The usually staid *The Economist* asked, "Who Is Afraid of Huawei? Security Threats and China's New World-Beater."[22] And in the world's largest smartphone market – China – Huawei is ahead of Apple.

Huawei has joined ZTE, another Chinese company, in the handset business. ZTE also started out as a contract manufacturer, but has become the fourth largest handset-maker in the world by volume. ZTE initially sold its cheap phones unbranded to telecom operators. Over time, ZTE evolved the model. By 2012, more than 80 percent of its handsets shipped overseas were either as ZTE-only or ZTE-plus-operator brand.[23] While it sold the ZTE-only branded handsets mainly in emerging markets, its managers informed us of their global brand ambitions. The ultimate target: the more lucrative North American and Western European markets.

MANAGERIAL TAKEAWAYS

Managers of business marketing firms that seek to move into global consumer markets can follow this general approach to brand-building:

- Run a profitable B2B business that throws off enough cash to invest in end-user insights, R&D, and product development.
- Set up an effective R&D network to develop products for end users, potentially through joint innovation centres with customers (e.g., HTC) and ultimately a globally located network (e.g., Galanz and Huawei).
- Operate a dual model of being both an OEM (private label supplier) to major brands from the developed world as well as selling its own brand, with the ultimate objective of exiting the former business (e.g., HTC, Galanz, and Huawei).
- Get co-branding on the OEM and private label sales (e.g., "Intel Inside") to build low-cost awareness for the brand with end users.

- Link the organization's core competencies to an unmet B2B or B2C need as Galanz did with microwaves, HTC did with Android handsets, and Huawei did with phones.
- Develop and launch the consumer brand initially in the domestic market before going to international markets. Domestic competition strengthens branding capabilities at lower cost.
- Enter "softer" markets (domestic versus international, emerging versus developed markets) to hone the organization's branding skills before moving to advanced countries.
- Launch major marketing campaigns to build brands only on the back of unique products.
- Confront the organization's business model and how the B2B model differs from the B2C model so as to plot the transformation needed.

THREE

THE DIASPORA ROUTE

FOLLOWING EMIGRANTS INTO THE WORLD

The word *diaspora* comes from Greek διασπορά, meaning "scattering, dispersion." It is "the movement, migration, or scattering of people away from an established or ancestral homeland."[1] As professors based in London and Chapel Hill, North Carolina, we belong to the Indian and the Dutch diasporas, respectively. We are among 215 million first-generation migrants around the world, roughly 3 percent of the world's population. If migrants formed a nation, it would be the world's fifth largest between Indonesia and Brazil. The numbers of second-generation migrants are even greater.

People have migrated from their homeland to other parts of the world at least since the Greeks and Phoenicians started to establish colonies overseas around 1000 BC. And business has followed. Traders regularly sold goods to their diaspora, ranging from Phoenician vases in North Africa, to European furniture in the Americas. The international expansion of banking giant HSBC

– founded in Hong Kong in 1865 to finance the growing trade between China and Europe – followed the Chinese diaspora around the world.[2] While catering to the diaspora is an old practice, companies can now harness the purchasing power of emigrants more effectively than ever before.

Why? First, there is greater financial power in the numbers. Over the past 20 years, the number of first-generation migrants has grown by 40 percent. Over 30 million Chinese and 22 million Indians are scattered across every continent, while 32 million Mexican-Americans make up 10.3 percent of the US population. Four million Turks live in Germany, and 1.5 million Japanese live in Brazil. In the past, migrant groups were often among the poorest in a society. Today, the median income of Indian-Americans, Chinese-Americans, and Vietnamese-Americans is $90,528, $67,331, and $53,579 respectively compared to an overall US median income of $51,222.[3] Forty-five percent of the students at UC Berkeley are Asian-American.

Second, the opening of India's and China's economies has inverted the importance of two of the world's pre-eminent diasporas – overseas Chinese and Indians – as desirable target markets for products from their countries of birth. Now that both countries have become economic powerhouses, the Indian diaspora connects India to global entrepreneurial talent and knowledge workers, and overseas Chinese individuals act as vital conduits between China and their various countries of residence.

Third, historically, sheer geographical distance between the home country and its diaspora complicated contact. If you migrated to another continent, your family did not expect to see you for decades. Not any more. Cheap air travel and nearly free telecommunications services such as Skype allow migrants to stay in constant contact with relatives and friends back home.

In theory, these developments render the diaspora quite viable for launching home-country products into the host country. In practice, success depends on the diaspora's mindset. If migrants assimilate, emulating host-country consumption patterns, life-styles, and brand preferences, they offer no prospects to be a potential foothold. On the other hand, if migrants desire to preserve elements of their home culture, its products, and its brands, they can provide not only a market opportunity in their own right, but also a beachhead to penetrate Western markets more deeply. So, using the diaspora depends on how migrants relate to both home-country and host-country cultures. Cross-cultural psychology helps us to understand migrant behavior, and to gauge the potential to leverage the diaspora in becoming a global consumer brand.

UNDERSTANDING THE DIASPORA

The culture in which people grow up plays an important role in shaping their self-identity. No matter where they live, people have a sense of themselves as, say, Chinese, Brazilian, Indian, or American. When a person moves from one culture (called the "home culture") to another (called the "host culture"), they modify aspects of self-identity in response to information about, and experiences with, the new culture. This process, commonly referred to as *acculturation*, involves changes that result from continuous and direct contact with individuals from the host culture.[4] Marketers can observe these changes in a host of domains, including attitudes, lifestyle, and values, as well as purchase and usage behaviors.[5]

In the past, observers deduced that the host culture absorbed migrants in a process called assimilation. Consider the "American melting pot":

> The fusing process goes on as in a blast-furnace; one generation, a single year even—transforms the English, the German, the Irish emigrant into an American. Uniform institutions, ideas, language, the influence of the majority, bring us soon to a similar

complexion; the individuality of the immigrant, almost even his traits of race and religion, fuse down in the democratic alembic like chips of brass thrown into the melting pot.[6]

Social scientists long viewed acculturation as a unidimensional process in which migrants progressively resembled the dominant culture of their new country. More recently, however, more sophisticated research has revealed reality to be considerably more complex: some people cling to their home country, others straddle cultures physically, linguistically, and behaviorally, and some relinquish both home and host culture altogether. Why? Consider two basic challenges that migrants must confront.[7] One pertains to the maintenance of their own cultural distinctiveness in the host society. The other challenge refers to their willingness to affiliate themselves with the host culture. The migrant must decide (1) whether their original cultural identity and customs are beneficial or detrimental to prosperity in the host country, and (2) whether to participate in the host-country's customs, to what extent, and for what purpose. Combining a migrant's responses to these questions, we get four modes of acculturation (Figure 3.1).[8]

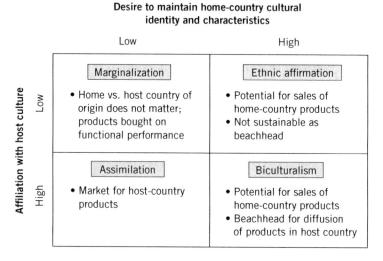

Figure 3.1 **Modes of acculturation for the diaspora**

Assimilation refers to the process by which the migrant dons the host culture while closeting his own, that is, blends in with the new culture. Assimilators are disinclined to keep old customs and are adverse to purchasing products from their homeland because they would stand out again. In fact, these migrants are prone, perhaps hyperprone, to purchase host-country brands, as an affirmation of the host's culture. For example, some Korean-Americans show higher ownership of American products than Anglo-Americans; in another study, some Mexican-Americans consumed more host-country breakfast products (high-sugar dry cereals and packaged pastries) than Anglo-Americans did.[9]

Then there are those migrants who believe – and whose marginal economic and educational opportunities reinforce this belief – that society in general has marginalized them. Cultural *marginalization* often goes hand in hand with economic marginalization. They are frequently relatively poor, and neither home nor host culture factors into their purchase decisions; instead, they weigh affordability and functionality. Home-country firms can sidestep these two diaspora segments – assimilators and the marginalized – and instead target the other two segments, *ethnic affirmers* and *biculturals*, both interesting prospects for products and services from emerging markets.

ETHNIC AFFIRMERS

The opposite of assimilation is *ethnic affirmation*. These migrants consciously separate themselves from the host culture and think little of – even reject or deride – its lifestyles, values, products, and brands. Ethnic affirmers cling to their home culture, sometimes more fervently than its current residents do, as means of retaining their self-identity. It is a self-preservation mechanism for minorities among a dominant host culture. Migrants who affirm their ethnicity are an attractive market segment for home-country products. However, they socialize primarily with others from their own country, so they do not make for a tenable beachhead for home-country brands. In general, their behavior has limited social demonstration effects on the host country's native population.[10]

RELIANCE MEDIAWORKS

India's Reliance MediaWorks, a member of the Reliance Group, tapped the ethnically proud segment of the Indian diaspora in the US who affirm their ethnic identity by consuming cultural goods, most notably Bollywood movies.[11] Other groups may consume these goods as well, but Reliance targets people who look to affirm their ethnic identity. Most US cinema chains do not carry Bollywood movies; those that do often cannot offer an adequate customer experience given the mismatch between the cultural needs of an Indian audience and the profit demands of the largely American executive team. As result, Bollywood movies usually run in second-rung theatres and art houses.

In response to this consumer void, Reliance acquired local theaters in regions with a high Indian diaspora, rebranded them, and launched BIG Cinemas in 2008. Reliance purchased facilities from mom-and-pop operators and renovated them with new digital projectors and sound systems, computerized accounting controls, stadium seating, and concession stands of Indian food. Its theatres show Bollywood movies, regional Indian films in languages like Tamil and Telegu, as well as Hollywood movies.[12] (After all, many Hollywood movies have global appeal.) Reliance adjusts the mix of the films screened based on local demographics.

These theatres act not only as entertainment centers, but also as social points for Indian-American families. To upgrade the experience, Reliance has invested significantly in building new theatres and upgrading the acquired ones. In areas where the demand is really high, it has adapted its theaters to treat the South Asian diaspora with amenities. For example, a refurbished 12-screen multiplex in North Bergen, New Jersey, features a Bombay Café that serves such treats as samosas, *papdi chaat,* and mango *lassi*. Some of the other theatres have fully equipped kitchens to cook South Asian cuisine.

MAYBANK ISLAMIC

While ethnic groups are usually defined in terms of nationality and language, they can also coalesce around religion: Hindus and Muslims, Shiites and Sunnis, Catholics and Protestants. Islamic banks cater to those whose religious beliefs prescribe certain practices not supported by the host-country banking system.[13]

Based on the religious laws of *shariah*, Islamic finance is not allowed to charge *riba*, or interest, on securities.[14] Instead, it backs securities with tangible assets, and both borrowers and investors share the risk. Thus, traditional securities such as bonds and real estate investment trusts take the form of structured loans, leases, or risk-sharing contracts to become *shariah*-compliant. Islamic finance also cannot engage in such forbidden activities as gambling, liquor, tobacco, and financial services that profit from interest. In the last decade, Islamic banking has grown 15–20 percent a year globally, with Malaysia at the forefront. Worldwide, the Islamic financial market has crossed the $1 trillion mark, and some estimate it will grow to $4 trillion by 2020.

Clearly, Islamic banking differs dramatically from traditional Western banking, so it cannot serve everybody's financial needs. However, people who seek to adhere to the dictates of *shariah* will value its products. Malaysia's Maybank Islamic caters to this segment. Maybank Islamic is currently the largest Islamic banking player in the Asia Pacific, and its products are fully *shariah*-compliant. Maybank Islamic has expanded not only to other Muslim countries, such as Indonesia and Bahrain, but also to countries where Muslims form a minority, including Singapore, Hong Kong, Philippines, and the United Kingdom.

Islam and other religions also prescribe strict diets, and businesses have sprung up to serve those religious requirements. For example, all food products of the Pran-RFL Group are halal certified and comply with Islamic dietary guidelines. Founded in 1980 in the city of Dhaka, Pran-RFL Group is Bangladesh's largest food and nutrition company and the largest exporter of processed agro products (under the Pran name), which reach more than 80 countries. The company told us they love the Bangladeshi diaspora, who are critical in their success.

BICULTURALS

As we noted, ethnic affirmers are great targets but not beachheads for home-country products, because they do not mingle much with the host-country natives. Migrants who exhibit biculturalism are more promising beachheads because they try to accommodate both home and host cultures. These people have a sense of belonging in two cultures without compromising their cultural identity. They can alter their behavior to fit a particular context, and they integrate elements of both cultures into their behavioral repertoire.[15] For example, one study among Indian-Americans found that many preferred Indian food and dress at home but American food and dress outside the home, often referred to as *situational ethnicity* by sociologists.

Biculturals are the best diaspora prospect for emerging market firms. Compared to ethnic affirmers, they are typically better educated, have higher socioeconomic status, income, and self-esteem, and are more integrated in the host-country social networks. They also have more local friends and higher participation in host-country organizations and clubs. Moreover, their social relations with host-country natives make them promotional conduits to the wider population.

ICICI BANK

The Industrial Credit and Investment Corporation of India (ICICI), a leading Indian bank, has successfully used the bicultural diaspora to expand internationally.[16] It observed that as much as

10 percent of its global remittances came from the Indian diaspora, who typically paid excessive fees to Western Union or other
wire transfer services. ICICI initially leveraged its relationships
with banks in the Middle East, where it could offer a large Indian
worker population a new low-cost remittance service. ICICI
launched comparable services through subsidiaries in the UK,
Russia, and Canada; branches in the United States, Singapore,
Bahrain, Hong Kong, Sri Lanka, Qatar, and Dubai; and representative offices in the United Arab Emirates, China, South Africa,
Bangladesh, Thailand, Malaysia, and Indonesia. By engineering
cheaper and better remittance products, ICICI encouraged existing
customers in India to keep their deposits in the bank, thereby
providing an inexpensive source of capital for the bank to develop
and to cross-sell higher value products such as mutual funds and
other India-based investment services.

Consumers liked these innovations – and told their friends.
ICICI was signing up not just members of the diaspora, but also
non-Indians in countries like Canada, where Indians are well integrated into society. According to Lalita Gupte, managing director
of ICICI, "The idea of using the diaspora as a beachhead to enter
a new market had proven viable."[17]

To diffuse further from the diaspora to the general population,
ICICI in the UK launched a marketing program where, if a
customer refers a friend, the customer gets a calling card with 500
free minutes to India, a promotion aimed squarely at friends and
families of the Indian diaspora.

These activities began to show up in ICICI's performance.
With revenues of 44 billion rupees, foreign operations now
account for 11 percent of ICICI's total revenue. Total deposits
grew fivefold from 482 billion rupees in 2003 to 2550 billion
rupees in 2012. In the same period, net profit after taxes increased
from 12.1 billion to 64.7 billion rupees.[18] And in 2012, ICICI was
ranked at number 63 in BrandZ Top 100 Global Brands.[19]

DIASPORA AND REVERSE DIASPORA

Thus far, we have focused on how emerging market brands can use the diaspora to enter overseas markets. However, emerging market brands can also use what we call the "reverse diaspora." In a reverse diaspora, expatriates or tourists from the developed nations visit emerging markets and consume the brands there. They like the experience and want to replicate it when they return to their home country. That is how the Mediterranean kitchen (olive oil, pasta, tomatoes, zucchini, and so on) conquered Northern Europe in the 1970s and how Thai food has recently become popular in Scandinavia.

The reverse diaspora has provided a platform for the global expansion of the Mandarin Oriental hotel chain. Mandarin Oriental started with the opening of The Mandarin in Hong Kong in 1963, which soon built up a reputation for luxurious service. Western business people experienced its superb quality first hand and its fame spread. Our personal experiences reinforce this. In 1983, one of us visited Hong Kong with his father, who insisted on staying at the Mandarin Hotel because he had heard that it was the best hotel in the world. And indeed, it was! For the other author, despite visiting 60 plus countries, the Mandarin Oriental Bangkok is still his favorite hotel in the world. It is based on such guest experiences that Mandarin Oriental has subsequently expanded into Western Europe and North America. Today, it has hotels in such international business hubs as London, Paris, New York, Geneva, and San Francisco. Mandarin Tokyo is the first official six-star hotel in the world and has been voted the World's Best Hotel.[20]

Today, the brand is so strong that it proudly uses its name around the world. Originally opened as the Hyde Park Hotel in 1902, Mandarin Oriental Hotel Group purchased the property in 1996 and reopened it as the Mandarin Oriental Hyde Park, London in 2000. Its long-running successful advertising campaign astutely features both Western (e.g., Frederick Forsyth and Helen Mirren), and Asian (e.g., Sa Dingding and Lin Chiling) celebrity "fans."

The flow of people, especially from neighboring countries, is a two-way street. The emerging market of Mexico and the mature market of the US have an extensive border over which Mexican brands, especially in the beer industry, have exploited both diaspora and reverse diaspora effects to penetrate the US market, and subsequently go global.

MEXICO AND THE US

The US is home to the world's largest Mexican migrant community in the world. The 32 million Mexican-Americans comprise about two-thirds of all Hispanics in the US, and the total Hispanic community is expected to grow from 52 million in 2012 to 125 million in 2050. Mexican companies such as baker Grupo Bimbo, broadcaster Televisa, and beer brewer Grupo Modelo see this diaspora as hugely attractive. As Carlos Madrazo, head of Televisa's investor relations, has said, "The person who goes to the US still shows a preference for Mexican brands. The Hispanic market is very loyal."[21]

Beer is one product category for which the Mexican (Hispanic) diaspora is very important. The percentage of drinking-age adults of Hispanic ethnicity is expected to grow from 16 percent in 2010 to 23 percent in 2030, and beer is by far the alcoholic beverage of choice. US beer brands account for about 75 percent of the Hispanic market, helped by their size, massive advertising spending, and sizable segment of "assimilators." Despite these powerful incumbent marketing and cultural forces, Mexican brands have captured 25 percent of Hispanic beer consumption.

Recognizing that they can never match the overwhelming marketing budgets and clout of the US brands, brands like Modelo Especial, Tecate, and Victoria make overt appeals to Hispanic sensibilities. For example, Tecate (the fourth-largest import brand) has traditionally reached out to first-generation blue-collar Mexican-Americans with advertisements emphasizing immigration perseverance. Victoria beer avoids a head-on collision with US brands by pursuing a limited distribution strategy. It is only available in those US cities with a large Hispanic population. These are "conventional" diaspora examples. In contrast, Corona exploits the reverse diaspora.

Corona

The best known Mexican brand of beer, Corona, is the only brand from emerging markets in the Interbrand top 100 list of most valuable global brands. Its brand value even exceeds Heineken's. But how?[22] Grupo Modelo, the parent company of Corona, started exporting to the US in 1979, but initial sales were low, reaching only 800,000 cases in 1983. Then sales exploded, reaching 23.5 million cases in 1988.[23] What happened? Two words: spring break. In the 1980s, students from all parts in the US (but especially from Texas, Arizona, and California) traveled to the resorts of Mexico – for wonderful beaches, great weather, and low prices.

These vacations "were carnivals of excess: 24/7 drinking, wet T-shirt contests, dirty dancing, and sexual escapades, real and imagined." Corona, quite unintentionally, fitted well into this pattern of debauchery. It cost only $4 per case, and its distinctive, simple package design made it appear an authentic Mexican beer. A stroke of luck never hurts either. US students started to put lime in their long-necked Corona bottles, analogous to another favorite college ritual: licking some salt, drinking a shot of tequila, and sucking on a lime wedge.

As college students returned to campus, they sought Corona to relive the wild fun of Mexico. Then when the students entered their professional lives in major metropolitan areas, distribution followed. And why not? If anything, the contrast between the carefree college life and the stressful life of long work days made them prone to exaggerate the stories of Corona-steeped debauchery. Corona became the drink of choice among young professionals (called "yuppies").

The reverse diaspora was a windfall for Corona.[23] Corona's smart marketing campaign took maximum advantage of this opportunity by focusing its advertising campaign on pleasant memories of Mexico (its tag line between 1984 and 1987 being "Cross the Border"). Over time, through consistent advertising and marketing campaigns, Grupo Modelo established Corona's premium image. "Fun, Sun, and Beach" were guiding messages behind everything that Corona did in the US market. Most recently, in its Corona Beach Getaway campaign, Grupo Modelo has highlighted the fact that the beach is not necessarily a physical place, but a state of mind. But remember: while a company can opportunistically leverage the reverse diaspora effect once the ball gets rolling, as Corona has done, the initial reverse diaspora effect is more serendipitous.

Corona has complemented its success by emphasizing its roots among Hispanics. But its Hispanic campaign differs significantly from the campaign to the US Anglo population. This features the "Corona bleachers," a sort of a Greek chorus for beer-drinkers who remind acculturated Latinos of their roots. In one ad, the diaspora berates a man for touching a ball with his hands *como fútbol americano*. Says Jose Molla, co-chief creative officer of La Comunidad, Corona's Hispanic agency, "We are Latins – we kick the ball." Today, springboarding on its success in North America, Corona has a worldwide reach using Mexican sun and fun as the image, and raking in over $7 billion in sales annually.[24]

USING THE DIASPORA AS A BEACHHEAD TO BREAKOUT

ICICI and Corona demonstrate how companies have successfully employed a two-pronged diaspora-based strategy in their internationalization process. They start by catering to the demand of the ethnic affirmers and biculturals of the diaspora. Next, they use this foothold to launch the brand to the majority population. What are key conditions for using the diaspora successfully as a beachhead to conquer a majority population in the host country? We maintain that four conditions are critical to this process (Figure 3.2).

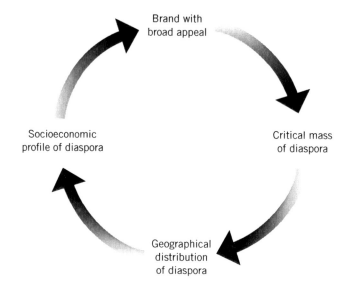

Figure 3.2 **Key success factors leveraging the diaspora**

BRAND APPEAL

The brand's product characteristics and cultural imagery should appeal to the mainstream population. Those home-country brands that fail to break out beyond the diaspora usually strike a negative chord or no chord at all with mainstream consumers. For example, even though Islamic banking prohibits investing in or financing the kind of instruments that contributed to the global financial crisis of 2007–09, the religious associations interfere with a wider receptivity of products that might have spared the main street population such pain.

Now compare the typical Bollywood movie to Western films. Bollywood plots tend to be melodramatic and formulaic, employing such stock elements as star-crossed lovers, disapproving parents, corrupt politicians, kidnappers, wealthy villains, long-lost relatives, sibling rivals, convenient coincidences, and lots and lots and lots of songs and dances.[25] Regardless of the movie theatre experience, the cultural world of these movies requires suspensions of disbelief beyond the cultural repertoire of most Westerners.

Emerging market brand managers must either find product attributes that connect with consumers outside the diaspora, or associate the brand with aspects of home culture that give it credibility, if not increase its appeal. For example, ICICI banks offer depositors high interest rates on their term deposits. So good is this offering that *Euro* magazine in Germany ranked ICICI first among 38 banks, and ratings agencies such as Moneyfacts in the UK named ICICI "Best Fixed Rate Account" provider in 2010.

CRITICAL MASS OF THE DIASPORA IN THE HOST COUNTRY

In military strategy, the most difficult and critical phase of invading an overseas country is gaining a beachhead. It must be easily accessible and sufficiently large for the invader to amass and organize its forces. Once the emerging market brand has secured a beachhead of sufficient size, it can then march into the hinterland. Best to come ashore where the diaspora, especially biculturals and ethnic affirmers, live and shop; they provide the easiest entry in the market. But the diaspora must be large enough to generate the sales volume required for operating control systems and processes, advertising, and other marketing investments. While the costs of marketing to the diaspora will be comparatively modest, reaching the mainstream population will require mass marketing activities, including expensive advertising and the building of distribution channels.

In evaluating the potential, rather than the absolute size of the global diaspora, it is more relevant to look at its size relative to specific countries. For example, while the global Chinese diaspora is about 50 percent larger than the Indian diaspora, with 1.5 million people, the size of the Indian diaspora in the UK is five times the size of the Chinese diaspora.[26] Similarly, the Mexican diaspora exists mainly in the US but is so large that Mexican brands have been very effective in exploiting it.

GEOGRAPHICAL DISTRIBUTION OF THE
DIASPORA IN THE HOST COUNTRY

Ideally, the diaspora should be regionally concentrated and nationally dispersed. Concentration of large numbers in a few geographical areas reduces market entry costs, a plus for companies with limited marketing resources. However, further expansion in the country is greatly facilitated by concentrated groups of diaspora people – especially biculturals – in other regions, situated like stepping stones. Nationally dispersed smaller groups of biculturals act as contact points or nodes through which information and product usage spreads in different localities to the mainstream population (Figure 3.3). This model has proven useful in understanding a wide range of phenomena, from the working of human memory to the retrieval of documents.

Pollo Campero, a fast-food chain from Guatemala, has over 50 restaurants in the US. Founded in 1971, it promises "A Taste of Latin America," blending spices from all over Latin America together "for an ensemble of rich, bold flavors that is uniquely us." In selecting the sites, it uses the geographical distribution of Hispanics across the US, focusing on areas with a heavy Hispanic population. It has 12 restaurants in Los Angeles, seven in New York, and four in Houston.[27]

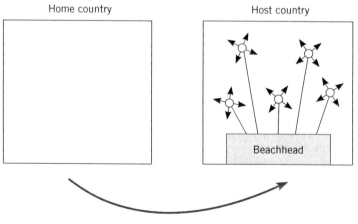

Figure 3.3 **Diffusion of the brand in the host country**

SOCIOECONOMIC PROFILE OF THE DISPERSED DIASPORA

Spreading activation works only if a substantial proportion of the diaspora kernels are biculturals. How can the company assess this? – by determining whether the socioeconomic profile of these diaspora members resembles that of the larger market. People tend to socialize mostly with people who are like themselves. Sociologists call this tendency *homophily*, the universal tendency of people to associate with others of a similar socioeconomic status.

Philippines-based fast-food company Jollibee used the principle of homophily when it entered the US market. It targeted relatively affluent Filipinos in California and used this base to reach the mainstream population. The Filipino diaspora in California was more favorable to spreading activation than that in Hong Kong, where the Filipino population consisted mainly of domestic workers with relatively lower status in the eyes of the mainstream population.

Another example comes from the Brazilian diaspora in Japan.[28] Brazilians love drinks based on guarana, an Amazonian red berry. Arco Iris offers the brand Cotuba – a fizzy, intensely sweet, caffeine-filled soft drink made from guarana. It began exporting Cotuba to the 300,000 members of the expatriate community in Japan and since then has expanded its appeal to native Japanese. Not a mean feat in a market described by Arco Iris' marketing director as "closed and nationalist." And at 380 yen for a 2-liter bottle, the product does not come cheap. It now uses its success in Japan to increase its appeal in the domestic market: with the new slogan: "Success in Brazil and in Japan."

One firm that analyzed its diaspora on the above four factors – brand appeal of the product, critical mass, geographical distribution, and socioeconomic profile – and determined that the diaspora could help its efforts to go mainstream in the host country is Dabur.

DABUR: FROM DIASPORA TO MAINSTREAM

Founded in 1884 by Dr. S.K. Burman, Dabur has become a leader in herbal, nature-based products. Its products derive from *Ayurveda*, the ancient Indian system of medicine based on natural and holistic living. The word *Ayurveda* comes from two Sanskrit words – *ayu* or life, and *veda* or knowledge – and addresses body, mind, and spirit. Set up originally as a manufacturer of herbal medicines, Dabur extended the principles of *Ayurveda* to personal care. It based its new product development on strong internal research and development, identifying plants with therapeutic power and combing through 3,000-year old *Ayurvedic* texts.

In the 1980s, Dabur cautiously started selling its products abroad, focusing on the Indian diaspora in the Gulf region. Many Indian migrants knew of Dabur as a brand and preferred its products. Internationalization accelerated after 2003. On the one hand, Dabur became more aware of international opportunities; on the other hand, it became more concerned about threats at home, as foreign packaged goods companies pursued "a piece of the action." Dabur CEO Sunil Duggal observed:

> People are signing blank checks to get a foothold and presence and scale in the Indian market. And I am worried that 80 percent of my business is in India. There is vulnerability, because at the end of the day, I am competing with multinationals, the big boys, in every category.[29]

In the international division, Dabur's key categories are hair oils, hair creams, shampoos, and toothpastes. Its international product portfolio revolves around two brands, Dabur and Vatika.[30] Dabur targeted the mainstream population in the host countries only after gaining ground with the local Indian diaspora, especially in the Middle East. Soon after selling its brands to the Indian diaspora in the Middle East, Dabur realized that its personal care products also appealed to many Arab women. And not surprisingly – after all, India and the Middle East have interacted for many centuries, as early as the fourth millennium BC.[31] More recently, Bollywood had associated Indian beauty care products with Indian film stars.

Dabur is now explicitly moving beyond the diaspora. Targeting the mainstream population in host countries makes eminent sense for Dabur. While host-country consumers are probably not familiar with *Ayurveda* per se, the interest in "natural" personal care and medicinal products is universal and booming. Moreover, people around the world have at least a vague notion of how old the Indian culture is. Using texts originating over 3,000 years ago has a mythical quality, as if consumption taps into a world of undiscovered secrets. Dabur's strategy is characterized by:

- a high level of localization of the supply chain, manufacturing, sales, and marketing to enhance flexibility and reduce response time to changes in market demands;
- leveraging a global preference for "natural" products among local consumers to increase the company's share in personal care categories;
- a product focus: Dabur's key categories in the international division are hair oils, hair creams, shampoos, and toothpastes;
- a brand focus: its international product portfolio is largely organized around two brands – Dabur and Vatika;[32]
- a geographical focus: the focus markets are the Persian Gulf countries, Egypt, Nigeria, Turkey, Bangladesh, Nepal, and the US.[33]

The combination of product, brand, and geographical focus has allowed a medium-sized company such as Dabur to give its brands some marketing punch in a world dominated by giants like

L'Oréal, Unilever, and Procter & Gamble. Duggal summarizes the three key ideas behind their international business initiatives:

- tailing the Diaspora as a means to generate business among the mainstream consumer;
- providing a geographical hedge against any possible disruption in the home market;
- leveraging our understanding of consumers and the supply chain in developing markets to build businesses there. In particular, Dabur's understanding of traditional trade channels in Africa is perhaps superior to that of many Western companies.[34]

In sum, Dabur possessed a value proposition that resonates with people beyond the Indian diaspora. And success followed. The overseas business has been growing at a compound annual growth rate of 32 percent since 2004, and international sales in 2012 accounted for over 30 percent of Dabur's overall sales of over $1 billion.[35] International growth has not hurt profitability either – in the same period, the margin for earnings before interest, taxes, depreciation, and amortization increased from 13.3 percent to 17.9 percent.[36] Presently, Dabur feels it has exhausted the diaspora potential for foreign market entry and it is now increasingly looking at market entry via acquisitions. Acquisitions as a route to global branding success will be discussed in the next chapter.

MANAGERIAL TAKEAWAYS

Applying cross-cultural psychology to the global branding strategy of emerging market companies, we have teased out key success factors for leveraging the diaspora in launching global consumer brands.

First, managers should gather and evaluate data on the four dimensions below to determine whether their brand will benefit from the diaspora strategy:

- *Brand appeal.* Will our brand's product characteristics and cultural imagery appeal to the mainstream population? Be wary of religious associations or cultural stereotypes.
- *Critical mass of the diaspora in the host country.* What is the size of the diaspora relative to the host country's overall population? Where is the percentage highest? What are the demographics of the diaspora within a country, and do a substantial number of these migrants fall into our target audience?
- *Geographical distribution of the diaspora in the host country.* Do members of the diaspora live in close proximity to each other and to points of distribution? In which cities or regions of the host country? Can we leverage word of mouth in these communities?
- *Socioeconomic profile of the dispersed diaspora.* To what extent do migrants associate with people outside the diaspora who share their socioeconomic status?

Second, implementing a diaspora-driven strategy works best when firms:

- segment the diaspora into four types – assimilators, marginalized, ethnic affirmers, and biculturals;
- target the ethnic affirmers as an attractive market and the biculturals as a beachhead, but ignore the other two segments;
- study tourism patterns and demographics at home to determine whether the number of tourists from a foreign country is substantial enough to leverage a reverse diaspora effect.

FOUR

THE BRAND ACQUISITION ROUTE

BUYING GLOBAL BRANDS FROM WESTERN MULTINATIONALS

Jaguars are the largest of the South American cats. In native language, *jaguar* means "he who kills with one leap,"[1] a description that fits such characters as James Bond and the winners of Le Mans, the world's oldest sports car race of endurance and efficiency. The jaguar figure fixed on the hoods of automobiles has become iconic and, for a time, was the world's most coveted automotive brand. No wonder Ratan Tata said that the Tata Group's chance to own the Jaguar brand was "irresistible." Overnight, for $2.3 billion, Jaguar came to belong to Tata Motors and India.

The previous three strategies – Asian Tortoise, business to business to consumer, and the diaspora play – are slow, deliberate approaches to building a global brand that require patience, perseverance, large investments, and a minimum of one or two decades, sometimes even longer. As a result, impatient firms and entrepreneurs from emerging markets opt to acquire an existing global brand from the developed world. Business leaders in China and India believe that they must achieve in 20 years what Western Europe and the United States have accomplished in the 200 years since the Industrial Revolution.

Historically, companies from developed countries bought brands and firms from developing countries. A recent report indicated that, in the 6,500 deals struck between 2006 and 2011, 78 percent of acquirers came from developed countries.[2] However, of the 194 deals that exceeded £1 billion, 41 percent of acquirers came from emerging markets.[2] The number of deals in which firms from emerging markets are buying assets from developed countries has increased at an average rate of 17 percent per annum since 2002.[2]

To determine who was acquiring whom, *The Economist* analyzed World Bank data: between 2000 and 2010, China led outbound cross-border mergers and acquisitions (M&As) deals from emerging markets, and the acquired firms were most frequently located in the US.[3] Clearly, China is exploiting the large trade deficit with US to buy American assets. China is investing aggressively elsewhere too. In 2011 alone, despite the continued Eurozone's economic crisis, China's investment in Europe reached $10 billion, up from less than $1 billion in 2008.[4] "A starved camel is still bigger than a horse," says Wang Hongzhang, Chairman of China Construction Bank, with RMB 100 billion ($15.8 billion) set aside in 2012 for foreign acquisitions.[5]

The Chinese state actively supports the rush to acquire assets overseas. Over the past decade, China's capital outflow has grown 10-fold, to about $60 billion in 2012, making it the fifth largest outward direct investor in the world. Given China's growth and its $3.5 trillion in capital reserves, experts estimate that the country's total foreign direct investment will range somewhere from $500 billion to $5 trillion by 2020.[6] If "Made in China" characterized the past two decades, "Owned by China" may characterize the next.

The numbers above include the activities of sovereign wealth funds (e.g., China, Dubai, Qatar, and Singapore), natural resource firms (e.g., Sinopec's acquisitions) and business to business firms (e.g., Tata Steel's buying Corus). This chapter spotlights global consumer brands for which separate data are unavailable. Instead, we have identified some of the developed world brands acquired by emerging giants over the past decade (Table 4.1). True, China initially focused on natural resources deals, but the "latest five-year plan contemplates a broader range of deals to acquire brands, strengthen market share and buy advanced technologies. Western companies will be on the shopping list more often."[7]

Table 4.1 **Examples of recent acquisitions**

Acquired (country)	Acquirer	Country of acquirer	Year of acquisition	Amount ($)
Heinz (US)	3G Capital/ Berkshire Hathaway	Brazil/US	2013	23.2 billion
AMC Entertainment (US)	Dalian Wanda	China	2012	2.6 billion
Weetabix (UK)	Bright Foods	China	2012	1.2 billion
Putzmeister (Germany)	Sany	China	2012	525 million
BEA (US)	LCBC	China	2012	140 million
Ferretti (Italy)	Weichai Group	China	2012	228 million
Aquascutum (UK)	YGM Trading	China	2012	24 million
Saab (Sweden)	Pang Da and Youngman	China	2011	100 million
Volvo (Sweden)	Geely	China	2010	1.8 billion
MG Rover (UK)	Nanjing Automobile	China	2005	87 million
IBM PC Business (US)	Lenovo	China	2004	1.75 billion
Thompson (France)	TCL	China	2003/2005	211 million
Ritmüller (Germany)	Pearl River Piano Group	China	1999	Unavailable
Gieves & Hawkes (UK)	Trinity Ltd	Hong Kong	2012	51.7 million

Acquired (country)	Acquirer	Country of acquirer	Year of acquisition	Amount ($)
Sonia Rykiel (France)	Fung Brands	Hong Kong	2012	Unavailable
Cerruti (France)	Trinity Ltd	Hong Kong	2010	70 million
Pringle (UK)	Fang & Sons	Hong Kong	2000	8.8 million
Escada (Germany)	Mittal	India	2009	Unavailable
Jaguar/Land Rover (UK)	Tata Motors	India	2008	2.3 billion
Whyte & Mackay (UK)	United Breweries	India	2007	1.2 billion
Aston Martin (UK)	Investment Dar	Kuwait	2007	960 million
Eight O'Clock Coffee (US)	Tata Coffee	India	2006	220 million
Pierre (US)	Taj Hotels	India	2005	50 million
Tetley Tea (UK)	Tata Tea	India	2000	450 million
Sara Lee (US)	Grupo Bimbo	Mexico	2010	959 million
Valentino (Italy)	Qatar	Qatar	2012	858 million
Harrods (UK)	Qatar	Qatar	2010	1.5 billion
Orascom/Wind (Italy)	VimpelCom	Russia	2011	24.8 billion
Miller (US)	SAB	South Africa	2002	5.6 billion

THE RATIONALE FOR ACQUIRING GLOBAL BRANDS

A few decades ago, who would have imagined that firms from emerging markets would acquire such Western brands as IBM's Think Pad, UK cereal maker Weetabix, the very British Jaguar and Land Rover, Swedish Saab and Volvo, London's Harrods, or the quintessential US company Heinz? Acquiring existing global brands has always taken less time and money than building new global brands. So why did these emerging market giants wait so long to buy?

The most important driver is economic growth. Firms in rapidly developing economies, especially China and India, grew at unprecedented rates. Even during the height of the Industrial Revolution, the United Kingdom did not sustain annual growth rates close to what we have witnessed over the past four decades in China and the past two decades in India. Increased demand from these massive countries has upped the prices of natural resources. The ensuing natural resource boom has benefited other economies – Brazil, Russia, Indonesia, and countries in the Middle East and Africa that are rich in minerals, oil, or agricultural production. Riding on this growth, emerging market firms have grown larger, more profitable, and cash flow positive. This cash, combined with their recent access to global capital markets, is fueling their acquisition spree.

The collapse of the dotcom bubble in 2000–01 followed by recession in the West facilitated these acquisitions because Western asset prices have been relatively depressed over much of the new millennium. The sales and profits of many European companies with heritage brands slumped. For example, German Putzmeister was the world's biggest maker of concrete pumps until its sales fell from more than a billion euros a year before the crisis to €570 million by 2011. Putzmeister's assets now belong to Sany of China. Similarly, Mexico's Carlos Slim increased his stake in Dutch telecom Royal KPN from 9 percent to 21 percent by purchasing shares in the open market for less than the €8 a share that he had previously offered KPN.

Do emerging market buyers tend to overpay for their acquisitions?[8] Perhaps, from a Western or Japanese point of view.[9] American and European companies, inhibited by slow-growing home markets, acquire rivals primarily to grow bigger and to create efficiencies of scale. After every merger, executives identify synergies, create efficient processes, and reduce headcounts to decrease costs and enhance margins – the only way to boost profits in a slow-growing market. By contrast, emerging giants want unique capabilities. They buy these companies to gain complementary competencies – assets such as technologies, products, brands, or distribution networks, and capabilities like new business models and marketing and innovation skills – the value of which outweighs the high operating costs and stagnant domestic market (Table 4.2).

Table 4.2 **Two approaches to M&As**

	Traditional approach to M&As	**Emerging giants' approach to M&As**
Rationale	The aim of a takeover is usually to lower costs, although some companies use acquisitions to obtain technologies, enter niches, or break into new countries	The aim is to obtain new technologies, brands, and consumers in foreign countries
Synergy levels	The acquirer and the acquisition usually have the same business model. Even when a company takes over a startup, the approach to market is the same	The acquirer is often a low-cost commodity player, while the acquisition is a value-added branded products company
Integration speed	The buyer makes several changes in the acquisition soon after the takeover. It slows the quest for synergies thereafter	Integration is slow-moving at first. After a while, the buyer starts pulling the acquisition closer
Organizational fallout	High executive turnover and headcount reduction are likely at first. Culture clashes occur and productivity declines, but things settle down over time	Little interference, executive turnover, or headcount reduction occurs right after the acquisition. Although it is as yet too soon to tell, tensions could simmer over the long run and blow up
Goals	The buyer has clear short-term aims but may not have thought through long-term goals	The acquirer's short-term objectives may be fuzzy, but its long-term vision for the acquisition is clear

Source: Adapted from Kumar (2009); see Note 9.

Emerging giants can create some value from takeovers by switching to the low-cost resources and business processes in their home country. On the revenue side, emerging markets will increasingly absorb Western companies' output of technologically superior products, thereby generating post-acquisition growth. For example, Bright Foods of China attempted to acquire Western brands such as GNC, Yoplait, and Jaffa Cakes, before succeeding with Weetabix. Like many acquiring companies from emerging markets, Bright Foods dominates in its domestic market. With an extensive distribution network, the firm can leverage this distribution to introduce Western brands to Chinese consumers whose tastes are rapidly changing. Ultimately, this process may also work in the reverse as Pan Jianjun, Bright Food's spokesperson, said, "We hope to introduce China's dining culture to the world."[10] In other words, Bright Foods may introduce its domestic brands such as Dabaitu toffee and Maling canned meat to Western consumers via the distribution channels of the acquired firm, thus changing slow-growing acquired companies with low margins into fast-growing, high-margin enterprises after their acquisition.

RETAIN OR MIGRATE?

If you grow organically, you can wait for value to increase over time. If you grow through acquisitions, you pay a premium to acquire foreign brands. One manager told us during a personal interview, "The money paid for that goodwill stares you in the face all the time you look at the balance sheet. You need to create value real fast, which increases the chances of a failed acquisition." In the final analysis, what a firm paid for an acquisition matters far less than what the acquiring firm does with its acquisition. Specifically, should the emerging market company retain the acquisition as a separate brand in its brand portfolio or merge it into a single brand?

In the vast majority of cases, the acquiring firm retains the brand from the developed country for its unique brand positioning and especially its association with the developed world. Several of its features distinguish it from the acquirer's own brand or brands. The acquired brand remains a standalone when, compared to the acquirer's existing brand, it:

- is strong in different regions and channels;
- is reaching different customer segments;
- has a unique brand image and distinctive heritage;
- is substantially different in perceived positioning and pricing;
- suffers from few product overlaps.

If the post-acquisition strategy is to retain the acquired brand as part of its brand portfolio (e.g., Land Rover, Volvo, and Weetabix), the acquiring firm must develop a sound strategy to grow the acquired brand and to manage the synergies between the brands without losing their distinctive positioning. If the post-acquisition strategy is to merge the acquired brand with the existing brand (e.g., Taj Hotels and Lenovo), the acquiring firm must decide which brand to delete (the acquired or acquirer) and how to manage the brand migration process without losing too many of the existing customers of the brand being deleted.

ACQUIRE AND MIGRATE

For an emerging market firm acquiring a brand from a developed country, over time deleting the acquired brand and migrating its customers and capabilities to its own brand is a valid strategy under three conditions:

- The acquiring firm has considerable control because customers face substantial exit barriers, as with telecom operators where consumers are tied by contracts and have limited number portability, and with banking and retail industries where location is a key driver of the customer's brand choice.

- The acquirer believes that its own brand is stronger than the acquired brand from the developed country, as when Taj Hotels acquired hotel properties in Boston and San Francisco.
- The acquisition agreement or a strategic decision (e.g., economies of scope or desire to have a single global brand) mandates a discontinuation of the acquired brand and a migration of its business to the acquirer's brand. For example, Lenovo had the right to use the IBM brand logo for only five years under rather stringent conditions.

Of the three scenarios above, only the third is challenging. When the acquiring brand controls its clientele or is stronger than the acquired brand, the change in brand name takes place relatively swiftly after completion of the deal. However, instead of simply changing the name, the acquiring firm must bring over some new attributes or values so that customers view the change as more than cosmetic rebranding.[11]

If the goal is to migrate the business to the acquirer's brand and to discontinue the acquired brand, brand migration usually entails a three-part process that we call "maintain, link, build." Consider Lenovo, an excellent example of maintaining IBM's value, linking it to Lenovo's brand, and then building upon the business.

LENOVO–IBM

In 1984, Legend Holdings began with $25,000 and 11 computer scientists, to deliver information technology to consumers and businesses in China. In 2003, Legend began marketing its products under the Lenovo brand – a hybrid of the "Le" from Legend with "*novo*," the Latin word for "new." The company officially changed its name to Lenovo a year later. By 2005, Lenovo had revenues of about $3 billion and the financial power for a high-profile $1.75 billion acquisition of IBM's PC division that marketed the ThinkPad line of notebooks. At the time of the acquisition, IBM had a strong brand franchise in notebooks; Lenovo was, however, relatively unknown, especially in the largest market of the US.

As part of the deal, Lenovo acquired the rights to the ThinkPad brand and negotiated permission to use the IBM logo for a period of five years with increasing restrictions. Lenovo intended, over this time, to phase out and replace the IBM name with its own. Lenovo's marketing team managed this brand migration aggressively, allowing Lenovo to terminate its right to the use of IBM logo two years earlier than the agreement stipulated.

Figure 4.1 maps out the process that Lenovo used to migrate from IBM ThinkPad to Lenovo ThinkPad and become the world leader in personal computers. The challenge of "killing a brand" is keeping its consumers within the acquirer's own brand. Sales managers must maintain the present sales revenues while marketing managers create the future brand reality. As a result, after the acquisition, Lenovo had to maintain the momentum of the IBM ThinkPad sales, even though its ultimate objective was to disassociate with IBM and replace it with Lenovo.

In the PC industry, product life-cycles are short and new products are the lifeblood. In the "maintain" stage immediately after the acquisition, Lenovo had to ensure that the stream of great IBM ThinkPad products kept coming. Lenovo leveraged the IBM sales-force, IBM's strong relationships with corporate customers, and the IBM logo in all its advertising. Concurrently, Lenovo launched an extensive public relations campaign to introduce Lenovo in the general press in the Western world. During this phase, it closely monitored metrics on customer satisfaction, the brand equity of ThinkPad, sales revenues, and positive press mentions.

In the "link" stage, begun in 2006, Lenovo's objective was to strengthen the ThinkPad brand and to start linking it to Lenovo. Besides introducing new ThinkPad products, the company launched a major "ThinkPad Unleashed" campaign that included advertising at the Turin (Italy) winter Olympics and other Lenovo branded product launches. In fact, the four television spots that

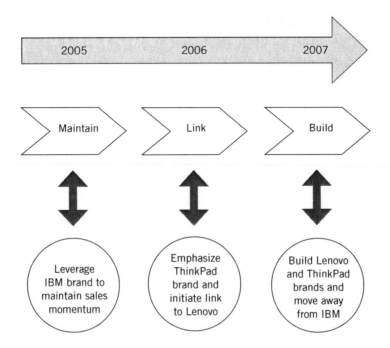

Figure 4.1 **Lenovo IBM ThinkPad migration**

ran during the Olympics never mentioned IBM, but the IBM logo appeared on the Lenovo ThinkPad laptops. Lenovo's metrics demonstrated that ThinkPad brand equity remained strong, and there was a growing awareness of the Lenovo brand. The firm was succeeding in communicating that Lenovo was improving the ThinkPad brand. The IBM brand played more the role of an endorsement brand.

In the "build" stage, starting in 2007, Lenovo launched the IdeaPad line of consumer-branded PC products and dropped the use of the IBM logo on all its products two years ahead of schedule. Lenovo used the 2008 Beijing summer Olympics to launch Lenovo as a global brand. While not as famous as Dell and Hewlett-Packard, Lenovo's revenues have increased 10-fold in seven years to $29.5 billion in 2012. Lenovo's net profits in this notoriously volatile industry stand at half a billion dollars. The Lenovo brand business has gone truly global. Lenovo's sales for the year ending March 2012 were split 42 percent from China, 42 percent from developed countries, and the remainder from other emerging markets.

Recent acquisitions have continued Lenovo's growth. In 2011, Lenovo formed a joint venture with NEC to create the market-leading PC group in Japan. As a result, Lenovo became the leader in two of three of the largest PC markets in the world (Japan and China). It also acquired Germany's Medion, its largest acquisition since IBM. Medion doubled Lenovo's market share to 14 percent in Germany, Europe's largest PC market, while giving it a 7.5 percent share of the Western European PC market.

Lenovo continues to look for local brands to acquire in Russia, India, South-East Asia, Eastern Europe, and Latin America. In September 2012, Lenovo agreed to acquire the Brazil-based electronics company CCE, thereby doubling its PC market share in Brazil. Yuanqing Yang, Chairman and CEO of Lenovo, said that the deal has laid the foundation for the company's "PC+ vision," including products such as tablets and smartphones.[12]

Beyond cost synergies and brand migration, Lenovo's acquisition of IBM's PC business also brought supply chain efficiencies: Lenovo expected these to save between $150 million and $200 million annually on procurement; and sharing best practices, consolidating vendor lists, increasing the use of standardized parts, and consolidating product lines would yield an additional savings of $10 million to $30 million.[13] Given the size of the acquisition, these are not dramatic.

But revenue enhancement primarily drives the acquisition strategy of emerging giants. Lenovo's big opportunity was selling its products through IBM's extensive distribution network, especially in the developed world. IBM PC operated in 160 countries across the globe, and ThinkPad had a very strong franchise in the enterprise laptop market. Sales of the combined group outside China after the acquisition were expected to be 72 percent of total sales, versus 2 percent for Lenovo alone prior to the acquisition.

ACQUIRE AND RETAIN

Emerging market giants acquire developed market firms for their complementary capabilities and brands. The acquired brand brings benefits that would take considerable time to build internally and with uncertain chances of success. As Figure 4.2 illustrates, a successful post-acquisition strategy would combine the complementary capabilities of the two brands and find a common glue that keeps them together. Therefore, acquiring firms face two major challenges post acquisition if they want to retain both brands (e.g., Geely *and* Volvo, Tata Tea *and* Tetley Tea):

- how to keep the two brands in distinct positions so that they reach different segments rather than just cannibalize each other;
- despite the distinctive positioning of each brand, how to drive synergies between the two brands, so that the acquiring firm is not simply duplicating costs across the value network.

Without distinctive positioning and operational synergies, why have two brands in the portfolio? Let us explore these dilemmas by contrasting the Geely–Volvo acquisition with the Tata Motors–Jaguar Land Rover (JLR) deal.

GEELY–VOLVO

The purchase by China's Geely of Sweden's Volvo for $1.8 billion was one of the most high-profile global brand deals in 2010. Volvo, a global upscale brand, sold about 450,000 cars around the world, generating $16.8 billion, or about $37,000 per car.[14] In contrast, Geely sold about 432,000 cars primarily in China and generated $3.2 billion, about $7,400 per car.[15] On paper, these brands appear to have complementary target customers – high end and low end – and harmonious strengths in different parts of

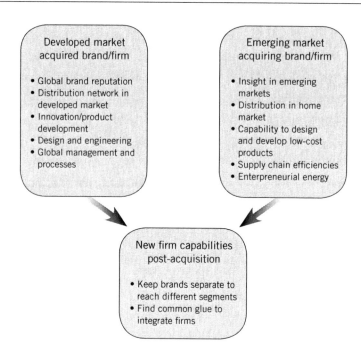

Figure 4.2 **Complementary brand capabilities**

the world. Volvo was not as successful in China as other upscale automakers such as BMW and Mercedes were, and Geely was struggling against foreign competitors in China. Furthermore, both companies sold fewer than a million cars annually, often considered the minimum efficient scale in the industry. But when we combine their sales, they approach a million cars sold.

Theoretically, if we examine Figure 4.2 and each party's strength, we might suggest this post-acquisition agenda. Volvo should (1) leverage Geely's insights into Chinese consumers to increase Volvo's sales and service footprint in China; (2) deploy and develop a more efficient global supply chain that taps into China to reduce costs; as well as (3) investigate whether Geely has low-cost product development capabilities to create China-specific Volvo models and entry-level Volvo models for the rest of the world. On the other side of the deal, Geely should use (1) Volvo technology, design, and engineering capabilities to improve the quality of its own cars; as well as (2) use Volvo's global management savvy and contacts with distributors to penetrate other parts of the world with the Geely brand. Finally, as Volkswagen did with its brands of Audi, Volkswagen, and Seat, both Volvo and Geely should find where they could combine product platforms, suppliers, and parts to lower costs without diluting the brands.

Yet, two years after the acquisition, press reports suggest that the integration is moving slowly. *China Daily* quoted an insider with knowledge of internal meetings, "I've never in my whole career seen such a huge gap between the management of the acquirer and the acquired company."[16] That the press reported these differences signals post-merger trouble. The *Wall Street Journal* reported that executives "are fully aware that it is easy to talk about technology sharing, but difficult to execute correctly."[17] Volvo saw the benefits as immediate and obvious for Geely, but wanted to ensure that sharing technology would not dilute the Volvo brand. In such cases, the more upscale brand in the portfolio usually wants to keep its distance from the other brands, while the more mass market brand wants to close the distance. The trick is to find the right distance between whatever distinguishes the brands for the two segments, and to integrate and rationalize the rest for scale and scope synergies. Ultimately, Geely and Volvo have the management talent to negotiate these challenges, but with how much organizational pain and brand damage?

TATA MOTORS–JLR

In contrast to Geely–Volvo, Tata Motors' acquisition of JLR has fared much better. When Tata bought JLR from Ford in 2008, most observers considered it an expensive purchase and doubted whether Tata, a mass market player, could manage upscale brands in developed markets. British commentators were skeptical. After all, Ford and BMW had previously failed in their turnaround attempts. Furthermore, Tata was seen as being primarily associated with buses and trucks. Its down-market passenger cars, like the Safari 4×4, were ranked among the worst cars in Britain. A *Daily Telegraph* columnist argued: "So what, apart from cash, can the Indians bring to the party? With the best will in the world, I can't think of a single thing."[18]

To make things worse, at the time of the acquisition, the demand for luxury cars was plummeting in JLR's two largest markets, Europe and North America. But the Tata Group had a long history of acquisitions including global ones. As a result, it knew how to manage Western firms and global brand portfolios. For example, it had acquired Tetley Tea in 2000 and kept the Tetley brand separate from the Indian brands (e.g., Tata Tea, Chakra Gold, Kanan Devan, and Gemini) in its portfolio. As is Tata's custom, its executives preserved JLR's existing management team, adding few executives from India. Of course, Tata worked hard to reduce JLR's costs. The automobile unions agreed to much-needed labor flexibility in pay and work schedule. Tata also invested £7.5 billion over five years, with over £1 billion drawn from the general group's resources, which has been subsequently repaid. Phil Popham, global operations director for JLR, observed: "The acquisition has worked because the investment has been carefully targeted and effective."[19] Over the past two years, the workforce at the Halewood plant in UK trebled to 4,500 as new models came online and increased sales.[20]

The declining demand in traditional mature markets prompted JLR to focus heavily on China. The division's percentage of sales from China grew from around 5 percent in 2005 to 17 percent in 2012. To avoid China's steep tariffs, JLR is planning to build its first factory there. It already assembles Land Rover's Freelander from kits in India, and is exploring the same in Brazil. To protect the cherished heritage of the brands, Tata is maintaining their connection with the UK. In many ways, JRL is now where Mercedes and BMW were some years ago, when they started manufacturing in the US but worked to maintain the "German-ness" of their cars.

Four years after the acquisition, the Jaguar and Land Rover brands were flourishing. Sales for the year ending 2012 reached around $22 billion, with profits of almost $2.5 billion, a remarkable turnaround for a firm that, in 19 years under Ford ownership, reportedly accumulated losses exceeding $10 billion.[21]

MANAGING ACQUISITIONS AS A LEARNING CAPABILITY

Acquisitions and mergers are always challenging. Even though this book focuses on brands and not M&As, the acquisition of a global brand brings with it the challenges of successfully integrating not only the acquired brand, but also the acquired firm, especially when the culture of the acquiring firm differs from that of the acquired firm. Learning how to integrate acquisitions from other cultures takes time.

When compared to their Chinese counterparts, Indian firms like Tata have much greater experience managing brands, brand portfolios, and the integration of foreign companies. More importantly, Chinese firms are still learning to manage employee diversity. In this respect, companies from other emerging markets such as India, South Africa, and Brazil benefit from private sector credentials, a lower language barrier, and a more cosmopolitan culture.[22] Acquiring firms should not underestimate these softer facets. Many M&As look good on paper but fail because the corporate cultures clash and the best and the brightest of the acquired firm leave.

Our visits to Lenovo in China reinforced the view that its success with acquisitions is because it has evolved to become quite "unChinese."[23] English is now the official language of the firm. Two foreigners were tried as chief executives before a Chinese national was installed in 2009 to turn around the firm's profitability. The performance culture of Lenovo makes it less political and hierarchical than a typical Chinese firm. More impressively, meetings and executives are rotated between the two headquarters of Beijing and Morrisville (North Carolina).

In contrast, TCL Corporation was one of the first Chinese companies to acquire major European and American brands. In the early 2000s, it entered the European and US markets by acquiring Thomson's TV business and Alcatel's mobile phone business. Why? The hope was to obtain brand recognition, clients, technology, and the manufacturing facilities associated with them. But integrating the two organizations did not proceed smoothly as Chairman and CEO, Li Dongsheng explained:

> In retrospect, we did get what we wanted, but with a price that was much higher than we expected. We were not prepared for the challenges in terms of management, resources, and experience; we were not able to manage the risks associated with them.[24]

TCL could easily have folded up shop, but – like many Chinese firms – it endeavored to master the globalization and branding game. TCL's globalization went through four phases including some untimely brand acquisitions.[25] In the first stage, between 1999 and 2002, TCL stayed close to home: it acquired Lu Shi in Hong Kong and entered the Vietnamese market. In the second stage, between 2002 and 2004, TCL acquired GO (US), Schneider (Germany), Thomson (France), and Alcatel (France) to become the largest television manufacturer in the world. In the third stage, between 2005 and 2006, integrating the acquisitions resulted in significant losses. Consequently, TCL adjusted its globalization strategy to increase product quality and control over the global supply chain. In 2011, when Japanese manufacturers such as Sharp, Sony, and Panasonic were struggling with losses in their television business, TCL was profitable. Now in its fourth phase with sales approaching $10 billion in 2012, TCL says it is striving to build TCL into the "most creative brand in China in ten years."

As Chinese firms gain experience in M&As, one observes that they are getting smarter at it. At Bright Foods, which has completed four major acquisitions in three years, they shared with us their five relatively simple questions for evaluating a target firm:

1. Is the target in our main business area?
2. Can the company be integrated?
3. Is the price reasonable?
4. Is the company healthy and running well, with acceptable financial risk?
5. What is the quality of the management team?

While the questions may seem obvious, the more interesting part is a company's ability to walk away from deals that do not pass muster after having spent considerable time on them. For example, Bright Foods looked at an Australian sugar company that the target valued at $1.75 billion but Bright Foods valued at $0.75 billion. They walked away, as they also did from United Biscuits because of very high pension obligations.

Bright Foods also recognized, after buying a French wine merchant, a dairy company in New Zealand, a food producer in Australia, and most recently Weetabix in the UK, that the cultural differences are large. Instead of trying to bridge the cultural chasm, they spend their integration efforts on developing a common vision to which incentive plans are aligned. This allows them to work together despite differences in cultural backgrounds and values.

MANAGERIAL TAKEAWAYS

The era of emerging giants as acquirers of Western brands and assets is here. Tata–JLR is a harbinger of the things to come. The *Financial Times* described this post-colonial turnaround story in the following unforgettable words:

An ageing dowager of an SUV brand (Land Rover) and an older gentleman who makes executive limousines (Jaguar), wards of a penurious uncle (Ford), are given a new lease on life by an Indian benefactor (Tata) who revives them.[26]

However, historical data on acquisitions, mostly on developed market companies, indicate failure rates of two-thirds. There may be reasons to expect that the failure rate for emerging giants may be lower since they do not search for traditional synergies or cost reductions, but rather for unique and proven capabilities. Still, they have the additional burden of cross-cultural acquisitions, which usually suffers from higher failure rates.

If firms grow through acquisitions, they pay a premium to acquire foreign brands and must create value very fast, but integrating cultures quickly is difficult and increases the chances of a failed acquisition. What can executives do to mitigate the chances of failure? Executives must ask themselves, "Should we retain the acquired asset as a separate brand in our brand portfolio or merge it with our own assets into a single brand?"

BRAND RETENTION

If we retain the acquired brand in our brand portfolio (e.g., Land Rover, Volvo, and Weetabix), we must:

- develop a sound strategy to grow the acquired brand and to coordinate its operations with indigenous brands without blurring their distinctive positions;
- establish guidelines for keeping the two brands in distinct positions so that they reach different segments rather than cannibalize each other;
- identify and drive operational synergies, so as not duplicate costs across the value network.

BRAND MERGER

If we merge the acquired brand with the existing brands (e.g., Mandarin Oriental Hotels and Lenovo), we must:

- decide which brand to delete (the acquired brand or our indigenous brand);
- manage the brand migration process without losing the deleted brand's existing customers;
- implement a three-part process, "maintain, link, build." This requires an acknowledgment of existing consumer connections, a transference of those emotional ties, and the introduction of new attributes or value rather than simply the announcement of a new brand name or design.

Most importantly, learn from every merger and acquisition. Document the problems and solutions of integration, retention, and migration. The more we study and reflect upon the process as a management team and an organization, the stronger and more likely the acquisitions capabilities will grow into a competitive advantage.

FIVE

THE POSITIVE CAMPAIGN ROUTE

OVERCOMING NEGATIVE COUNTRY-OF-ORIGIN ASSOCIATIONS

Some time ago, we held a seminar at a large emerging market car manufacturer. We began by displaying pictures of identical Volkswagen cars captioned as "made in Germany" and "made in Mexico." When we asked executives which of the two cars they preferred, the room filled with laughter. The German one, of course! Their own reaction summarized 10 slides of statistics, that the country of origin can be a brand asset – or a liability.

Marketing research has conclusively demonstrated that country of origin elicits powerful consumer reactions, the reactions depends on how the consumer views the country.[1] For example, over the last century, Germany has built an enviable global reputation for high-quality engineering and product reliability. In fact, in seminars around the world, when we ask the audience to indicate which country uniformly delivers superior engineering, the majority invariably respond, "Germany." Not bad for a country that was originally forced by Britain's Merchandise Act of 1887 to mark its products with "Made in Germany" as a sign of low-quality imitations of the British quality standard!

People automatically perceive German car brands and other highly engineered German products as "premium." Similarly, people associate France with style, fashion, elegance, and tradition, and these associations enable French wines, perfumes, skin care products, and clothing to command a premium. People no longer associate "shoddy" and "shabby" with Japanese goods. Instead, Japan has forged a strong reputation for process innovation and product quality. US companies benefit from universal perceptions of the United States as being innovative in technology (especially when creating entirely new product categories), creative in the arts, and trendsetting in consumer culture, with positive halo effects on lifestyle categories such as clothing and entertainment.

Table 5.1 shows the results of a survey conducted by the Japanese advertising agency Hakuhodo in six major cities.[2] The figures refer to the percentage of respondents in each city who perceive products from a particular country or region to have excellent quality and features. Some observations are that:

- there is a home-country bias – a country's own people perceive it more positively than foreigners do, especially on other continents;
- products from developed countries generally have a high-quality image;
- consumer perceptions lag behind reality; for example, independent testing agencies give high ratings to South Korea's consumer electronics and cars, but consumers themselves do not;
- products from the leading emerging economy, China, possess a poor quality image.

Numerous other studies corroborate Hakuhodo's study: emerging market brands generally suffer from a country-of-origin

Table 5.1 **Quality image of products made in various countries or regions**

	Seoul	Bangkok	Mumbai	Shanghai	Moscow	Frankfurt
1	Japanese (30%)	Japanese (54%)	Japanese (32%)	Japanese (50%)	Japanese (70%)	European (64%)
2	Korean (29%)	American (46%)	Korean (14%)	American (39%)	European (43%)	Japanese (39%)
3	American (19%)	European (34%)	European (14%)	Chinese (34%)	American (25%)	American (24%)
4	European (12%)	Korean (20%)	Chinese (13%)	European (27%)	Korean (15%)	Chinese (9%)
5	Chinese (3%)	Chinese (12%)	American (12%)	Korean (16%)	Chinese (1%)	Korean (8%)

Note: Data are the percentages of respondents that rate country/region producers as having excellent quality.

Source: Adapted from Hakuhodo (2008), see Note 2.

disadvantage. Hailing from India, China, or Russia generally decreases the brand's equity. Why? Why do consumers care about a brand's country of origin? Why do the images of countries differ so much? How does country-of-origin image affect consumer decisions? Most importantly, what can emerging market brands do to overcome their inherent country-of-origin disadvantage? This chapter addresses these questions, which are, in our experience, top-of-mind for the executives of many emerging companies.

COUNTRY-OF-ORIGIN IMAGE

Why do consumers care about a brand's country of origin when they can evaluate the product on its true merits and act accordingly? Because most consumers are either *unwilling* (because the incentives are low) or *unable* (because they lack the capabilities to analyze information) to evaluate a brand on its true merits. Instead, they rely on informational shortcuts or "cues" that in their perception reveal something about the qualities of the product.[3]

The most important cue is the product's *brand name*. Consumers understand that they reduce risk by purchasing a well-known, successful brand instead of an unknown brand. After all, a well-known brand has more brand equity to lose if it does not fulfill its promises. Think of all the advertising and promotion money wasted, let alone the future sales lost. A second very important market cue is the brand's *country of origin*. Country-of-origin image refers to the perceptions consumers have about products from the country associated with the brand. For example, Toyota, Volkswagen, and Hyundai represent Japanese, German, and Korean origins, even though they manufacture products beyond their own borders.[4]

In summary, when consumers are uncertain about product attributes, they rely on brand and country-of-origin perceptions to assess the product's attribute levels and to increase confidence in its claims. The reduced uncertainty lowers information costs and the risk perceived by consumers, thus increasing consumer value.

DIMENSIONS OF COUNTRY-OF-ORIGIN IMAGE

Although we might think simply in terms of a favorable or an unfavorable country image, country image is a multifaceted construct with six dimensions that influence the consumer's willingness to purchase products from that country:[5]

1. *quality*: reliability, durability, craftsmanship, workmanship;
2. *innovativeness*: use of new technology and engineering advances, pioneer of products, ideas, and concepts;
3. *aesthetics*: a well-designed, stylish, attractive appearance, pleasing to the senses, flair;
4. *prestige*: exclusivity, status, upper class, pride of ownership, heritage, sophistication;
5. *price/value*: low price, economy, value for money;
6. *social responsibility*: labor conditions, care for the environment, environmentally friendly production, safety.

Few, if any, countries rate favorably on all six dimensions. The country that comes closest is Germany; it is not known for low price, but it does not *have to* excel on price, given its strengths on all other image dimensions. For other developed countries, associations are more nuanced. For example, Italy generally rates high on aesthetics and prestige but not on quality, and the US excels on innovativeness but less so on some other aspects of image.

What differentiates developed countries from emerging markets is that *emerging markets tend to rate low on all aspects except price.* Even that is not an unambiguous strength. If quality falls short of consumer expectations, a low price will not mean high value for money. To illustrate this tension, Figure 5.1 contrasts the image of the largest emerging market – China – with the second largest developed market – Japan – among US consumers on six country-of-origin aspects related to quality (workmanship, reliability), innovativeness (technologically advanced), aesthetics (color and design), and price/value (value for money).[6] Even on the aspect with the strongest price connotation – value for money – Japan outperforms China. In light of such research, brand strategists have concluded, "One key challenge for ambitious Chinese brands looking to grow in Western markets is that the idea of brands from China still conjures up a one-dimensional image: Low Price."[7]

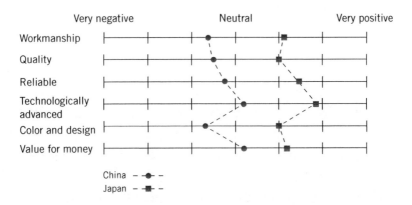

Figure 5.1 **Country image of China and Japan among US consumers**
Source: Adapted from Carter (2009); see Note 6.

WHY DO COUNTRY IMAGES DIFFER SO MUCH?

Why do the images of countries differ so much with respect to brands and products? A nation's image is gradually built over time. It results from a myriad of different influences, some of them idiosyncratic to a particular consumer's interactions with a country or its people. Rather than focus on specific differences, we identify four factors that generalize across consumers and give rise to a relatively homogeneous image of a country: economic development, culture and heritage, governance, and people.[8]

ECONOMIC DEVELOPMENT

Economic development encompasses the standard of living, infrastructure, education system, healthcare system, and investment climate. By definition, developed countries rate higher on this dimension than emerging markets. The ability to manufacture products requires a certain level of skills and technology closely related to the country's level of economic development. More developed countries have more accumulated capital, better education, and superior research and development (R&D) facilities, all of which facilitate more advanced production processes. Consequently, a brand hailing from an emerging market usually connotes poorer quality to Western consumers.

CULTURE AND HERITAGE

A nation's ability to communicate its cultural assets – from history and language to art and natural beauty – fully, authentically, and positively affects consumers' perception. Claims must be valid. Are its buildings, products, and cultural monuments real or imitations? Claims that are not substantiated by reality can backfire as they will be associated with state propaganda. It reminds Western consumers of the Cold War days when dubious "accomplishments" of the Soviet Union or German Democratic Republic were frequently touted to the world's media.

Of all the countries in the world, France and Italy rate highest on this aspect with Western consumers. As a result, their products often sell largely on aesthetics and prestige in categories such as clothes, foods, and cosmetics. After conducting a survey, one brand consultancy put it thus, "France has history, culture, gastronomy, fashion, wine, landscapes – and timeless romance."[9]

GOVERNANCE

Government competence and fairness, political freedom, tolerance, a stable legal environment, freedom of speech, individual rights, and environmental concerns – all of these factor into consumers' perception. When consumers view a country as a place governed by rule of law, where people can live openly, where business can operate freely, and where institutions are trustworthy, the country's image grows stronger. The Scandinavian countries rate highest on this aspect.

Lack of good governance negatively impacts country-of-origin image. If the country suffers from lax enforcement of food and drug regulations or bribery of regulators, Western consumers will wonder whether its products might pose health hazards. China has suffered from highly publicized safety hazards, relating to both domestic and exported products, including unsafe construction, toxic toys, faulty tires, contaminated foods, and dead pigs in the Yangtze River. News reports of Chinese consumers going to great lengths to obtain foreign brands that are deemed safer, or even traveling to Hong Kong to buy infant formula feed, reflects negatively upon the country's image.[10] Indeed, China ranks 99 out of 113 countries on governance.[11] Chinese industrialists acknowledge their battle to change the global perception of China as the source of shoddy, possibly dangerous goods, from cars to infant milk powder.[12] It is actually in the best interests of the Chinese economy to enforce product safety and intellectual property rules more vigorously. Ultimately, it is the overwhelming majority of honest and careful manufacturers that are hurt more by these scandals.

PEOPLE

The reputation of a country's citizens for such traits as competence, education, openness, friendliness, and perceived levels of ethnocentrism, hostility, and discrimination all factor into consumers' perceptions, often reflected in stereotypes. National stereotypes are broad, consensually shared beliefs and judgments related to a country and its citizens.[13]

Stereotypes of other nationalities tend to be richer and more detailed (although not necessarily more correct) the closer that a consumer is to the foreign country, either geographically or culturally. While Chinese, Korean, and Japanese people see numerous differences among themselves, Western consumers tend to lump them together. Similarly, Middle Eastern nations may see few differences between Scandinavians, while Scandinavians see few differences between Syrians, Jordanians, and Egyptians.

This makes stereotypes about people from distant emerging markets shallow and not held with high certainty. As such, stereotypes of emerging markets on the part of Western consumers are more malleable, subject to strategies to alter them.

THE ROLE OF COUNTRY OF ORIGIN IN CONSUMER DECISION-MAKING

How does country-of-origin image affect consumer decisions? Brands associated with a favorable country-of-origin image do not necessarily command higher consumer preference. In fact, the role of country-of-origin image in consumer decision-making is complex and nuanced. Figure 5.2 identifies the key conditions under which country of origin plays a larger or smaller role. These factors are economic development (developed versus emerging markets), consumer knowledge of and involvement with the product category, consumer animosity vis-à-vis the country in question, and the product–country match.

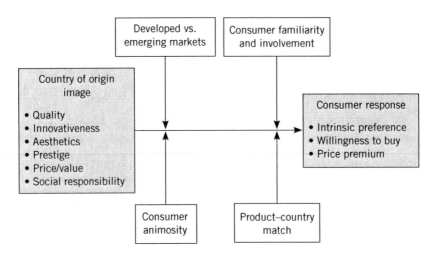

Figure 5.2 **The role of country of origin in the consumer decision process**

DEVELOPED VERSUS EMERGING MARKETS

For developed countries, the country-of-origin effect depends on the product category (e.g., Italy rates high for shoes but not for watches, while the reverse is true for Switzerland). For emerging markets, the country-of-origin image is universally negative – that is, the image of a country does not differ much between product categories (e.g., Pakistan rates low for shoes and watches). However, the negative image of emerging markets weighs more heavily (1) in categories with a high probability of product failure, and (2) for weak brands than for strong brands. Unfortunately, most emerging market brands still have low brand equity.

CONSUMER KNOWLEDGE AND INVOLVEMENT

The effect of country-of-origin information on consumer decisions systematically depends on the consumer's degree of knowledge of and involvement with a product category.[14] Although they are related concepts, there is a subtle difference: knowledge deals with the *ability* of consumers to process detailed product-related information, while involvement deals with the *motivation* to process detailed product-related information.

Product knowledge

Consumers with poor knowledge of the category have difficulty evaluating brands on their actual merits and will more likely use country of origin to infer product performance. For example, a consumer may know little about washing machines. When purchasing one, he may prefer a German brand because of his belief that German products are of high quality. The German appliances brand Bosch understands this when it emphasizes in its advertising: "The #1 Kitchen is German-Engineered."[15] Conversely, knowledgeable consumers are less affected by the country of origin of the brand as they are more capable of comprehending and weighing the technical specifications of brands of various washing machines more or less independently of the country of origin.

Product involvement

Product involvement refers to the general level of interest in and perceived relevance of the product category based on the consumer's needs, values, interests, and ego structure. Highly involved consumers are more motivated to exert the necessary cognitive effort to evaluate all available information, while less involved consumers will base their evaluation more on salient and readily accessible information cues, such as country of origin. Thus, for less-involved consumers, country-of-origin image will have a greater effect on product evaluations than it will for highly involved consumers.

CONSUMER ANIMOSITY

Consumers may hold strong emotions or feelings toward a specific country. For example, many Jewish people around the world feel a strong connection with Israel and prefer to purchase Israeli brands beyond what quality dictates. Anglophiles have an intrinsic preference for everything British that supersedes rational quality considerations. More often though, when people have strong feelings toward other countries, those feelings are hostile rather than friendly.

Consumer animosity – the anger deriving from historical or ongoing political, military, economic, or diplomatic events – profoundly influences consumer behavior.[16] This animosity does not drive product attribute judgments. Rather, consumers separate their anger towards a country from their assessment of that country's products. These people may very well acknowledge that the reviled country can produce high-quality products – but will not buy them. For example, many Jews still will not buy German cars because of the Holocaust. US brands suffered in the aftermath of the 2003 Iraq invasion: in 2004, Coca-Cola sales in Germany declined by 16 percent, while Marlboro sales in France and Germany declined by 25 percent and 19 percent, respectively.

One of the best documented cases of consumer animosity relates to Chinese feelings toward Japan after the Japanese occupation and Nanjing massacre, which is accentuated by Japan's lack of willingness to acknowledge these crimes. Animosity toward Japan shapes Chinese buying decisions, regardless of the perceived quality of Japanese products.[17] For example, analysts blame the large drop in Chinese sales for Japanese companies such as Nissan (–35 percent from a year earlier), Honda (–41 percent), and Toyota (–49 percent) on a September 2012 dispute over a group of uninhabited islands (known as the Diaoyus in China and the Senkakus in Japan).[18] One influential blogger wrote, "Recommended actions: Make no missteps, absolutely do not buy Japanese products, not even those that were designed in Japan."[19] The financial markets correctly anticipated the adverse effects as the stock prices of Honda, Nissan, and Toyota declined by 7.3 percent, 10.3 percent, and 3.1 percent, respectively, between 12 and 26 September.

A recent study has documented the animosity effect on PC sales.[20] Figure 5.3 shows the quality perceptions related to PCs from different countries of origin among Chinese consumers. The perceived quality of Japanese PCs is second only to that of American PCs. Without animosity, we would normally assume that this should translate into a high preference for Japanese PCs. However,

Japanese PCs garner a lower intrinsic preference than PCs from any other country (Figure 5.4). Consequently, their combined market share is negligible, at less than 3 percent. Improving quality is not the route to success – reducing animosity among Chinese consumers is. Note that the intrinsic preference for Chinese brands increases over time.

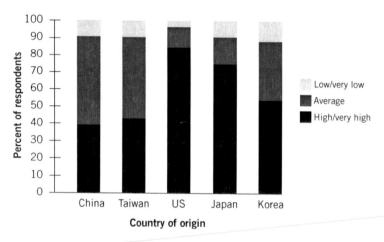

Figure 5.3 **Quality perceptions of PCs in China**
Source: Adapted from Chu (2013); see Note 20.

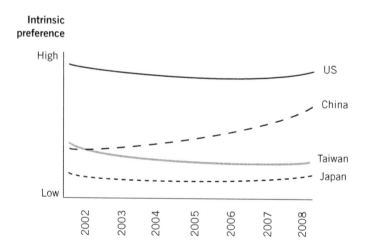

Figure 5.4 **Intrinsic preferences for country of origin in the PC industry among Chinese consumers**
Source: Adapted from Chu (2013); see Note 20.

Currently, consumer animosity hurts brands from developed market more than it does brands from emerging markets, most likely because developing countries have offended far fewer people in other countries. This state of affairs may change as emerging markets increasingly assert themselves both politically and economically.

PRODUCT–COUNTRY MATCH

A country may excel on some attributes, but these particular attributes may be irrelevant to the category in question. For example, consumers associate Italy with the good life (*dolce vita*) – a plus for foods but less so for cars, where choice rests on work-manship and engineering. In 2011, when Italian car-maker Fiat returned to the North American market after a 30-year absence, sales of its new Fiat 500 subcompact fell far short of expecta-tions. CEO Sergio Marchionne explained, "We thought we were going to show up and just because people like gelato and pasta, people will buy it. This turned out to be nonsense."[21] US consumers read the signs correctly. In the 2012 J.D. Power Survey of Initial Quality, Fiat finished dead last out of 34 brands on the US market.[22]

To understand the role of country-of-origin image in a specific product category, let's look at four scenarios (Figure 5.5).[23]

In cell 1, a country rates low on an unimportant product attri-bute. For example, Italy scores low on innovativeness, but innova-tion matters little in the beer category, where tradition and workmanship dominate. Thus, an Italian beer brand can ignore this aspect in its marketing strategy.

In cell 2, a country rates favorably on an attribute unim-portant to the category. Consider cosmetics, traditionally sold on prestige and aesthetics, an attribute of France. But Japan may leverage its high score on innovativeness to sell a market segment on the most advanced antiaging technology. Advertising should focus on analytical studies and laboratory research, rather than on prestige imagery. And indeed, it appears that Japanese

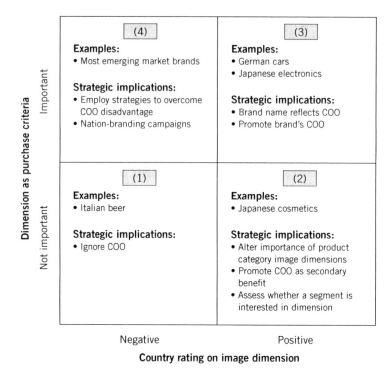

Figure 5.5 **Product–country match**
Note: COO, country of origin.
Source: Inspired by Roth and Romeo (1992); see Note 23.

cosmetics brands like SK-II and Shisheido pay significant attention to the science of cosmetics.[24]

In cell 3, a country rates high on an important attribute critical to a category. It is the ideal scenario for a brand in that category from that country. German car companies utilize brand names that reflect their Germanity and promote the brand's country of origin. Volkswagen does this adroitly. Its name is as German as can be (meaning "People's Car"), and in its foreign advertising uses German words like "Auf Wiedersehen, Sucka," "Fast as Schnell," and "Das Auto."

In cell 4, the country rates low on an attribute critical to a category – the worst situation for a brand in that category from that country. Unfortunately, emerging market brands find themselves here, where the negative rating extends to all country-image attributes (except price). Consumers around the world accept that a Western brand's country of origin may be a plus on some aspects, but not on others. For example, Japanese cars brands rate high on quality and innovativeness, but score lower on design than Italian cars, and on prestige than British cars. Not so with emerging market brands. Research has shown that, regardless of the product category, the brand is less attractive than its Western competitors.[25] *The Economist* summarized this situation: "One of the biggest challenges many Asian companies face as they globalize is the perception that Asian brands are inferior."[26] Of course, this challenge faces non-Asian emerging markets too.

OVERCOMING COUNTRY-OF-ORIGIN DISADVANTAGE

What can emerging market firms do to overcome this branding problem? Here we outline seven different strategies to confront the negative country-of-origin image:

- Disguise the origin in choosing the brand name.
- Confront negative associations.
- Focus on favorable "nuggets."
- Offer extra guarantees.
- Emphasize aesthetics.
- Utilize reverse-manufacturing.
- Invest heavily in marketing.

DISGUISE THE ORIGIN IN CHOOSING THE BRAND NAME

In its early period of international expansion, Japanese car-maker Nissan sold its cars under the Datsun brand name in Europe and the US because Nissan sounded too Japanese. Only in the early 1980s, after Japan's image had turned positive, did it rebrand itself as Nissan. Some emerging market brands have taken their cue from Nissan. Nothing in the name of TCL, Lenovo, or ZTE suggests that these brands come from China. In fact, their names are so nondescriptive that they could be from any country. This strategy can hurt too, as it is not easy to load nondescriptive acronyms with positive associations and emotions, a hallmark of strong brands.

Emerging market firms can go further by adopting foreign brand names. This strategy entails using, pronouncing, or spelling a brand name in a foreign language, such that the name triggers favorable foreign cultural stereotypes and influences product perceptions and attitudes. For example, the cosmetics brand Lasante suggests France, but it is actually Korean.[27] The piano brand Kayserburg uses advertisements with German phrases like "Klassik im Original" ("classic in the original") and "Klank der Welt" ("sound of the world"); but it comes not from Germany but from the Pearl River Piano Group. Similarly, fashion brand Stella Luna suggests Italy, but originates from China.

A variation on the foreign branding approach is to highlight that technology or critical components are sourced from developed markets. Germany is the country where piano-building started about three centuries ago. Pearl River Piano (discussed in Chapter 1) emphasizes the use of German components and German technology. On the inside of its Ritmüller pianos, one can read "Built with German Technology Fine Quality Piano for the World" and "Designed by L. Thomma."

To demonstrate the power of foreign branding over consumer perceptions, marketing professor France Leclerc and her colleagues conducted a series of experiments in which they compared French and English brand names.[28] They argued that French names invoke more aesthetic (hedonic) brand associations while English brand names invoke more utilitarian (performance and quality) associations. They chose two products for which aesthetic considerations were important (fragrance and nail polish) and two products bought on quality (foil wrap and gasoline). For each product, consumers listened to either English or French pronunciations of the same fictitious brand names, and rated the attitude toward the brand. They found that when the brand name was pronounced with a French rather than English accent, attitudes toward the aesthetic products were significantly more positive. In contrast, English pronunciation had an advantage for utilitarian products. These results explain why, in Europe, US cosmetics brand Estée Lauder markets itself using a French pronunciation rather than its English pronunciation (that is, *Estée Laudèr* rather than *Estay Lawdur*). The evidence from research is clear: using a foreign brand name is effective in overcoming bias against the country of origin of emerging markets.

CONFRONT NEGATIVE ASSOCIATIONS

For Fiat to convince Europeans or American consumers that Italy is a hotbed of engineering prowess is an uphill battle, to say the least. The attitudes and stereotypes of Italy and Italians are based on direct interactions, creative interpretations (e.g., movies), media exposure, and so on. Persuading consumers to change strongly held stereotypes is difficult. As mentioned previously, emerging markets are so new that consumers often have little knowledge, let alone a stereotypical view, of the countries in question. A recent study of Brand China concluded as much about China:

> Lack of information, or negative hearsay, about working practices and principles played a major part in why people either wouldn't consider buying Chinese brands or were unable to give a strong view ... The overwhelming picture for both groups is of lack of information.[29]

In such situations, strategies to confront and change negative attitudes have a decent chance of success. Ospop, the Chinese footwear-maker, combines humor and foreign beliefs about the poor working conditions in China. On the opening page of its website, Ospop presents a very different China:

> China is a nation of industrious, optimistic people creating opportunities for themselves and for their future. Here in the Middle Kingdom and all across the globe, people rise each morning and leave home ready to put in a good day's work for a fair wage. PROUDLY MADE IN CHINA.

FOCUS ON FAVORABLE "NUGGETS"

While emerging markets may suffer from an overall unfavorable country image, it may still be possible to find some positive "nuggets" of strengths to use for brand development. Two "nuggets" that stand out are credible products and favorable cities.

Consider China's cookware company ASD as an example of using credible products to crack open a market. Cookware from China does not have great credibility in the world markets. ASD considers this a substantial barrier to taking its brand to Western markets, dominated by brands such Le Creuset and Calaphone (although, incidentally, both source products from ASD). However, China is actually a credible source for products that are associated with the Chinese cuisine – rice cookers and woks, among others. After all, rice has been a staple in the Chinese diet for 2,500 years, whereas it became widely accepted in the West only in the last few decades. ASD can enter Western markets with these products, expand to cookware for the Oriental cuisine, and finally offer a full range of ASD-branded assortment.

Alternatively, a city might have more favorable associations than the country, and the brand might link itself with this city. In 2008, China's Shanghai Jahwa United introduced its cosmetics brand Herborist (discussed in more detail in the next chapter) in Europe, and decided to be open about its Chinese origins. It felt it was necessary to be honest, authentic. Its tag line was "The Chinese Beauty Remedy." Initially, it got a boost from the superbly organized 2008 Beijing Olympics. But shortly afterwards, a number of product scandals such as contaminated milk rocked Westerners' confidence in Chinese quality. That was when the brand's city identity was introduced. Jahwa instructed its overseas salespeople to emphasize that Herborist comes from Shanghai. As Zhuo (Joe) Wang, CEO of Jawha, explained to us, Western perceptions of China revolve around such words as old, low quality, low trustworthiness, and unsafe. In contrast, Shanghai is associated with cosmopolitan, dynamic, fashionable, fresh-looking, and energetic.

Jahwa decided to make this connection even more explicit when it revived one of its famous nostalgia brands, Shuang Mei, or "Two Sisters." With a logo redolent of 1930s Shanghai, when the city was labeled as the Paris of the Orient, the brand has been renamed Shanghai Vive – a fusion of the East and the West (the French word Vive literally meaning "live!" in the imperative form). The packaging and advertising conjures visions of old Shanghai, in all its decadence. The brand ranges from Pride of Shanghai soap at RMB 220, to skin creams priced at more than RMB 1,000, with a top price of RMB 1,500 – at or above those of foreign luxury cosmetics.

OFFER EXTRA GUARANTEES

The biggest country-of-origin hurdle of emerging market brands is an association with low-quality manufacturing. An effective counterstrategy is to offer additional guarantees above industry norms. This serves two purposes. First, it reduces purchase risk: consumers can get redress if the product malfunctions. Second, it signals to the market that the company stands behind its products. After all, if a brand breaks its promise, warranty costs will go through the roof. Consumers reason that an emerging market brand would offer exceptional guarantees only if it believes in its product quality.

Hyundai has employed this strategy to overcome the considerable reluctance of US and European consumers to purchase its cars. Hyundai rose to prominence over the last decade, as its country transitioned to developed status; but Korea still has a lingering unfavorable country image – as mentioned earlier, changes in consumer perceptions typically lag behind changes in the "real" world. Hyundai was the first in the industry to offer a 10-year/100,000 mile powertrain protection covering the repair or replacement of powertrain components (that is, selected engine and transmission/transaxle components) that are defective in material or factory workmanship. Its "America's Best Warranty" program earned consumers' trust and much free publicity. The company communicates its warranty:

> To make sure we deliver automobiles worthy of a 10-year warranty, Hyundai initiated the Drive Defects to Zero plan. ... America's Best Warranty does more than give you peace of mind, it's a commitment from Hyundai to maintain a high degree of quality, dependability and reliability.[30]

Its message to consumers? That Hyundai cars are well built, reliable, and durable. The result? In slightly more than a decade, Hyundai's market share in the US increased fivefold from 1 percent in 1999 to 5.1 percent in 2011.

Hyundai's strategy offers a blueprint for emerging market companies, when there is indeed a gap between perceived and actual quality. For example, the European safety agency Euro NCAP recently awarded high marks (four stars out of five) in crash tests to models of Chinese car-makers SAIC and Geely. Michiel van Ratingen, Euro NCAP Secretary General, says "These results mark a milestone for the Chinese automotive industry. It is a clear sign that Chinese car makers are building on recent experiences and rapidly investing in better vehicle safety. Even with the upcoming increased demands, five stars are expected to be within reach soon."[31] Offering a higher tread-wear warranty might be an option for South China Tire & Rubber Co., which has to convince

US consumers to switch from trusted brands like Michelin and Goodyear to Wanli. Of course, to be able to do that, it is important that the durability of Wanli tires is commensurate.

But do not expect results overnight. After all, Hyundai took about a decade to change motorists' perceptions of the inferiority of Korean cars.

EMPHASIZE AESTHETICS

Pleasing aesthetics cannot compensate for poor manufacturing quality but it can certainly accelerate brand acceptance. Nonexperts (that is, most consumers) cannot easily assess aspects such as reliability, workmanship, and durability; therefore, negative stereotypes may take a long time to change. On the other hand, even the most naive consumer can observe aesthetic qualities. Furthermore, aesthetics are becoming increasingly important in the consumer goods industry, where the threat of commoditization is ever present. While selling a low-quality product only on great design is nearly impossible, good quality is not enough to conquer the hearts of consumers. For this, a brand needs pleasing aesthetics.

Consider Hyundai's effective use of aesthetics. While experts called Hyundai's early designs "boring," brand perceptions changed dramatically when it adopted its hallmark "fluidic design." Sales followed. Industry analyst Jesse Toprak noted, "If Hyundai hadn't taken chances with their design, they would be nowhere near where they are in terms of sales."[32] Again, Chinese car companies are taking a page from Hyundai's book. BAIC hired Leonardo Fioravanti who designed the Ferrari Daytona as chief design officer, while Brilliance China Automotive lured Dimitri Vicedomini from the famous Italian design house Pininfarina.[33]

But why reinvent the wheel when a company can simply acquire design? This is what China's SAIC did to develop Roewe, one of the few indigenous Chinese luxury vehicle marques.[34] Roewe vehicles are largely based on technology and design acquired from the defunct British car-marker MG Rover. For example, the Roewe

750, its first model, is very similar in design to the famous Rover 75. In one stroke, SAIC had solved its design challenge.

REVERSE-MANUFACTURING

State-controlled company China Garments created China's first luxury men's apparel brand 社稷/Sorgere by combining Chinese aesthetics with European manufacturing quality. The brand name provides the best of two worlds – China and Italy, 社稷 ("Sheji") means "nation" and "Sorgere" means "to rise." According to China Garments CEO Zhan Yingjie, "We want to turn round the old thinking that we can only do processing. China has the ability to create its own luxury brand. ... China isn't just a global manufacturing center and Italy a global design center. These roles can be mixed."[35] Similarly, Marisfrolg is China's answer to Max Mara, an Italian women's wear house. It designs its products in Asia but sources 80 percent of the textiles, including cashmeres, cottons, and silks, from Italy, France, and Japan.[36]

Even if Shenji/Sorgere and Marisfrolg stumble, others will succeed in reverse-manufacturing. With the growth of China, India, and other emerging markets, we can expect a growing acceptance of non-Western aesthetic styles in the West and elsewhere. After all, 17th-century Qing China and Mogul India rivaled the France of Louis XIV (*le Roi-Soleil*) in taste and sophistication.

INVEST HEAVILY IN MARKETING

The previous six strategies are smart and mostly relatively inexpensive ways to overcome the country-of-origin disadvantage. A more straightforward strategy? Spend heavily on marketing to increase brand awareness and to create positive brand associations, regardless of the country of origin. Next to innovation, the second key component of Samsung's rise to global esteem was prolonged heavy spending on advertising and other marketing efforts. Samsung's worldwide media spending is around $1 billion per year.

Thai Beverage is Thailand's largest and one of the largest beverage alcohol companies in South-East Asia, with distilleries in Thailand, Scotland, Poland, Ireland, China, and France. The ThaiBev's flagship brand, Chang Beer, has won a Gold Quality Award in the Beers, Water & Soft Drinks category in 2008, 2009, and 2010 at the prestigious World Quality Selections, organized yearly by Monde Selection Bruxelles, and in 2011 won "Asia's Best Premium Lager" at the World Beer Awards 2011. Chang Beer's international expansion is focused on Western Europe and the US. It has been the official shirt sponsor of England's Premier League club Everton since 2004. In 2010, the two parties signed a £12 million deal, extending the existing commercial relationship for three years in the biggest sponsorship deal in the soccer club's history. The move aimed to strengthen brand awareness among target consumers around the world.[37] In 2012, Chang Beer signed three-year sponsorship deals with Spanish soccer giants Barcelona and Real Madrid for $16.5 million, and has committed to spending the same amount again on activating the deals across Asia. Part of that sum will be used to bring both clubs to play friendly games in the region.[38] These and other heavy investments in marketing appeared to have paid off. In 2011, Chang Beer international sales grew by over 50 percent. In the next few years, marketing activities for Chang Beer in overseas markets will continue to emphasize sports and music marketing under the concept of "Live Like You Mean It" to accentuate their brand presence and identity in consumers' minds.[39]

The challenges of Chinese athletic apparel brand Li-Ning are an interesting contrast. The company, founded by the legendary Olympic gymnast Li Ning, seeks global expansion, not just for foreign sales, but also for credibility against its competitors in China, where it is squeezed by higher end Nike and Adidas and by cheaper domestic challengers like Anta. Like Huawei and ZTE, Anta executed Mao's strategy of encirclement (see Chapter 1), first by focusing on smaller cities, and then by entering the first- and second-tier cities. Says Ray Grady, general manager of Digital Li-Ning, about the rapidly evolving Chinese consumer:

> [If] the brand is a true global brand, a cool brand, it goes from being 'It's not Nike' to [the fact that] there's pride around that. Being cool in the West is going to be strategic to getting them to demand a higher price point in the larger markets.[40]

Li-Ning must clear three hurdles to enter the US market. First, it must build awareness. Americans are not as familiar with the Li-Ning brand, its founder, and his sport (gymnastics) as they are with the sports and celebrities associated with other foreign athletic brands, such as Europe's Adidas and Puma. Second, Li-Ning must invest in marketing and event promotion to compete in Nike's home market. Small marketing budgets with occasional appearances at events generally support only an e-commerce distribution strategy. Third, Li-Ning must compensate for China's lack of prominence as a brand. Says David Srere, CEO and head of China operations at New York based Siegel+Gale, "There is a real lack of well-regarded global Chinese products and company brands and that's a problem. The first brand I'd like to build ... is Brand China."[41]

NATION/REGION-BRANDING CAMPAIGNS

A strategy to brand a nation or region differs qualitatively from the seven strategies for overcoming negative country-of-origin perceptions. Nation (or region) branding involves applying branding and communication techniques to alter or enhance the behavior, attitudes, identity, or image of a nation (or region).[42] For brevity, we will use the term *nation-branding* but the principles apply equally to regions. Ontario (Canada) and Wallonia (Belgium) are two examples of long-running region-branding campaigns.[43]

Since all companies from a country suffer because of the country's negative image, joining forces and budgets makes sense to carry out collective campaigns. Because of what economists call the "free rider problem," where companies that abstain from a collective activity (nation-branding) will still benefit from its outcome (the positive image), industry organizations or the government often organize collective campaigns, financed by general revenues or levies on companies.

In the last 10–15 years, national leaders have become increasingly aware of the importance of their nation as a brand and have launched nation-branding campaigns to increase awareness and knowledge of the country, create favorable associations around one or more country-image dimensions, build preference for the country, and persuade people to consider products from or travel to that country. Consider these nation-brand slogans: "Malaysia: Truly Asia," "Dubai: The Jewel in the Desert," "Incredible India," or "Sri Lanka: The Pearl of the Indian Ocean." While some of these slogans may help tourism, they do little to change the nation's image as a producer of quality goods and services.

To brand an emerging market, the brand strategist and government agency must think outside the box. What is credible and what resonates with Western consumers? Consider Bangladesh. Except for failed states such as Somalia and mad regimes like that of North Korea, there are few countries for which nation-branding looks less propitious. What are Western associations with Bangladesh? Natural calamities, political instability, grinding poverty, and corruption. Not a country to invest in, go to as a tourist, or buy products from. So what can be done about this?[44]

The famous Dutch soccer player Johan Cruyff said, "Every disadvantage has its advantage." So find it! Highlight the ability of the Bangladeshi nation to overcome obstacles to activate positive associations. Demonstrate the courage, commitment, and resilience of the Bangladeshi people, who continue to develop their country with some remarkable achievements despite such disasters. Show how Bangladesh has addressed poverty through financial innovation, specifically microfinance. Mention Nobel Peace

Prize recipients Muhammad Yunus and Grameen Bank and their contributions to other impoverished pockets of humanity. Using an *Economist* article, document the "extraordinary improvements in almost every indicator of human welfare" and that "girl education has soared" in the past two decades. Link these as responses to the dream on which the nation was founded when it liberated itself from Pakistan: religious tolerance, justice and equal opportunity for everyone, and a commitment to change the fate of the deprived.

South Korea and Taiwan have made the transition from emerging market to developed status and have launched campaigns that have helped the world to view them more positively.

NATION-BRANDING: SOUTH KOREA

South Korea has established a "Presidential Council on Nation Branding" that hosts trade fairs, organizes large events, and encourages close collaboration between the public and private sectors.[45] It invests millions of dollars to upgrade the country's national image and smartly uses big events to accelerate the improvement of its country brand. For example, local leaders regarded the 1988 summer Olympic Games as South Korea's coming out party because the city of Seoul showcased Korea's impressive economic progress after decades of war, dictatorship, and poverty. The country successfully hosted the G-20 summit in 2010, thereby improving its image, said nation-branding chairwoman Lee Bae-yong: "Likewise, if we successfully host the 2018 Pyeong Chang Winter Olympics, South Korea's nation-brand will be elevated." Its stated goal is to reach the global Top 10.[46]

Several South Korean brands – most notably Samsung, Hyundai, Kia, and LG – are well known and highly regarded around the world. But Korea still ranks only 42nd globally and eighth in the Asia/Pacific region. Its history, language, culture, and people are less known outside the Western Pacific Rim and are sometimes confused with those of Vietnam and Cambodia, both remembered for political conflict and war.

Governments and industry alliances should leverage their nation's strong corporate brands: "what makes these brands great makes our country great." While the improved image of South Korea will not improve Samsung, Hyundai, or Kia, it will help *new* Korean brands to enter the global marketplace.

REGION-BRANDING: TAIWAN

Taiwan is relatively small, and primarily engaged in contract manufacturing for large Western branded companies. For example, Taiwan's Asus designed the hardware for Google's Nexus 7 tablet launched in 2012. At the mega launch event, a Google executive introduced Jonney Shih, Chairman of Asus, who stood up and briefly waved at the crowd from his seat among Google's leadership team. According to the *Financial Times*, the choreography of the Nexus launch typifies how many Taiwanese companies struggle to move from producing components for other brands to building their own consumer brands.[47]

In the 1980s, Taiwanese companies poured billions of dollars into new product development and innovation, but international customers still demanded discounts from Taiwanese contract manufacturers. Western consumers equated Taiwan with cheap labor and especially cheap electronics. In 1990, Taiwan's Ministry of Economic Affairs (MOEA) launched a long-term ambitious campaign to create a new image for the "Made in Taiwan" badge. Using external consultants, officials came up with the unique positioning "Innovalue" for the Made in Taiwan label. Innovalue stood for the common brand essence of Taiwan's companies: "we use innovation to create great value in leading edge products."[48]

Despite the initial skepticism that one word could capture the unique strength of all Taiwanese companies, the region's branding effort has made progress. Over time, Taiwan has used different but related slogans such as "It's Very Well Made in Taiwan," "Excellence, Made in Taiwan," "Taiwan: Your Partner for

Innovalue." In 2006, the MOEA launched the "Branding Taiwan Plan" and incorporated its Image Enhancement Plan into branding, to expedite the globalization and market-competitiveness of Taiwanese businesses. The goal of this campaign is to enhance the image and brands of Taiwanese enterprises and to foster an even more favorable environment for international branding efforts.[49]

Local government involvement makes eminent sense. Lack of money to invest in global marketing inhibits most Taiwanese companies. Asus's 2012 operating margin was 5.5 percent (on sales of $14.7 billion) and Acer's was 0.4 percent (on sales of $16.2 billion), compared to Samsung's operating margin of about 10 percent and Apple's operating margin of over 30 percent, both on sales greater than $150 billion. Collective efforts through regional or national branding campaigns can assist by attacking negative region or country image.

MANAGERIAL TAKEAWAYS

Nation-branding may be a fad now as the elites of emerging markets seek to attract tourists, top talent, foreign direct investment, a lower cost of capital, and foreign operations (e.g., regional headquarters, R&D facilities, and services centers) in both the corporate and nonprofit sectors. That said, country of origin matters, and consumer perceptions lag behind reality on the ground, as we have demonstrated using South Korea as an example. To overcome the negative country-of-origin associations, brands from emerging markets need to think out of the box. They need to think creatively about what is credible and what resonates with Western consumers. Here are seven strategies.

- *Choose a brand name that disguises the country of origin.* Use, pronounce, or spell a brand name in a foreign language to trigger favorable foreign cultural stereotypes and influence product perceptions and attitudes. Highlight that key components or technologies come from developed markets.

- *Confront negative associations.* Where there is lack of information, persistent media stereotypes, or overexposure of negative events and national figures, acknowledge existing perceptions and then challenge them. Give counterevidence. Poke fun at stereotypes.
- *Focus on favorable "nuggets."* Consider whether there are credible items within the broader product category where your country of origin is a plus. Associate your brand with a cosmopolitan, dynamic, fashionable city in your country. Work with local authorities on city marketing.
- *Offer extra guarantees* and other types of warranty and services over and above industry norms to reduce purchase risk as consumers can get redress in case the product malfunctions, and to signal to the market that the company stands behind its brands and is committed to quality.
- *Emphasize aesthetics and invest in design*, since even the most naive consumer can readily observe and experience aesthetic qualities. Aesthetics are more fluid and increasingly important in consumer goods sectors where commoditization looms large. Learn from the fashion industry, where consumers choose products to communicate identity. Purchases are forms of self-expression.
- *Reverse-manufacturing.* Open a factory in your target market, hire its citizens to run manufacturing, and praise these people as essential to the quality of your brand.
- *Invest heavily in marketing.* The previous strategies are less inexpensive and indirect means to overcome the country-of-origin disadvantage. The more expensive and straightforward way is to spend heavily on marketing to raise brand awareness and to create positive brand associations, regardless of the country of origin.

In this chapter, we have looked at the most common situation, that the country of origin is a liability to the success of an emerging market brand, rather than an asset. However, there are situations, albeit a minority, where the emerging country *adds* to the equity of the brand. These situations have in common that the brand draws on resources that set the emerging market in question apart from others. We distinguish between two types of resources: *cultural* resources and *natural* resources. Chapter 6 will discuss strategies to leverage *cultural* resources for global advantage, while Chapter 7 will deal with strategies to brand a nation's *natural* resources.

SIX

THE CULTURAL RESOURCES ROUTE

POSITIONING ON POSITIVE CULTURAL MYTHS

In Chapter 5, we looked at how emerging market brands generally suffer from the negative image of their country of origin. That is, a brand's roots in an emerging market reduce its appeal on such dimensions as quality, innovativeness, aesthetics, price/value, social responsibility, and prestige. There are, however, exceptions. In certain product categories, originating from a particular emerging market *adds* value to the brand. In this chapter, we map out how brand stewards can leverage aspects of their home country's culture to go global.

When we talk about culture, we are not just, or even mainly, speaking of Rembrandt's paintings, the Bolshoi ballet, or the London Philharmonic Orchestra. A nation's culture refers to all the beliefs, attitudes, aspirations, values, and myths held by most people in a society, as well as the characteristic behaviors, rules, customs, and norms that most people follow. It includes aspects of the social and physical environment, including institutions (e.g.,

145

labor organizations, political parties, and religions) objects (e.g., products, tools, buildings, and landmarks), and their history.[1] Culture is all around us. That is why anthropologists like to talk about the "culturally constituted world."

Marketers have long known that they can imbue brands with elements of a country's culture. Indeed, some brands have become veritable icons, representative of a culture or a movement. Consider the Harley-Davidson motorcycle. With its prominence in the Hell's Angels motorcycle club founded in 1948 and its role in such movies as *The Wild One* (1953, starring Marlon Brando) and *Easy Rider* (1969), Harley-Davidson emerged as a symbol of counterculture.[2] It is not just a motorcycle – it stands unequivocally for rebellion, machismo, and lawlessness. The Hell's Angels connection turns off some consumers but attracts others who ride to escape from their drudgery of routines and rules. The Harley Owners Group (HOG) is "the granddaddy of all community-building efforts," promoting not just a consumer product, but a lifestyle. It has over one million members.[3]

Cultural brands exhibit the characteristics of strong brands described by conventional branding models. They have distinctive and favorable associations, they generate buzz, and they have a core following with deep emotional attachment. But what really "carries" the brand, what makes it stand out and stick, is its *cultural myth-making*.[4] But how can marketers imbue their brands with cultural meaning? How can emerging market firms leverage the cultural resources of their country of origin in the global marketplace? We will address these questions in this chapter.

A FRAMEWORK FOR CULTURAL BRANDING

Companies can work with existing cultural meanings associated with their country of origin. Cultural meanings represent the shared knowledge, symbols, and beliefs by which people represent significant aspects of their environment and through which they perceive the world. Let us look at a few examples to highlight different cultural meanings.[5]

The color black signifies death in Western countries, while white connotes death in China. The number 666 signifies the devil in Christian countries but has no cultural meaning in other countries. For 3,000 years, many cultures, including India and China, have used the swastika symbol to represent life, the sun, power, strength, and good luck. The word *swastika* comes from the Sanskrit *svastika* – with "su" meaning "good," "asti" meaning "to be," and "ka" as a suffix.[6] In the West, however, people associate this symbol with Nazi Germany.

The number four symbolizes bad luck in Japan, while 13 connotes it in the United States; eight is a lucky number in China. The color green means *disease* in countries with dense jungles but *nature* in countries without them. Flowers have different cultural meanings too. For example, many Western countries use white lilies for funerals, while Mexicans use them to lift superstitious spells.

But instead of calling out the diversity of cultural meanings behind numbers, colors, and symbols, our interest is in the uniformity of associations that consumers make with particular countries. For example, around the world, bright colors signify joy. As we will see, the Brazilian footwear brand Havaianas uses this significance to convey youth, joy, and fun – characteristics widely associated with Brazilian culture.

Figure 6.1 presents a model of the cultural branding process.[7] Globally recognized cultural meanings associated with the brand's home country are the building blocks of cultural branding. While we acknowledge that some brands – including some of the examples below – acquire cultural meanings not as part of a conscious branding strategy but due to a confluence of incidental factors not under the control of the marketer (e.g., Harley-Davidson probably did not choose its association with Hell's Angels), we use these case studies to illustrate how marketers can use cultural branding theory in a proactive manner.

The task of the marketer is to select particular cultural meanings to associate with the brand, and then to develop strategies that will transfer these particular cultural meanings to the brand. The meanings must be globally recognized, unique to the country, relevant to the category, and consistent with the brand. To achieve this transfer, the marketer can use three interrelated and mutually supporting pathways: brand development, brand communication, and brand reinforcement. We will now discuss the process (Figure 6.1) in more detail.

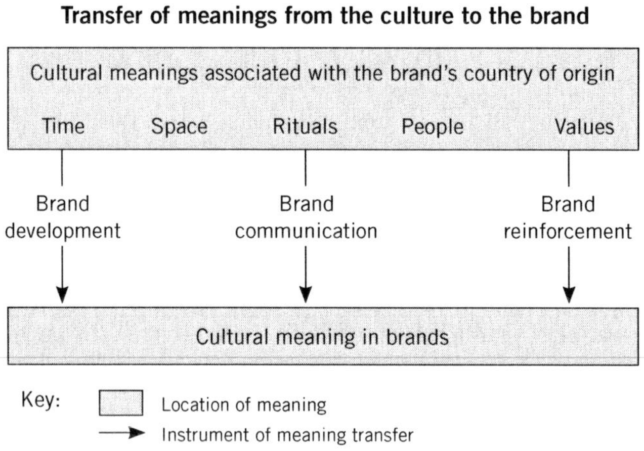

Transfer of meanings from the culture to the brand

Cultural meanings associated with the brand's country of origin				
Time	Space	Rituals	People	Values

Brand development	Brand communication	Brand reinforcement

Cultural meaning in brands

Key: ☐ Location of meaning
      → Instrument of meaning transfer

Figure 6.1 **A model for cultural branding**

CULTURAL MEANINGS

We begin by surveying the different types of cultural meaning and then provide guidelines for selecting which of these to associate with the brand. Finally, using two examples of Chinese brands, we will illustrate this process in practice.

SURVEYING THE CATEGORIES OF CULTURAL MEANING

To operationalize the somewhat mushy concept of cultural meanings, we distinguish here between five categories of cultural meaning and provide a number of examples/subcategories within each of them:

- *Time*: the concept of time (monochromic versus polychromic), time centrality (e.g., "time is money"), separation of work from leisure, punctuality, temporal orientation (past, present, future).
- *Space*: private versus public, urban versus rural, man-made landmarks (e.g., the Taj Mahal or the pyramids), natural landmarks (e.g., the Saudi desert or the untamed Amazon tropical forest), water versus land, rivers (e.g., Egypt being "the Gift of the Nile"),[8] high mountains versus wide plains (the Himalayas versus the Argentinean pampas), crowded versus empty (Singapore versus Mongolia).
- *Rituals*: festive versus somber events, life-cycle events (e.g., weddings, graduations, births and adoptions, rites of passage, retirements, funerals), religious practices and holy days (e.g., the Hajj pilgrimage to Mecca), social norms (e.g., degree of formality, greetings, formal versus familiar language), festivals and national commemorations.
- *People*: ethnicity, personality, physique, family units (nuclear versus extended), tribe, native tongue versus national language, popular sports, distinctions of class or caste, status or rank, gender, age, and occupation.
- *Values*: gender roles, autonomy (independence, individualism) versus social embeddedness (collectivism, *guanxi* in China, *ubuntu* in Africa), hierarchy versus egalitarianism, achievement, success, and materialism versus wellbeing, caring for the weak, humility, tradition versus modernity, rights of the individual versus the role of the government.

SELECTING CULTURAL MEANING FOR TRANSFER

No brand will be imbued with all cultural categories. In fact, "owning" one cultural meaning is better than relating to many cultural meanings. Some brands become cultural icons more by accident than by design. Initially, at Harley-Davidson, marketers were responding to consumption rather than actually creating it. However, the marketer can actively work to imbue the brand with cultural meanings. The Marlboro Man is created, calling on the myth of the Wild West, its open spaces, and the mythical Marlboro Country. The marketer must choose carefully among all the possible aspects of the nation's culture. Here are guidelines:

- Choose cultural meanings that the target segment will *recognize* anywhere in the world. Otherwise, the company must spend significant amounts of resources to educate foreign consumers about the cultural aspects in question.
- Choose those meanings that the target segment regards as *credibly* linked to the nation's culture. For example, US brands can credibly draw upon a culture of individualism, something not credible for Chinese brands. Advertisements featuring wide spaces make little sense for a brand from cramped Bangladesh with its 2,500 inhabitants per square mile.
- *Pre-empt* cultural meanings that no other brand has claimed. Here, there is a clear first-mover advantage in categories with multiple brands from the same country. The first brand to appropriate a cultural meaning effectively "owns" that position, and dislodging it is costly.
- Select cultural meanings that are *relevant*, or that the marketer can make relevant, for the product.

Shanghai Tang

Shanghai Tang is an international clothing company, founded in 1994 by David Tang. He practices the art of Chinese haute couture. The fundamental design concept is inspired by traditional Chinese clothing combined with the modernity of the 21st century. Table 6.1 provides an analysis of the cultural signs and symbols used by Shanghai Tang.

Table 6.1 **Semiotic analysis of Shanghai Tang**

Signs	Meanings
Traditional Chinese cuts	"Chinese heritage," historical meaning, luxury/chic
Chinese themes	A proud reminder of Chinese culture
Colors: bright, colorful	Modern "cool"/provocative unusual colors in Asia
Stretch/short/sexy variations	Signalling modernity/Western lifestyle, sex/celebrity symbol
Silk	High-quality luxury product

Source: Inga Katharina Radziejewski, personal communication, October 14, 2012.

Edward Tang (David's son) says that nostalgia – the styles and artifacts of China's culture, specifically from Chinese fashion of the 1920s and 30s – was his father's starting point. Shanghai Tang follows the finest tradition of imperial tailoring with attention to detail, craftsmanship, luxurious fabrics such as Chinese silk, and typical Chinese fit. These associated cultural meanings are credible. After all, Shanghai was called the "Paris of the East," with its range of chic restaurants to dark opium houses, its luxury hotels to dirty, bug-infested cheap hotel rooms, as well as its studios and dance halls.

Whether these cultural meanings are relevant depends on whether people like Chinese fashion of the 1920s and 30s and view the mandarin collar as a modern, chic alternative to the traditional neck tie. According to Shanghai Tang Executive Chairman, Raphael le Masne de Chermont, the Mandarin Collar Society "is a club with the goal to promote an elegant Chinese-inspired style for men. It's an alternative that allows you to reorient yourself, to be stylish while being yourself."[9] Men forgoing their shirts and ties for Mandarin collars would be the most important revolution in Western men's clothing since the adoption of the zipper. Unlikely, but perhaps appeals to a segment.

Kweichow Moutai

Kweichow Moutai Co. Ltd, is a state-owned Chinese liquor company founded in 1999, with a catchy slogan "Kweichow Moutai, Legendary Spirit of China." In its print advertisements, it claims that "There is more to China than calligraphy," and explains its roots as follows:

> Kweichow Moutai Legend. From the village of Moutai, in the Guizhou province of China, Moutai has acquired through the centuries the well-deserved status of National Liquor, and its reputation of one of the world's finest spirits. Its great aromatic presence and complex aftertaste are a tribute to China's age-old craftsmanship.

The problem is that the legend is not explained. Furthermore, we suspect that few Westerners (in fact, few non-Chinese individuals) will have any association, cultural or otherwise, with either the village of Moutai or the Guizhou province. Perhaps it will be a great success (although an article in the *Financial Times* doubted whether non-Chinese individuals will ever be able to appreciate the taste). But its marketing team may want to select cultural meanings that Westerners more readily recognize and understand or can be convinced of.

TRANSFER OF CULTURAL MEANING TO CONSUMER BRANDS

Marketers can transfer cultural meaning to their brand through three interrelated activities: brand development, brand communication, and brand reinforcement.

BRAND DEVELOPMENT

The first step is to choose the brand name, logo, slogan, and writing style that convey the intended cultural meaning. An effective cultural branding strategy creates a storied brand – a brand that has distinctive features (mark, design, and so on) through which consumers experience identity myths.

Shanghai Tang logo says "Shanghai Tang" in both Roman letters and Chinese characters.[10] For the Chinese characters, it uses complex Chinese, which is in line with its pre-World War II inspiration. They are written right to left and therefore read "Tang Hai Shang." If written left to right, these characters could mean "at the beach" together, or individually "superior," "ocean," and "beach or shoal." Collectively, they have several meanings, such "Shanghai nostalgia," "Shanghai panoply," or "Shanghai kaleidoscope." It claims to be the only Chinese luxury brand. "Brand China" does not convey luxury or quality as yet, so the labels inside say "Made by Chinese" instead of "Made in China." Other slogans that we have observed include "East Meets West" and "No More Ties." However, the brand clearly needs some more development work before it "owns" a slogan.

BRAND COMMUNICATION

Advertising is a key instrument in all branding efforts. However, the role and purpose of advertising in cultural branding differs from that in mainstream branding.[11] According to marketing professor Douglas Holt, mainstream branding models assume that the primary purpose of advertising is persuasion, influencing consumer perceptions about the brand (e.g., the functional and emotional benefits of the brand, or user imagery). Communications should use whatever creative content will best persuade consumption. But consumers are likely to discard this rhetoric once they believe what marketers intended them to believe.

In cultural branding, marketing communications are integral to brand value. Consumers buy the brand to experience the cultural stories and myths. The brand is the conduit through which the consumer can participate in the brand stories. To ride a Harley is to rebel like James Dean. The Marlboro man is a cowboy – the epitome of rugged masculinity – and importantly, he is by himself, which expresses the core US value of individualism. The Marlboro man is on his own, which aligns with that other important US value – independence, making your own way in life. By smoking a Marlboro, you become a little like this mythical idealized man.

Thus, advertising is crucial in charging a brand with the intended cultural meaning through the setting (whether it is urban or rural, fantasy or real life, inside or outside, and so on), people (their gender, age, occupation, clothing, and body postures, celebrities, "experts," the "common man"), and media used (type of media such as print, and specific outlets such as the *Financial Times* versus *People*). Each of these elements should reinforce the cultural meaning associated with the brand.

Shanghai Tang advertises in magazines in Asia and (less frequently) in Western magazines such as *GQ*. Shanghai Tang is only for the connoisseur. To buy it, you need a tip from an insider. According to a Shanghai Tang executive, "So many people like it that word of mouth spread it far. Also celebrities like Kate Moss, Angelina Jolie, and Sienna Miller wear clothing and handbags from Shanghai Tang and that raises brand awareness."[12] Note that it does not pay them to promote the brand. They bought the products for themselves – which provides good free publicity for the company.

BRAND REINFORCEMENT

The third role of marketing in transferring meaning from the wider national culture into the brand is to reinforce the association through other elements of the marketing mix – various elements related to pricing, distribution, and packaging.

Shanghai Tang reinforces its positioning as a luxury and lifestyle brand in at least three ways. First, it employs a selective distribution strategy. It currently has about 25 stores outside China, in cosmopolitan cities like Bangkok, Honolulu, London, Miami, New York, Madrid, Paris, and Tokyo. It locates stores in well-known areas such as Bangkok's Sukhumvit Road and Shanghai's Xintiandi to underpin its exclusive brand image. In April 2012, it opened its largest store, "Shanghai Tang Mansion," on Duddell Street in Hong Kong. Shanghai-based firm Design MVW designed the mansion's 1,400-square-meter shopping experience.

Second, Shanghai Tang sells furniture, porcelain, and clothing accessories. It also has lifestyle restaurants in Shanghai and London that showcase the furnishings and glassware available at Shanghai Tang stores.[12]

Third, it prices all items consistent with the upscale image. Women's blouses sell in the $125–270 range, men's sleepwear upward of $170, and children's jackets between $130 and $265 (Table 6.2).

Hitherto, Western firms have used cultural branding more often than have emerging market brands. While in a taxi from Beijing Capital International Airport to downtown Beijing, we heard nothing but contemporary US hits on the radio. Long-standing US brands introduce themselves to new generations of consumers by incorporating elements of popular culture into advertisements. For example, in the 1980s, Pepsi featured singer Tina Turner to transfer the energy, independence, and vitality of the American (pop) culture, but she would not resonate with today's teenagers. Therefore, in its latest global campaign, Pepsi used rapper Nicki Minaj.[13]

Where does that leave emerging markets? Just as the center of economic gravity is shifting from the West to the East, there is every reason to assume that, in the coming decades, the cultural center of gravity will shift to the East. In fact, cultural creativity and international appeal have historically followed economic ascendance. We are going to look at two distinct ways in which emerging market brands can leverage their home country's cultural resources – using either ancient myths or contemporary myths. We will discuss the former route to cultural branding using China's

Herborist and illustrate the latter type of cultural branding with Brazil's Havaianas.

Table 6.2 **Product and price analysis of Shanghai Tang**

Women's	Men's	Children's	Accessories	Home
Coats $435–625	Jackets $290–770	Jackets $130–265	Pouches and cases $25–50	Candles and fragrance $25–50
Jackets $170–880			Handbags $155–430	Bed and bath $65–1350
Blouses $125–270			Belts $90–265	Tableware $40–205
Tops $65–240	Shirts/T-shirts $60–155	Shirts/tops $40	Wallets $40–125	Frames and albums $125–270
Dresses $295–515		Dresses $155	Footwear $70	Travel $55–155
Sleepwear $170–295	Sleepwear $170–295	Sleepwear $75–150	Hats and caps $30	CDs $25
Sweaters $140–550	Sweaters $120–675	Cardigans $125–360	Scarves $110–290	Boxes $45–610
Beachwear $235–545	Pants $235–355	Baby wear $45–220	Watches $90–315	Stationery $40–50
Pants and skirts $255–315	Cufflinks $60	Toys $20–35	Jewelry $70–750	Wine accessories $70–190
			Umbrellas $65	Games sets $1295–2035
				Key rings $85–100

Source: Inga Katharina Radziejewski, personal communication, October 14, 2012.

CULTURAL BRANDING BASED ON ANCIENT MYTHS

Few countries have richer ancient cultural resources to draw from than China. Yet there are few Chinese companies that draw upon these cultural resources. This is starting to change, with Shanghai Jahwa United leading the way.[14] In 1995, a senior executive from a Western cosmetics giant implied that Shanghai Jahwa's products lacked originality and authenticity. Its Chairman, Ge Wenyao, was so embarrassed that he decided to do something different, something special. After three years of preparation, he launched the brand Herborist, based on the theory and practices of traditional Chinese medicine. The first Herborist store was opened in Shanghai in 1998 because department stores refused to carry the brand. Initial sales were lackluster. On the first day, they sold one item. The customer? Mr. Ge himself. In 2012, sales exceeded $200 million and were growing by 30 per cent annually. Its international sales, while still small, are also growing rapidly. So how did Shanghai Jahwa do it?

According to Shanghai Jahwa's CEO Joe Wang, the key to understanding Herborist's success is its brand essence. It is organized around the concept of Chinese beauty, which it delivers through modern Western technology. Chinese beauty is focused on the ancient Daoistic philosophy of balance and taking a holistic view of life. It focuses on what is inside of human beings, not just the outside. You are beautiful when you feel good. Western advertisements communicate the message that you feel good when people look at you. Herborist turns the logic around – people look at you when you feel good.

Herborist draws from two ancestral traditions of equilibrium: the balance between Man and Nature as the source of vitality, and knowledge of the healing powers of plants in restoring balance. According to legend, around 2800 BC the Emperor Shennong inventoried the therapeutic properties of 365 plants in a treatise, the *Ben Cao Jing*, organized according to the flow of energy that they release in the body. Generations of herbal scientists have studied this work, and it remains an authoritative reference in Chinese herbal science today. Herborist chooses its slogans – "Herborist: The Chinese Beauty Remedy" and "The Middle Empire Discloses Its Beauty Secrets" – to support its cultural heritage.

From 2008, Herborist started to expand internationally. It is currently available in a number of European countries, including France, Spain, Italy, the Netherlands, Poland, and Turkey. How was it able to leverage it Chinese message abroad? First, it used a simpler message. Most Western consumers do not have a detailed knowledge of ancient Daoist principles and traditions, but the principle of yin–yang and balance are understood. Consequently, its message is that Herborist is a modern cosmetics product rooted in traditional Chinese medicine and plants, balancing the yin and yang of the skin. The packaging exudes Western technology and manufacturing, while the product itself is based on the ancient Chinese traditions. According to Wang, the target segment is highly educated, cosmopolitan, 40-something women, who are culturally sensitive, looking for something exotic, bored with using the established Western brands, and skeptical about chemical ingredients. Herborist's price positioning is in the middle to high entry level prestige segment, similar to say France's Biotherm. It sells primarily through Sephora, a French international chain of cosmetics stores.

Shanghai Jawha is an example of a small but growing number of Chinese (and non-Chinese) companies that find inspiration in ancient cultural myths. Take luxury fashion brand Shang Xia. It gets its inspiration from old Chinese notions about aesthetics, which emphasize outer serenity and inner sumptuousness. Rather than accentuating the wearer's contours, their clothes serve to hide the female curves. Chinese aesthetics are claimed to be more subtle than Western aesthetics; there must be a moment of interaction between the person and nature for the magic to take place. Explains CEO Jiang Qiong'er: "when the women move, especially in the wind, the draping fabric clings temporarily to their body, to give a suggestion of their sensuality."[15] The company plans its international launch with an opening of a boutique in Paris.

Another example is the fashion brand Zuczug, which is influenced by Chinese culture such as traditional food markets, by the

Tibetan plateau, and by its "ultra-wired, tech-obsessed youth."
Now that Western luxury brands have opened stores everywhere
in China, it is aimed at wealthy Chinese shoppers that are looking
for something new, distinctive, and high end but that requires the
eye of the connoisseur. Zuczug sells Popsicle-orange riding pants
for $185 and camel-wool jumper dresses for $315 (2012 prices).
Its vibrant hues and patterns lend themselves to photo- and video-
sharing on social media. Currently sold through a network of over
70 Zuczug stores in China, founder and master designer Wang
Yiyang claims that he has "every intention of making Zuczug a
global brand."[16]

CULTURAL BRANDING BASED ON CONTEMPORARY MYTHS[17]

An alternative way to leverage cultural resources is to draw on
contemporary cultural myths. Alpargatas S.A.'s brand Havaianas
provides a good example how to build your brand this way.
Brazilian-Argentinean Alpargatas is the largest public footwear
company in Latin America, with sales exceeding $1 billion. Inter-
national operations are responsible for about 30 percent of
revenues, and its main brand is Havaianas.[18] Since its launch in
1962, Havaianas has grown into a blockbuster brand for primarily
flip-flops (slippers), positioned across all social classes in Brazil
and in the mid to upper classes in international markets. How did
Havaianas go global? Through cultural branding.

HAVAIANAS IN BRAZIL
The old Havaianas: a product
In 1962, Alpargatas launched Havaianas made of rubber. Within
a year, Havaianas was selling more than a thousand pairs a day
in small shops and local markets. But their simple design and very
low prices insinuated that Havaianas were for poor people,
housewives, and laborers. As economic conditions began to

improve in the late 1980s, people's disposable income grew appreciably, and consumers began deserting the "cheap" Havaianas brand. In the early1990s, sales of Havaianas declined by a disastrous 35 percent – from 100 million pairs to 65 million pairs. This drop forced the company to change its thinking dramatically about a pair of rubber flip-flops – not as a commodity, but as a brand. The transformation process soon catapulted the company into brand leadership in Brazil and emboldened it to tap into international markets.

The new Havaianas: a brand

Alpargatas retained the core brand identity – "Havaianas is for everyone and everyone is for Havaianas" – but recognized that consumers have different needs. It revamped the entire marketing strategy to focus on the consumer, not the flip-flop. The product line grew from two to over 25 different models with numerous colors so that consumers could complement their own identity. Alpargatas packaged the higher end products in boxes – similar to those of shoes – and priced them five to six times higher than the basic flip-flops. Alpargatas invested heavily in marketing communication to associate Havaianas with relaxation and irreverence. It launched a series of funny, attention-grabbing advertisements using artists wearing Havaianas outdoors, at the beach, or shopping. Simultaneously, it launched a new media campaign featuring sophisticated and artistic actors. These celebrities reinforced the notion that consumers were no longer wearing flip-flops but Havaianas. None of the elements of Havaianas' new strategy had been offered before in the industry. Table 6.3 shows consumer associations with the "old" Havaianas versus the "new" Havaianas.

HAVAIANAS IN THE US

Alpargatas leveraged what it learned in rebranding Havaianas in Brazil to expand into neighboring countries whose cultural and

Table 6.3 **Havaianas: brand association pre- and post-1994**

Cognitive associations		Emotional and cultural associations	
Before 1994	**After 1994**	**Before 1994**	**After 1994**
Durable: don't deform, strips don't break Hygienic: don't smell Useful: comfort Traditional – only one model Excellent cost–benefit relation Limited colors Functional	*New association* The "sandal style" – fashion sandals (more than 80 models and 60,000 colors) 100% natural 100% Brazilian *Associations maintained* Excellent cost–benefit relation Accessibility Comfort Durability Hygiene	"Poor man's slipper" "Housemaid slipper"	Brazilian national identity Tropical nature Beach Heat Holidays Joy and relaxation Physical and emotional wellness Comfort

Source: Adapted from Niraj Khalpada et al. (2012); see Note 17.

geographical proximity catalyzed the expansion. But its aspirations did not stop there. Could Havaianas penetrate the US, even if Brazil were not well known as a manufacturer of footwear? Yes. To justify its premium positioning in a low-tech category, Alpargatas called upon several interrelated cultural meanings, primarily around the cultural categories of Brazil's people and values. This included association with vibrant colors, sensuality (dancing and carnival), youth, joy, fun, positivism, simplicity, and sense of humor. All of these are relevant to wearing flip-flops, as opposed to say, men's dress shoes.

Brand development

Alpargatas had chosen the brand name long before it launched Havaianas in Western markets,[19] so it focused on other brand attributes, such as the playful yet artistic visual display of the brand name and logo writing to emphasize joy and fun. The slogan, "Havaianas: Original as You," does not directly connect with the Brazilian culture, but with its emphasis on customization. In 2011, brand recognition in the US had already surpassed 30 percent.

Brand communication

Havaianas brand managers used all marketing and promotion channels, from print newspapers and magazines to digital and social media. Many of its print and billboard advertisements refer to Latin-American playfulness through images of tango dancing, Brazil's carnival, and beautiful young people having fun. Alpargatas also regularly arranged promotional events in different US locations to widen its community. It pairs limited editions of its products with special events, such as the FIFA World Cup. Recognizing that soccer equals Brazil and Brazil equals soccer, Alpargatas launched the "Teams collection," with a pair of flip-flops for each of the 32 countries competing in the 2010 World Cup. Each pair looked like a brightly colored team jersey in flip-flop form. It sent about 400 mailers with Teams flip-flops to opinion-formers in the US. Cleverly playing on the idea that Brazil is often a soccer fan's second favorite team, after their own country, each mailer contained a Brazil pair and a carefully researched second pair. Mexican-American actress Eva Longoria, for example, got Teams collection flip-flops from Mexico and Brazil, noted Jim Anstey, marketing director of Alpargatas USA/Havaianas.[20] Imagine the buzz such actions create.

Brand reinforcement

Havaianas' rich and varied product portfolio, as well as its use of vibrant colors and swirling designs, helps cater to many different customer segments. It boldly attacks the quality prejudice against cheap Brazilian-made footwear brands. Last time we checked, it offered Havaianas from $16 a pair, to $200 for custom-designed sandals studded with Swarovski crystal. To build credibility for the top of its line, the company aggressively and diplomatically cultivated the celebrity market. For example, it provided special edition Havaianas, hand-stitched and encrusted with Swarovski crystals, for Oscar swag baskets awarded to Academy Award nominees. By reaching the top strata of society, Alpargatas can generate "consumer pull" at the lower strata as the latter seek to emulate their idols. This is in contrast to the more traditional "channel push" by brand managers.

Alpargatas aligned its pricing strategy with the broader strategy to position Havaianas in the upper segment. The wide price range enables Havaianas to capture different customers with different expectations, from the casual fashion consumer to the "will-buy-at-any-cost" fashionista. Its relatively higher entry price point of $16 for a flip-flop differentiates Havaianas from the lower end market.

Its distribution strategy complements and supports the other elements of the marketing mix. Alpargatas distributes primarily through high-end chains like Marshall Field's, Saks Fifth Avenue, Bergdorf Goodman, Nordstrom, and more upscale West Coast surf stores. It also sells Havaianas through Amazon.com, where it maintains a "Havaianas Store." Finally, in 2010, it began opening its own retail shops, first in Huntington Beach, California. Alfonso Sugiyama, US Havaianas President, observed "Flip-flops are a staple of beach culture and Huntington Beach as the lifestyle hub of California is the perfect place for our first Havaianas outpost."[17]

Havaianas did not restrict itself to the US. It sells through international websites and has now also opened Havaianas stores in Europe and Singapore. In summary, Havaianas has successfully leveraged some of Brazil's cultural resources not only to change the attitudes of developed countries toward Brazilian products, but also to transform an unglamorous product line into a lifestyle brand. And the future is beckoning. Brazil is hosting soccer's FIFA World Cup in 2014 and the Olympic Games in 2016, thereby exposing more people to the Brazilian culture of fun, sun, beaches, and parties.

MANAGERIAL TAKEAWAYS

The Havaianas case demonstrates that relatively young emerging market nations in Africa and Latin America can use the cultural branding strategy. Other countries such India, Vietnam, Burma, Egypt, Iran, Turkey, and Indonesia sit upon ancient cultural resources, waiting to be unleashed. Here is a summary of the process for executives:

1. *Survey the categories of cultural meaning.* To leverage cultural meanings in global branding, managers should first survey five aspects of their country's culture: *time* (e.g., history and pace), *space* (e.g., geography and landmarks), *rituals* (e.g., life-cycle, religious and national festivals), *people* (e.g., demographics), and *values* (e.g., social systems).

2. *Select cultural meanings for transfer.* Managers should choose only one or two cultural meanings that the target segment will *recognize* anywhere in the world and will regard as *credibly* linked to the nation's culture, that no other brand has claimed, and that are relevant, or that the marketer can make relevant, to the product.

3. *Transfer cultural meaning to the brand.* Marketers can transfer cultural meaning to their consumer brand through three interrelated activities: *brand development* – developing the brand name, logo, slogan, and writing style that convey the intended cultural meaning; *brand communication* – determining the setting, the characters, and the media to use in story-telling and myth-making; and *brand reinforcement* – aligning the other elements of the marketing mix, such as pricing, product placement, promotion, distribution, and packaging, so that they amplify the cultural meanings.

We believe the potential for cultural branding is greatest for China and India. By any standard, these nations are very ancient, dating back to at least 2,000 BC – think about the Xia dynasty in China or

Harappa and Mohenjo-daro civilizations in the Indian subcontinent. Their contributions to world culture and learning are hard to overstate. Some of the oldest writings (the Mahabharata, Ramayana, Analects), philosophies (Daoism, Confucianism), products (paper, gun powder, compass, tea), man-made constructions (the Great Wall, Taj Mahal, Grand Canal), and the world's first global religion (Buddhism) originate from these two countries.

Companies such as Herborist and Shanghai Tang have tapped into China's ancient culture, just as Dabur has tapped into India's tradition of Ayurvedic medicine. This is just the beginning. We believe and predict that India and China hold the future of cultural branding.

SEVEN

THE NATURAL RESOURCES ROUTE

BRANDING COMMODITIES IN FOUR STEPS

Who has not heard of the bubbly beverage champagne? Why does champagne command higher prices and higher brand equity than other sparkling wines? Because France has branded this natural resource. Winemakers produce champagne from grapes grown in the Champagne region in the north-east of France; the process requires secondary fermentation of the wine in the bottle to create carbonation. The Champagne winemaking community, under the auspices of the Comité Interprofessionnel du Vin de Champagne (the trade organization established by statute to administer the common interests of the Champagne industry), has developed a comprehensive set of rules and regulations for all wine produced in Champagne, to protect the region's economic interests. It has codified the most suitable growing places, the most suitable grape types (most champagne being a blend of up to three grape varieties, although other varieties are allowed), and most aspects of viticulture, including pruning, vineyard yield, the degree of pressing, and the time that the wine must remain on its lees[1] before bottling. Only after meeting all these requirements may a winemaker label the product "champagne."

We attribute the popularity of champagne to the success of champagne producers in marketing. The leading manufacturers such as Moët & Chandon, Veuve Clicquot, and Piper-Heidsieck put considerable energy into creating a history and an identity for their sparkling wine and associating themselves and their beverage with nobility and royalty. Through advertising and packaging, champagne now conjures images of high luxury – and last time we checked retailed upward of £25, compared to Spanish sparkling wine (called cava), which sells in the £5 to £10 range at Britain's leading retailer, Tesco.[2] High prices do not deter champagne's success; it sells 340 million bottles annually, over 15 percent of the world's sparkling wine market of 2.15 billion bottles.[3] Of course, its value share (in US dollars) is even higher, given its premium price, and certain vintages appreciate in value over time.

While champagne is a great example of branding a natural resource – the grapes grown in the Champagne region – it is by no means the only one. At the opposite end of the spectrum is plain water. Evian Natural Spring Water is sold for a premium price because it is marketed as being "bottled exclusively at its protected natural spring source (Cachat Spring), which lies at the very foot of the French Alps, far from any urban or industrial development."[4] Similarly, Perrier is a brand of carbonated bottled mineral water made from a naturally carbonated spring in Vergèze in the Gard *département* of France. Both the water and natural carbon dioxide gas are captured independently. Then, in the bottling process, the carbon dioxide gas is added so that the level of carbonation in bottled Perrier is the same as the water of the Vergèze spring.[5]

Similarly, emerging market companies are branding their natural resources, such as Natura cosmetics (Brazil), Forevermark diamonds (South Africa), Café de Colombia, Habanos cigars (Cuba), and Premier cosmetics (Israel). How do these companies do this? How can an emerging market company upgrade an other-wise undifferentiated commodity to a global brand? Our research has identified a sequence of four steps, all of which add value to the commodity, thereby transforming an uncut stone into a shining diamond (Figure 7.1).

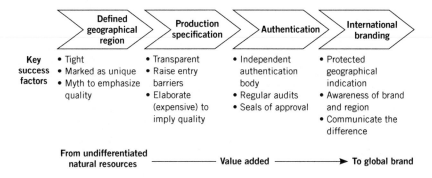

Figure 7.1 **Branding natural resources**

DEFINE THE GEOGRAPHICAL REGION

Successful branding of natural resources requires an association between the brand and a particular geography. Products from that geographical area should have certain unique (perceived) charac-teristics that set it apart from similar products from other regions. The geographical area must be fairly tightly defined, and either known for or marketed for its unique characteristics. Often the region is associated with certain myths that help to emphasize quality. For example, Brazil's personal care company Natura (with annual sales of approximately $3 billion) associates its Natura Ekos line with Brazil's unique biodiversity. Its products draw from traditional plant ingredients, amplifying Brazil's environmental heritage and promoting quality of life in those communities that cultivate or extract those ingredients.

PREMIER DEAD SEA
Established in Israel in 1990, the Dead Sea Premier Cosmetics

Laboratories is a major manufacturer of high-quality cosmetic products that leverage the healing properties of the Dead Sea – not a claim that such global giants as Shisheido or Estée Lauder can credibly copy.

The Dead Sea is a tightly defined salt lake in the Jordan Rift Valley, 67 kilometers long and 18 kilometers at its widest point. Compared to the 3 percent salt content of ordinary sea water, the Dead Sea's chemical composition is unique. It contains 32 percent salts, with a relatively high concentration of minerals such as magnesium, calcium, bromide, and potassium. Its high density of 1.240 kg per liter makes swimming in it similar to floating. And it is the backdrop to thousands of years of brand-relevant history and legends, such as being a refuge for King David, a health resort for King Herod, and a source of beauty for Queen Cleopatra.[6]

The Premier line consists of over 150 items, a full range of high-quality skin care products, hair and body care, toiletries, and cosmetics exported to over 62 different countries. The company claims that its Premier products benefit the skin because of their high concentration of minerals extracted from the salt of the Dead Sea. By replenishing the minerals depleted from the skin, Premier products allow the skin to hydrate naturally, rebuild itself more quickly, and take on a healthy appearance.[7] Premier states:

> Dead Sea water is uniquely acclaimed for nourishing the skin, easing rheumatic discomfort, activating the circulatory system, and relaxing the nerves. … The Dead Sea has been a health, rehabilitation and beauty spa since ancient times … Today, the Dead Sea is renowned for its unique, natural ability to regenerate the skin's own vital functions.[8]

SPECIFY PRODUCTION STANDARDS

A uniquely specified production system greatly enhances the equity of natural resource brands. Ideally, the production process should be transparent, because consumers increasingly care about the social and environmental impacts of their consumption. Such a production system distinguishes the product from more cheaply made items. Natura's concern for the environment directly translates into its production processes. To ensure that it extracts the Brazilian flora inputs according to proper social and environmental standards, Natura developed its Active Ingredient Certification Program for the Brazilian biodiversity used in the Natura lines. The program consists of six stages: (1) an audit of the ingredients' place of origin, (2) the development of a management plan, (3) an assessment of environmental and social impact, (4) implementation of the management plan, (5) certification of the extracts, and (6) a periodic monitoring of the process.

Natura does not test on animals. It sells refills, whose average mass is 54 percent less than the mass of regular packaging, resulting in a significant decrease in solid waste dumped in the environment. In its 2005 report, *Talk the Walk*, the United Nations Environment Programme identified Natura as one of the "pioneers in sustainable lifestyles marketing."[9] Recently, the company launched a Carbon Neutral Program, designed to reduce and offset all its emissions of greenhouse gases.

Moreover, an elaborate production system steeped in local tradition enhances brand credibility and consumer perception of quality. Finally, such production specifications also raise entry barriers for competitors. Clearly, Natura's green production is more than a strategy; it guides its business and increases costs for competitors.

FOREVERMARK

One company that draws strength from its production standards is South Africa's giant De Beers, with sales of around $7 billion, roughly 36 percent of the world diamond market. In 2008, it introduced diamonds branded under the Forevermark name, a radical step in an industry that defines quality of diamonds very precisely in terms of the four Cs: cut, clarity, color, and carats. How can De Beers brand a natural resource if origin does not matter?

In the 1990s, journalists began to report on horrible labor conditions, oppression, pillage, and murder in the diamond-mining operations of such African countries as Angola, Liberia, and Sierra Leone, where warlords and insurgents were mining and selling diamonds to finance their bloody activities. These stones became known as "blood diamonds" or "conflict diamonds." The 2006 political thriller *Blood Diamond* starring Leonardo DiCaprio raised Western awareness of the terror and tragedy associated with the production of diamonds. As a result, global consumers started to vet the origin of their potential purchase in search of diamonds that were "responsibly sourced."

At the same time, De Beers spotted a new competitor: the laboratory, where scientists cultured diamonds.[10] Recent technological breakthroughs had enabled the production of high-grade artificially made diamonds, vastly superior to cubic zirconia. For a typical wedding engagement-ring size of about 1 carat, consumers can save between 25 and 50 percent. Like cultured pearls and fake fur, cultured diamonds may gain in acceptance as naturally mined gems become more socially or environmentally costly to obtain. And nothing augments social acceptance more than celebrity endorsements. Dervla Cogan, co-owner of London-based Brilliant Inc. Ltd, boasts a long list of celebrity clients. Catherine, Duchess of Cambridge (the former Kate Middleton) wore cultured diamonds during part of Queen Elizabeth's *diamond* jubilee. What is the attraction of cultured diamonds? "Lab-grown diamonds are 'conflict-free,'" says Melissa Salas, director of marketing for Buy. com.[11] If Duchess Catherine feels comfortable wearing cultured diamonds during a diamond jubilee, then anybody can. Clearly, it was time to act. De Beers Forevermark embraced this opportunity; about its "mining sources," De Beers asserts,

Forevermark diamonds only come from a few carefully selected mines that are committed to high business, social and environmental standards ... These mines are located in various countries including Botswana, Namibia, South Africa, Australia and Canada.[12]

Forevermark addresses its lack of a tightly defined geography with its brand promise, "Consumers can be confident that Forevermark diamonds benefit the people, communities and countries from which they originate."[13] De Beers inscribes an icon and an identification number on the table facet of each diamond.

AUTHENTICATE INGREDIENTS AND PROCESSES

Each year in India alone, drinkers allegedly consume more Scotch whisky than the entire whisky production of Scotland and buy 30,000 more tons of Darjeeling tea than is actually produced![14] The most probable explanation is fraud in reporting and adulteration in production. That is why the authentication of products, preferably by an independent body, is important to natural resources branding. This authenticating body should conduct regular audits according to transparent standards and should communicate its authorization using some seal of approval. For example, to combat fraud in the Darjeeling tea market, the Tea Board of India administers the Darjeeling certification mark and logo.

No country is better at authenticating its natural resources than France. Roquefort is among the oldest examples; it was regulated by a parliamentary decree in the 15th century.[15] In the 19th century, the French took the lead by advocating for international protection of geographical indications by hosting and ratifying the Paris Convention for the Protection of Industrial Property of 1883. This took place after foreign inventors refused to attend the International Exhibition of Inventions in Vienna in 1873 because they feared that other countries would steal and commercially exploit their ideas.[16] The Convention applies to industrial property in the widest sense, including patents, marks, industrial designs, trade names, and geographical indications (indications of source and appellations of origin).[17]

The *appellation d'origine contrôlée* (AOC) – "controlled designation of origin" – is the French certification granted to certain French geographical areas for wines, cheeses, butters, and other agricultural products. It was set up by the government bureau Institut National des Appellations d'Origine, now named the Institut National de l'Origine et de la Qualité (INAO). The INAO guarantees that all AOC products hold to a rigorous set of clearly defined standards, covering both their territorial origin and their conformity to precise rules for production and processing that guarantee their distinctive character. Manufacturers of AOC-approved products may print the AOC seal on, for example, the labels of wines and the rinds of cheeses.[18]

The World Intellectual Property Organization, an agency of the United Nations, administers the Paris Convention and a number of other treaties that protect geographical indications, such as the Lisbon Agreement for the Protection of Appellations of Origin and Their International Registration (1958) and Articles 22–24 of the Agreement on Trade-Related Aspects of Intellectual Property Rights (TRIPS).[19] In any member country of the World Trade Organization, it is illegal to manufacture and sell a product under one of the AOC-controlled geographical indications if the product does not comply with the criteria of the AOC. To prevent any possible misrepresentation, manufacturers may not use an AOC name on the label of a product not qualifying for that AOC.[20] The effect? Anybody who purchases Haut Médoc wine or Roquefort cheese will have noted the price premium that these branded natural resources fetch compared to their lesser competitors and imitators.

SOUTH AFRICA'S WINE OF ORIGIN AUTHENTICATION PROGRAM

The French AOC authentication system has inspired other countries, although the criteria are often less stringent. Consider South Africa's "Wine of Origin" program, which defines the wine regions of South Africa. Wine regions under the Wine of Origin system fall into one of four categories: the largest and most generic are Geographical Units (e.g., the Western Cape region) which include smaller Regions (e.g., Overberg), followed by districts (e.g., Walker Bay), and finally wards (e.g., Elgin). The accreditation appears on wine labels together with the name of a production area, such as W.O. Stellenbosch, Durbanville, or Robertson. The aim is to assure the buyer that 100 percent of the grapes grew in a specific area, each of which should also produce wines with a distinctive character.[21]

HABANO OF CUBA

In some emerging markets, the rules are about as strict as in the AOC system. Consider Habano cigars. When we think of cigars, we usually think of Cuba. Corporation Habanos S.A. – a joint venture between the state-owned Cubatabaco and Altadis S.A., a Spanish company owned by the Imperial Tobacco Group PLC[22] – has leveraged this association to dominate the premium cigar segment, where it holds a global market share of 30 percent. The uniqueness of its cigars derives from Cuba's natural growing conditions, such as soil characteristics and climate, the different plant varieties of Cuban black tobacco needed to produce a high-quality cigar, and the elaborate production process.

The cigars are handmade under strict quality controls. A Cuban Habano requires five different types of leaves. The inner part forms the long filler and consists of three leaves with three different characteristics: Ligero for strength and flavor, Seco for aroma, and Volado for good combustion. A fourth leaf secures and wraps the long filler leaves. Together they form the "Bunche." The fifth leaf dresses the Habano and determines its appearance.

All this effort is worth protecting, and as a result, the company has devised a special Habano logo. It applies the Habanos Protected Denomination of Origin only to cigars made of 100 percent Cuban tobacco leaves selected from the island's best tobacco regions and manufactured in Cuba under the strictest quality control measures in the agricultural, curing, and manufacturing processes.[23] It affixes the Habano Cuban cigar trademark to boxes of brand names to indicate that the cigars receive the Habano Protected Denomination of Origin.

TAKE THE BRAND INTERNATIONAL

The final step is to leverage all international intellectual property protections in branding the natural resource. As noted, international treaties explicitly allow for legal protection of geographical indications. In the aforementioned TRIPS agreement, the World Trade Organization defines geographical indications as: "indications that identify a good as originating in the territory of a Member, or a region or locality in that territory, where a given quality, reputation or other characteristic of the good is essentially attributable to its geographic origin."[24] An appellation of origin is a special kind of geographical indication.

Emerging market firms can also seek protection of their natural resource brands under trademark laws in the form of collective marks or certification marks, laws against unfair competition, consumer protection laws, and specific laws or decrees that recognize individual geographical indications.[25] For example, state-owned Cubatabaco hired a New York lawyer to file a trademark infringement suit in federal court against a Michigan shopkeeper whose cigar store, "La Casa de la Habana," resembles Cubatabaco's retail franchise, "La Casa del Habano." Cubatabaco claimed that the average consumer would not be able to distinguish the Michigan retailer from the Habano trademarked stores.

The bigger challenge is to persuade consumers that a branded version of the natural resource – say, a Habano cigar – is not only distinguishable from, but also preferable to, the generic version. Natural resources are viewed more as commodities rather than as differentiated products. Thus, without an intensive branding campaign, consumers may not perceive any difference between the branded and the unbranded natural resource. To create strong natural resource brands, companies must file for international protection for their geographical origin.

While emerging market firms must obtain international recognition and protection for brand origin, they must also inform the Western consumer of the brand, its origin, and its unique benefits over unbranded varieties.

PURE CEYLON CINNAMON

Since time immemorial, human beings have prized cinnamon as a gift fit for monarchs and gods: an inscription in the temple of Apollo at Miletus (in present day Turkey) indicates that a devotee left an offering of the spice.[26] Now naturalized in South-East Asia, cinnamon – a spice extracted from the inner bark of several trees from the genus *Cinnamomum* – is native only to the island nation of Sri Lanka, the largest producer of cinnamon in the world. Sri Lanka has been taking steps to obtain "protected geographical indication" (PGI). On July 17, 2012, it announced that it had secured trademark rights for the "Pure Ceylon Cinnamon" brand name in the European Union. Sri Lanka has now two global PGI trademarks of natural resources – Pure Ceylon Cinnamon and Pure Ceylon Tea.[27] Manufacturers from other countries may not lawfully use Ceylon in their branding or marketing efforts.

Securing geographical indication rights is an important step forward for Sri Lankan producers. Another big step is educating Western consumers about real cinnamon, about its origins in Sri Lanka, and about the dramatic quality differences among the products sold as "cinnamon" in the West, for example the similar tasting and quite pervasive cassia, a spice that is inferior in terms of both health and sensory aspects according to experts. Pure Ceylon Cinnamon contains very low levels of coumarin (0.004%), considered safe for consumption. By contrast, cassia contains much higher levels of coumarin (5%), known to severely damage the liver. Further, Pure Ceylon Cinnamon has a smoother surface, is much sweeter, and has more flavor than cassia. Hence, consumers can reduce both the sugar and the amount of cinnamon needed in their recipes.[28]

CONCHA Y TORO

In the wine industry, especially French wines benefit from awareness of their geographical regions, and emerging market wines strive for that advantage. With annual sales of over $800 million, Chile's Concha y Toro has grown into one of the largest global wine brands. Two aspects of its branding strategy are noteworthy – its use of geography and its sophisticated use of sub-brands under the same Concha y Toro umbrella brand.

First, Concha y Toro promotes Chile's Central Valley, the geographical source of most of its wines:

> ... the Central Valley where the vineyards are naturally protected
> by the four frontiers of Chile:
>> To the north the Atacama Desert, the driest in the world.
>> To the south, the awesome Ice Fields.
>> To the West, the immense Pacific Ocean.
>> To the east, the majestic Andes Mountains.[29]

While consumers get no information about the valley itself, it sounds like an area that yields good grapes. Moreover, providing a geographical indication (e.g., "Central Valley") contributes to the quality image of the brand, even if consumers have limited or no knowledge of the area.[30] Geographical information shows that the brand belongs to a particular region, which gives it credibility. Finally, consumers may over time come to appreciate the region, based on positive product experiences and word of mouth.

Second, Concha y Toro produces 12 different wine sub-brands under the same umbrella brand, from basic Frontera – the best selling Chilean wine in the world – to premium Don Melchor, retailing at around $90 and highly praised by the world's most influential wine expert, Robert Parker.[31] This diverse portfolio allows for economies of scope and brand synergy. However, it may undermine consumer willingness to pay top dollars for super premium sub-brands as it is still "only a Concha y Toro."[32]

Concha y Toro taps into the super-premium segment in a joint venture with Baron Philippe de Rothschild. The brand Almaviva is marketed as "The recent synthesis of French tradition and American soil has delivered an exceptional wine embodying the best of both worlds." The label shows the two parents. Any association with Rothschild increases the credentials of the wine, which retails at $100 or more (dependent on the vintage). We encountered it at a tax-free shop at Hong Kong International Airport, chained against theft. The 2008 vintage is described by the Wine spectator as:

> Broad and muscular, boasting lots of dark currant and fig paste notes laced with loam, licorice snap and espresso flavors. The dense, fleshy finish lets a hint of roasted sage smolder. Very solid for the vintage. Cabernet Sauvignon, Carmenère and Cabernet Franc. Drink now through 2018.[33]

Now let's look at how Café de Colombia took all four steps – defined its geographical region, specified rigorous production standards, authenticated ingredients and processes, and then took the brand beyond Colombia – to create a brand in a highly commoditized category.

THE MAKING OF THE CAFÉ DE COLOMBIA BRAND

With a brand value of $11 billion, Nescafé is the strongest coffee brand in the world – in fact, it is one of the strongest brands period.[34] But Nescafé is a processed product sold by the largest food company in the world, Switzerland's Nestlé. How could a Columbian organization of coffee-growers successfully compete with its own brand of coffee? To make things worse, coffee is historically associated with Brazil, by far the world's largest coffee producer. When Federación Nacional de Cafeteros de Colombia (FNC) launched Café de Colombia, many Western consumers did not realize that coffee was grown in Colombia, a country better known for another crop. So how did FNC transform its beans into a premium-branded natural resource?[35]

It started with a crisis, as do many efforts that require a radical break with the past (recall the Havaianas example in the previous chapter). In the late 1950s, an excess supply of coffee in world markets led to a collapse in the price of Colombian coffee, from $0.85 to $0.45 per pound. To increase revenues, the FNC had to act. Its leadership team determined that building a global brand for Colombian coffee could yield increased demand, higher prices, and an improved standard of living for growers. This insight was truly radical. No one had branded coffee based on origin before.

The FNC decided to hire a world-class advertising agency, New-York based Doyle Dane Bernbach (DDB), to develop an international advertising campaign. DDB created the character of Juan Valdez, a fictional character like the Marlboro Man. He served to communicate to consumers and to represent the typical Colombian coffee-growing family traditions, the quality of Colombian mountain-grown coffee beans, and the labor-intensive process required to produce high-quality coffee. Television commercials showed Juan Valdez (initially a Cuban actor, later replaced by a real Colombian grower) hand-picking coffee beans in a coffee field.

The advertising campaign focused on educating trade and consumer audiences about the superiority of Café de Colombia. The Colombian coffee plant is of the species *Coffea arabica*, variety Colombian Milds, which grows only in Colombia, Kenya, and Tanzania (the latter two being minor producers). With its volcanic soil, tropical mountain climate, and high altitudes, Colombia provides an ideal *terroir* to grow high-quality Colombian Milds coffee beans. The production of high-quality beans is an elaborate process: growing, hand-picking, soaking, washing, drying, testing on aromas, color, size, and moisture, hulling, grading, sorting, and checking for imperfections. Only after this long process do the Colombian beans receive their stamp of approval for export.

The FNC's sustained advertising campaigns and related marketing efforts to brand Café de Colombia delivered results. In 1959, only 4 percent of all consumers in the United States knew that Colombians grew coffee; by 2005, awareness had increased to 92 percent. Awareness in other Western countries and in key emerging markets such as Russia, China, and South Africa was also very high (above 70 percent), as was awareness of Juan Valdez and identification of the Café de Colombia logo.

In 2007, Café de Colombia received the European Union's coveted Protected Geographical Indication certificate in recognition of the distinctive properties of Colombian Coffee uniquely associated to the geographical, topographical, and agroclimatic conditions under which the FNC grows it. It is the first non-EU product to receive PGI recognition.[36] The FNC pursued PGI for several reasons:

- To thwart coffee roasters' efforts to marginalize the country of origin of the coffee beans as a product characteristic. Roasters attempt to make origin irrelevant in order to gain sourcing flexibility, in which case they can switch at will between Colombia Arabicas and other Arabicas and in the process appropriate more of channel profits.
- To use country of origin as a differentiation tool that other coffee suppliers cannot copy, since geographical identification is intrinsically linked to the attributes and quality standards of the origin.
- To cater to the needs of younger consumers who demand more and better information about the supply chain (including origin and method of production) of food products (called "traceability" in agricultural marketing).[37]

As a consequence of the FNC's branding efforts, Western consumers began to grasp that not all coffee was created equal. People started to seek coffee from Colombia. Hence, Colombian coffee began to command a price premium over other Arabica coffees. Figure 7.2 shows the three-year moving average spot market prices (in $) per pound for Colombian Milds versus its two direct competitors, Other Mild Arabicas, and Brazilian and Other Natural Arabicas.[38] While coffee prices have always been very volatile, the figure shows that the FNC's branding efforts have allowed Colombian Milds to realize a price difference of around 8 percent over Other Mild Arabicas and 24 percent over Brazilian and Other Natural Arabicas[39] – very impressive for an agricultural commodity.

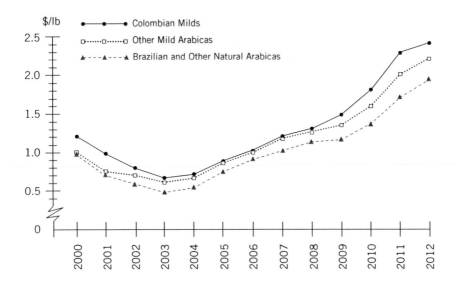

Figure 7.2 **Three-year moving average prices of three types of Arabica coffee**

Source: Authors' calculations based on data published by the International Coffee Organization.

MANAGERIAL TAKEAWAYS

It is "natural" to think of natural resources as undifferentiated commodities. Indeed, most economic textbooks treat them as such. But France more than any other country has shown how to turn natural resources into global brands. Why should emerging market companies not do the same, with their own many unique natural resources? In this chapter, we outline how executives of emerging market companies can brand their natural resources for global advantage, in a sequence of four steps:

1. The company must establish some association between the brand and a particular geographical area, which should be tightly defined, marketed as possessing unique characteristics, and associated with a myth.

2. The production process through which the natural resource is extracted and processed should be transparent, difficult to copy (to raise entry barriers), and elaborate (to imply quality).

3. To mitigate adulteration, if not outright fraud, emerging market firms needs authentication of the source and the process, ideally by an independent body. Authentication should involve regular audits and result in exclusive seals of approval.

4. To create a true brand, the company should try to obtain PGI from international organizations such as the EU or World Intellectual Property Organization. Ultimately, a strong brand resides in the mind of the consumer. Companies must overlay the preceding "reasons to believe" activities with marketing activities to make the branded natural resource more attractive than the unbranded (and cheaper) variety. For this, the branded resource must create awareness of the brand and the region, and communicate the difference.

EIGHT

THE NATIONAL CHAMPIONS ROUTE

LEVERAGING STRONG SUPPORT FROM THE STATE

What do Airbus, Michelin, Hyundai, NEC, Samsung, Singapore Airlines, Volkswagen, and LG have in common? They all started as national champions, companies supported by their governments at a time when their countries were emerging or recovering from the ravages of war. Their achievements in the global marketplace have inspired emerging countries to build their own national champions, with some notable successes.

For example, state-backed oil firms account for more than 75 percent of the world's oil reserves; the world's largest natural gas company is Russia's champion Gazprom. The largest cellular service provider is China Mobile, with 700 million customers.[1] Saudi Basic Industries Corporation is one of the world's most profitable chemical companies. Dubai Ports is the world's third-largest ports operator. Coal India is the world's largest coal-miner. State companies make up 80 percent of the value of the stock market in China, 62 percent in Russia, and 38 percent in Brazil.

Between 2003 and 2010, they accounted for one-third of the emerging world's foreign direct investment as well as a growing proportion of the world's very largest firms.[2]

Despite their ubiquity, many national champions have historically, from a financial perspective, performed poorly. For every success, there are multiple failures, national basket cases rather than national breadwinners. They usually tend to succeed in quasi-monopolistic industries such as energy and utilities, but rarely in hypercompetitive business to consumer (B2C) industries such as consumer electronics or packaged goods. Beyond financial failure, most national champions fall short on brand-building. Given this, why do governments attempt to create national champions? What are the benefits and limitations? More specifically, under what conditions can emerging market firms leverage state capitalism to create viable and profitable brands that consumers desire rather than creating just another inefficient Moloch, devouring state resources, extracting large rents from domestic consumers, and with no global potential?

A BRIEF HISTORY OF NATIONAL CHAMPIONS

A *national champion* is a business enterprise selected by the government of a nation-state to spearhead the national effort to compete internationally in a particular industry, such as natural resources (e.g., oil or iron ore), basic industries (e.g., steel or ship-building), intermediate goods (e.g., machine tools), energy (e.g., utilities or nuclear energy), consumer products (e.g., cars or computers), advanced technologies (e.g., telecommunication equipment, aerospace, or pharmaceuticals), and services (e.g., banks or airlines). The champion receives special treatment, including subsidies, market protection (e.g., tariffs and import restrictions), and firm-specific or industry-specific policies that foster their growth.

State-owned enterprises have existed since the Roman Empire. The modern concept of the national champion originated with

Jean-Baptiste Colbert (1619–83), Louis XIV's famous Minister of Finance. Envious of the manufacturing prowess of the Dutch Republic and England, Colbert pushed through *dirigiste* policies to foster manufacturing enterprises in a wide variety of fields. The government established new industries, protected inventors, invited workmen from foreign countries, and prohibited French workers from emigrating. It transformed the economically weak French kingdom into a manufacturing powerhouse, with a special emphasis on luxury goods. All of Europe sought French Gobelin tapestries and Sèvres porcelain. That France still leads in luxury goods attests to the long-term success of Colbert's policies.[3]

Contemporary scholarship, specifically the work of Andrew Shonfield, Stephen S. Cohen, and John Zysman on French economic policies has sparked a resurgence of interest in national champions.[4] The overriding theme of this scholarship is best summarized by the philosophy of *économie concertée*, which prescribes:

- the merger of small firms into a national champion;
- the close partnership between the state and big business, aimed at managing rapid but orderly increases in output and productivity;
- the support of exports in semi-competitive markets;
- the creation of internally protected markets for the national champions and outright subsidies for these firms.[5]

This philosophy, now referred to as *state capitalism*, has provided a blueprint for cultivating national champions.[6]

THE RATIONALE FOR NATIONAL CHAMPIONS

Governments usually advocate the creation of national champions on the basis of industrial policy, strategic trade, and national security.[7]

INDUSTRIAL POLICY RATIONALE

The industrial policy rationale holds that certain sectors of the home economy are particularly valuable because they provide high-paying jobs and/or high value-added business activities. Unless a country wants to remain a collection of screwdriver factories, the government must actively nurture home-grown firms. The industrial policy rationale raises a fundamental question about the linkage between corporate ownership structures and economic success.[8] The unstated assumption among Western policy-makers and executives – and one that we encounter all the time in our discussions with Western managers – is that dispersed ownership structures (many companies competing with each other) produce better economic outcomes than state capitalism, characterized by concentrated ownership structures around a small number of very large national champions. For example, then European Union Competition Commissioner Neelie Kroes said, "It is open, competitive markets that generate wealth – not politicians," and United States Federal Trade Commission Chairman Deborah Majoras gave a speech entitled "National champions: I don't even think it sounds good."[9]

Yet there is no denying that concentrated ownership structure around a small set of national champions has been the engine of development in emerging markets of the time, starting with the world's earliest emerging market, the US. In the late 19th century, the US adopted this approach to build its own industrial base in the face of overwhelming British economic might. In this so-called robber baron era, the economy was dominated by large, politically connected conglomerates operating in a weak institutional environment without anti-trust scrutiny. Later, this approach was used by Germany, Japan, and South Korea, and currently China is the most prominent (although certainly not the only) example.

So, what can we learn from the history of state capitalism and its main vehicle – national champions? It teaches us that:

- the corporation is a very effective organizational vehicle for promoting investment, productive enterprise, and economic development;
- dispersed corporate ownership is not a necessary condition for transformative economic development;
- national champions are an important and often (although certainly not invariably) viable approach to developing key industries;
- policies evolve over time – today's national champions can be tomorrow's private enterprises, in open competitive markets (cf. developments in Germany, Japan, and the US).

From this discussion, it should be obvious why tweaking industrial policy appeals to emerging markets. The leadership of these countries maintains that they need home-grown companies and their own ecosystem of suppliers to move the economy forward. For example, for every job created by a state-supported automobile plant in China, Chinese suppliers create four additional jobs, at relatively high wage levels. More broadly, in almost every major industry, China is building a world-leading company.

India also uses industrial policy to promote national champions. Its first Five Year Plan called for developing the Indian economy in general, and the rural sector in particular. The commercial banks of the country, including the Imperial Bank of India, however, confined their services to the urban sector. Consequently, in 1955, India nationalized the Imperial Bank of India, renaming it the State Bank of India, to offer retail services to the entire country and loans to critical developmental sectors. With assets of $360 billion and more than 14,000 branches, including 173 foreign offices in 37 countries, the State Bank of India has become a *Global Fortune* 500 company. However, that has not been without it being seen as a bastion of inefficiency and having unions go on strike frequently to protest issues such as the adoption of computers.

STRATEGIC TRADE RATIONALE

The strategic trade rationale argues that the state should maintain a home-grown presence in sectors where (1) economies of scale are exceptionally large – often larger than the ability of any single national market to absorb output efficiently; (2) barriers to entry are especially high; and (3) rent-seeking is especially prevalent. Without state help, such sectors are subject to pre-emption by foreign firms or rival states.

Consider the aerospace industry, characterized by huge economies of scale and high barriers to entry. Developing a new plane has large up-front associated costs and business risk. In the 1970s, three US giants – Boeing, McDonnell Douglas, and Lockheed Martin – dominated the market. Many European aircraft manufacturers innovated but had such small production runs that they could not compete with the US companies. As a result, state-owned airlines depended on US manufacturers that could charge high (oligopolistic) prices. To break into the market, European governments (especially those of France, Germany, and the United Kingdom) united to set up Airbus Industrie in 1974. Since these uncertain beginnings, the market for large (that is, over 150 passenger) planes has become essentially a duopoly – Airbus versus Boeing. Airbus makes great planes, but few experts believe that it could have broken into the market without very generous "launch aid" and other forms of government largesse. Today, about three-quarters of the Air France and Lufthansa planes are Airbus, and this cannot be a coincidence.[10]

Emerging market governments have noticed Airbus's success. Brazil's Embraer may not yet command the affinity among consumers that other brands do, but B2C national champions can learn from it. Founded in 1969 by presidential decree, Embraer benefitted from Brazil's tax policies, capital injections, and preferential purchase arrangements. It transformed its scientific and technological knowledge into marketing and engineering capabilities, trademarking its designs from day one, licensing technology from other aircraft manufacturers, patenting its own innovations, and applying for – and receiving – certification for its first wholly designed and manufactured aircraft, the Bandeirante, by the world's leading aviation authorities. However, political consider-ations began to trump business considerations, and Embraer required drastic restructuring to spare it from bankruptcy. In 1994 it began a privatization process, and in 2000 went public on both the New York and São Paulo Stock Exchanges.

Embraer is now a dominant player in the regional jet market, pushing such European companies as Fokker out of business. To date, it has delivered over 1,700 turbo-propeller and (more recently) jet airplanes, with a 1,000-order backlog and options.[11] Consumer response is also positive. Brett Snyder of Cranky Concierge (not an easy source to satisfy) calls the E-series more comfortable than most other aircraft of that size. America's largest newspaper, *USA Today,* reported, "The E-jets are roomy enough; fliers love them, small enough airlines need them."[12]

Airbus and Embraer provide a viable organizational model for the Commercial Aircraft Corporation of China (Comac). Comac's C919 jet, under development, is "the nation's multi-billion-dollar gamble to take on the Airbus and Boeing aviation duopoly, the first step in China's ambitions to become a global force in the aerospace industry."[13] With 168–190 seats, the single-aisle C919 is competing directly against the Airbus A320neo and the Boeing 737 MAX. It will be the largest commercial airliner designed and built in China. Its first flight is expected in 2014, with deliveries scheduled for 2016. General Electric (GE) will supply avionics in a joint venture with Aviation Industry Corporation of China. GE understood from China's five-year plan that if it wanted to sell avionics in China, it ought to produce them there.[14]

Breaking into a market characterized by large development costs, huge economies of scale, and high risk aversion among customers (airlines) and consumers (passengers) is extremely tough. However, even before the end of the design phase of the

C919, Comac has already secured 380 orders. The purchasing airlines were all Chinese, such as China Eastern Airlines, Air China, and China Southern Airlines. Interest abroad is slower to emerge, although Comac has signed nonbinding memorandums of understanding with a few international carriers such as the parent corporation of British Airways.[14]

Clearly, China is taking a leaf from the Airbus playbook, and then some. A person close to Airbus says, "Of all the newcomers, Comac will be the strongest – not because they have the best skills base today but because they have more financial firepower than anybody else. They can sink billions into aircraft projects without any concern for the bottom line." Boeing is not sanguine either. Its former head of the commercial aircraft division, Jim Albaugh, concludes, "Whether the C919 is a good aeroplane I don't know, but eventually they'll get it right."[15] All this bodes well for Comac's long-term viability, even though it faces competition in the narrow-body segment from Russia, which is developing its own modern passenger jet, the MC-21, manufactured by United Aircraft, expected to enter service in 2017 according to its President, Mikhail Pogosyan. But Comac is in a better position. After all, aviation experts expect China to be the most valuable aircraft market over the next 20 years. Airbus estimates that China will need more than 4,000 aircraft, worth half a trillion dollars.

NATIONAL SECURITY RATIONALE

The national security rationale holds that countries must avoid dependence on foreign firms that might delay, deny, or constrain the provision of goods and services crucial for proper functioning of the home economy or its security apparatus. Consider what happened to France in the 1960s. France left the North Atlantic Treaty Organization and pursued its own, independent nuclear arsenal, called the *force de frappe*. In response, the Lyndon B. Johnson Administration ordered IBM and Control Data to withhold advanced computer technology from France. At the time, these two US companies had a virtual monopoly on high-speed computational abilities, so Johnson's order seriously delayed French work on the hydrogen bomb. It also reinforced the notion that Europeans needed their own computer firms to serve their national needs, rather than depend on US firms.[16] Unfortunately, the results were disastrous. Who thinks of Italy's Olivetti, France's Bull Information Systems, or Britain's International Computers as a serious challenger to IBM in the computer market?

To us, government officials can more easily (although not always more legitimately) argue for national security in the business to business sector. Emerging markets do not want foreigners to control the exploitation and supply of their native energy and metals. That is why we find the largest national champions in the extractive industries (e.g., Coal India, Petrobras, Pemex, CNPC, Gazprom, ONGC, Vale, and Saudi Aramco). Their respective governments consider these industries to be fundamental to the country's sovereignty, wealth, security, and development.

But one could argue for national champions in *any* industry where foreign firms could withhold supply. Ambitious politicians or underperforming business people who look for state protection against more efficient foreign competitors obviously abuse this argument. Indeed, why only oil, minerals, and airlines, but not steel (for guns), footwear (for boots), textiles (for uniforms), or food? Not too long ago, the French government even declared the yogurt industry to be a national security interest.

THE LIMITS OF NATIONAL CHAMPIONS

Despite the arguments above for national champions, they suffer from several limitations.

LIMITS TO THE IMPORTANCE OF A FIRM'S NATIONALITY

How important a factor is nationality to a company's behavior or to the decisions of its executives? History shows that, over time, the leaders of national champions lose their ability – or willing-ness – to respond to the needs of local politicians and their constit-uents, if such a response runs contrary to corporate self-interest or sound business practices. For example, the French President regu-larly summons CEOs of French national champions to the Palais de l'Elysée for "a drubbing whenever they suggest closing a factory or offshoring production."[17]

Business strategists have noted that, in the long run, the global marketplace imposes consistent discipline upon similar companies of different nationality, and their behaviors converge. According to Berkeley professor Robert Reich, the market should favor any company that improves productivity in its use of domestic resources, pays higher wages, conducts local research and develop-ment (R&D), and generates spillovers and externalities that benefit the local economy, independent of who owns the equity shares.[18]

The British car industry is a case in point. The end of state ownership did not spell the end of the industry. On the contrary, production more than doubled from 837,000 in 1995 to about two million vehicles in 2012, with 80 percent of them exported. And, for the first time, the UK is making more money from exporting cars than it spends on importing them. Car makers such as Toyota, Nissan, and BMW recently announced investments in British plants totaling £4 billion. The industry accounts for 10 percent of Britain's exports and employs more than 700,000 people.[19]

LIMITS TO THE ECONOMIC-POLITICAL
USEFULNESS OF NATIONAL CHAMPIONS

Apart from the fundamental question about the substantive role of nationality in a firm's behavior in the long run, there are economic-political limits to the usefulness of national champions. The preferential treatment of national champions may be so strong that it stifles the competitive rivalry necessary for continuous product improvement and the development of brands vital for survival in the global marketplace.

Relatedly, national champions devour capital and human talent that private firms might have deployed more efficiently. For example, despite accounting for only 15 percent of employment, two-thirds of all bank loans in China go to the public sector.[20] Studies have shown that national champions use resources less efficiently than private companies. The Beijing-based Unirule Institute of Economics found that, once one corrects for hidden subsidies such as free land and lower interest rates, "the real return on equity of state-owned and state-holding enterprises from 2001 to 2009 is [negative] 6.3 percent."[21] China is not alone. The Organization for Economic Cooperation and Development (OECD) reported that the total factor productivity of private companies is twice that of state companies.[22] Government directions to national champions are also highly susceptible to political considerations. Take Coal India, the state-backed energy group. Critics have accused the Indian government of using Coal India for "politically convenient ends," "stacking its management and board of directors with former civil servants loyal to their political masters."[23] Given its deemed monopoly and consequent profits of $2.7 billion, Coal India may be too attractive to leave alone.[24]

Indeed, along with political cronyism and quasi-monopolies comes corruption. National champions receive resources and "enjoy rents in excess over their free market equilibrium value."[25] Economists Alberto Ades and Rafael di Tella studied the effect of industrial policy geared toward national champions and the level of corruption in a sample of 32 developed and emerging countries. They found that the existence of policies favoring national champions goes hand in hand with corruption. As a consequence, this leads to an inefficient use of public funds and allocation of resources.[25]

LIMITS TO THE WISDOM OF GOVERNMENT BUREAUCRATS TO CHOOSE WISELY

Finally, why would government bureaucrats be smarter than the market in selecting winners? Many countries have tried to create and maintain national champions in "sunrise" industries such as high tech. However, the historical record of Europe and Japan in the 1970s and 80s shows how difficult picking winners is. Emerging market bureaucrats have long regarded Japan as the model for industrial policy and national champion prowess. But careful retrospective analysis has failed to find consistent evidence that subsidies or preferential tax treatment contributed to the total productivity growth in targeted sectors. Japan's famous Ministry of International Trade and Industry helped Isuzu and Mitsubishi Motors and ignored Toyota and Honda. The latter two rose through the entrepreneurial energy of their founders, not through public aid.[26] To compound this issue, the political process favors the well-connected insiders over such innovative outsiders as Amancio Ortega (Zara), Steve Jobs (Apple), Bill Gates (Microsoft), Larry Page (Google), Li Ka-shing (Cheung Kong Holdings), Mark Zuckerberg (Facebook), Sam Walton (Wal-Mart), and Karl Albrecht (Aldi). Economist Michael J. Boskin summarized nicely, "Industrial policy failed in the 1970s and 1980s. Letting governments, rather than marketplace competition pick winners and losers is just as bad an idea today."[27] The failure of state capitalism argues for a policy of "let hundred flowers blossom," that is, let the invisible hand of the market reveal the winners.

If picking involves a new technology among rival technologies, then putting all one's money on a single national champion is very risky. After all, acceptance of new technologies depends on an entire ecosystem of domestic and foreign companies, and the trajectory of each alternative technology. For example, the state-owned giant China Mobile is the largest cellular phone operator in the world, with 698 million subscribers to date, accounting for two-thirds of the Chinese mobile market in 2012. It has a market cap of $200 billion, making it the most valuable telecom company in the world. But in fast 3G connections, the fastest-growing part of China's cellular industry, China Mobile is much less of a force and its market share is slipping.

What precipitated China Mobile's slide?[28] When Beijing issued 3G licenses in 2009, it asked the national champion to use a locally developed technology called TD-SCDMA. Chinese regulators hoped that China Mobile's adoption of the technology would boost domestic technologists and reduce royalty payments on the licenses of foreign-owned patents. But global chip-makers and phone manufacturers have been reluctant to design components for this domestic technology. As a result, China Mobile subscribers could not use the iPhone or many phones running on Android, and consider the carrier's own selection of handsets "boring." In contrast, in the same year, the state let China Mobile's two competitors start building their 3G networks using the world's two most common standards W-CDMA (China Unicom) and CDMA2000 (China Telecom).

WHEN CAN NATIONAL CHAMPIONS BUILD CONSUMER BRANDS?

Various experts have called the policy of bolstering national champions "a boulevard of broken dreams" or "usually an ill-advised attempt," but we take a more nuanced view. We believe that a state can successfully incubate national champions into global brands in consumer markets, provided that the government leaders consider these three conditions: community, competition, and company (Figure 8.1).

COMMUNITY

The state can play a positive role in the business community, such that it helps to launch healthy national champions that develop global capabilities. Here are the necessary traits.

Competent, not corrupt

State capitalism works well only when directed by a competent state, and not by one mired in corruption and cronyism. By

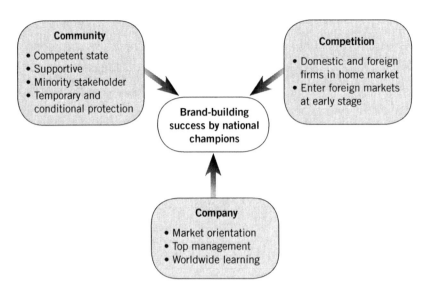

Figure 8.1 **C3 framework of factors determining the success of national champions as a global brand**

"competency," we mean a state that operates consistently and predictably, that is, with openness, accountability, and honesty in decision-making and action-taking, and manned by highly educated bureaucrats who have to pass rigorous exams. East-Asian countries have a decided advantage over other emerging markets on this front because of their strong Mandarin culture and long history of a reasonably well-organized, highly educated state bureaucracy inspired by Confucius. According to Confucianism, society is structured around hierarchical and *reciprocal* relations (e.g., between the government and the people). Ruthless rulers and disobedient citizens are both morally unacceptable. China's state employees are selected based on rigorous examinations testing applicants' knowledge on a wide range of subjects – a tradition that dates back to at least the Song dynasty, and before.

In contrast, the Middle East, Latin America, and Africa have neither a comparable cultural tradition nor a history of impartial courts and the rule of law to counter the arbitrariness of the state. Argentina is an example of a potentially rich country – it was the eighth most prosperous nation in 1909 – whose incompetent leadership has repeatedly destroyed its economy. In 2012, it grabbed control of oil and gas producer YPF from Spain's Repsol. Probably, it will run this company into the ground within the next 10 years – as Venezuela did with its state oil company PDVSA.

Supportive, not directive

The state should support rather than direct business activities. The state should set up economic and knowledge infrastructures in which national champions can seed and flourish. By "economic infrastructure," we mean a market mechanism that protects national champions for a short time against foreign encroachment, subsidizes R&D, and finances state purchases. By "knowledge infrastructure," we mean a rigorous primary and secondary education system for all citizens, both vocational and university options, and ongoing job training programs. For national champions to compete globally on quality rather than price, the state must cultivate scientists, technologists, and engineers to conduct first-rate R&D.

For example, Brazil recently took the initiative to improve its knowledge infrastructure. By the end of 2015, it will have sent more than 100,000 Brazilians, half of them undergraduates, half graduate students, abroad for a year to study such subjects as biotechnology, ocean science, and petroleum engineering that the government regards as essential for the nation's future as a manufacturing power. The initiative will cost $1.65 billion, a quarter of which will come from business and the rest from the state.

Minority, not majority, shareholder

If the state hold shares in the national champion, it should hold few. The minority-shareholder model, pioneered in Brazil, has been called "one of the sharpest new tools in the state-capitalist toolbox."[29] It limits the state's ability to use national champions for rewarding clients or pursuing social policies.[30] Private shareholders have just enough power to insist on greater fiscal and operational efficiency and managerial effectiveness. A McKinsey study found that companies in which the state holds a minority stake are 70 percent more productive than wholly state-owned ones.[22] Moreover, by taking a minority stake, the state can assist many more companies with the same amount of resources.

Temporary and conditional, not permanent and unlimited, protection

Finally, state support must be short term and conditional on market performance. Without clear limits on the duration and the nature of state support, the company will never learn to compete. Market-based performance metrics force the company to focus on its customers as well as its bureaucratic owners.

We are fans of "hard" metrics such as market share, profit, and return on investment (ROI), but these metrics can be misleading. Given cheap money and strong protection, even corporate sluggards can show a high market share and good ROI. For example, according to the Unirule Institute of Economics, the real interest rate for Chinese state-owned enterprises is only one-third of the market interest rate.[31] Under those terms, it is actually difficult not to turn a profit. A more useful metric is *customer satisfaction*, for which validated measurement instruments exist.[32] If the state applies such market-based measures, it will spot the national champion's failure to deliver desirable goods and services much earlier. After all, satisfying customers in the home market is a *conditio sine qua non* to compete for consumers in the global arena.

COMPETITION

Just like soccer teams in the English Premier League get better by playing each week against strong rival soccer teams, firms sharpen their skills by competing both in their home market and abroad.

Home market rivalry, not quasi-monopoly

If the national champion enjoys a quasi-monopoly in the home market, it does not learn to stand on its merits. Monopolies breed complacency and stifle innovation. Given its protected position, the company lacks incentive to develop innovative capabilities or to listen to the voice of the consumer. Such companies stand little chance outside their home market. Says *The Economist*: "At home, it is hard to argue that any of the really big firms – the banks, the telecoms firms and petrol companies – draw customers because of any special appeal rather than their ubiquity and lack of competitors."[33]

The national champion must face competition from other firms, including cutting-edge international firms on its home turf. And this competition should be fierce, not token, relegated to a niche. The government should encourage foreign competitors to put the national champion on edge. In the short term, the absence of competition may make the industry more attractive; but in the long run, more rivalry in one's home market puts pressure on national champions to innovate, improve, and move beyond basic advantages that the home country may enjoy, such as low factor costs. After cutting their teeth at home, national champions should take their brands abroad.

Foreign, not just domestic, markets

Andy Grove, the former CEO of Intel once said, "You have no choice but to operate in a world shaped by globalization …. There are two options: Adapt or Die." The trend toward globalization is very powerful, if not unstoppable. Industry boundaries no longer stop at national borders, and competition intensifies in industry after industry. Even national champions can no longer hide behind high tariff walls that work in the short run but hobble the champion in the longer run. They must go global, and the earlier the national champion faces the rigors of global competition, the sooner it will adapt its operations and adopt a customer-based brand-building approach.

COMPANY

Last but not least, the successful national champion should possess certain key characteristics to build strong consumer brands. Three traits stand out.

Market, not product/political, orientation

Too often, national champions focus on output (product orientation) or on the government (political orientation). Ajit Singh, India's civil aviation minister, charged with the turnaround of Air India, observed, "It is very difficult for the government to run any service sector business. For government employees, they are the kings; the customer is never the king. That's ingrained."[34] While this focus may serve a company without global ambitions, it is a handicap to the development of successful global brands and world-class service. The primary, if not sole, orientation of the B2C company should be toward the needs of the consumer. Which segment should we target? How can our brand serve this segment effectively using our marketing mix – our brand positioning, product assortment, pricing and promotion strategy, and distribution channels?

If market orientation does not guide the company's thinking, developing a brand will be difficult, because configuring the marketing mix depends on the needs and characteristics of the target segment. After all, strong brands originate in the minds of the consumer. Consumers love strong brands because they fulfill important needs: functional needs (what does it do for me or help me to do?), emotional needs (how does it make me feel?), and self-expressive needs (what does it say about me?). Numerous studies have shown that strong brands command higher consumer loyalty, reduced price sensitivity, higher advertising effectiveness, and greater trade leverage. But these benefits accrue to the firm only because the brand stands for something and delivers something that the target consumer group values.

That is why Russia's Lada is a weak domestic automobile brand while Hyundai has become a strong international brand. Lada fails to deliver on consumers' functional, emotional, or self-expressive needs (except perhaps that of national pride). Thus, it can compete only on price. In effect, it is what economists call an "inferior good," a product for which demand declines with rising income. In contrast, Hyundai successfully built its brand around the functional "value" proposition – good quality for a lower price, supported by its "Assurance" powertrain warranty, trade-in value guarantee, and job-loss protection plan. Its next challenge is to form a strong emotional connection with customers.

Business executives, not political appointments

While it is unavoidable that there are ties between the national champion and the government, this can easily result in the C-suite being filled by political appointments, bureaucrats rather than businessmen and entrepreneurs. After an in-depth study of state-owned enterprises, the Unirule Institute of Economics concluded, "Enterprise senior executives enter the government for policies and resources, while governmental officials enter enterprises to materialize their economic profits earned while in the position."[21] These people have little incentive to develop their companies' brands despite having access to vast resources and political pull, since their career is tied to the state, not to the vagaries of the marketplace.[35]

It is important to emphasize that cozy ties between business and politics, and political appointments are not restricted to emerging markets. The *Financial Times* criticizes the omnipresence of the Élysée (that is, the Office of the President) in pulling strings and nominating the heads of French industrial champions: "The politics of patronage often dictate the appointments of top managers in state-controlled or quasi state companies with inevitable disturbing results."[36] And some also see the common practice of US companies hiring former politicians as senior executives or corporate lobbyists to obtain regulatory favors, from tax breaks to other subsidies, in this light.

Worldwide learning, not home market knows best

To succeed in developed markets, national champions must develop an organizational capacity for worldwide learning, rather than adopting a home-centric (called "ethnocentric" in the strategy literature) view of the world. The company-wide generation of market intelligence pertaining to the current and future needs of existing and potential customers around the world, the dissemination of intelligence within the company, its responsiveness to this intelligence in its product development, marketing strategy, and organizational form, and the ability of the company to learn from its successes or failures in different markets are preconditions for the growth of brand-building capabilities.

Some analysts have argued that national champions have the potential to be "the corporate world's greatest learning machines."[37] Their CEOs often maintain they have the best of both worlds: the ability to plan for and invest in the future, but also to respond quickly to changing consumer tastes, without the shackles of meeting quarterly expectations. This is nice in theory, but learning takes a long time. What can these companies do to accelerate learning on a worldwide scale?

First, they can acquire foreign companies to gain rare technological and brand-building expertise. China's car company Geely gained access to cutting-edge car-making and brand-building skills when it took over Volvo for $1.8 billion. Organic learning of these crucial skills would have taken many years.

Second, listing the company on foreign exchanges (as Embraer did) introduces the brand to the world's most sophisticated bankers and analysts, although ongoing market scrutiny and expectation of returns may undermine a national champion's ability to plan for the long term.

Third, the national champion should hire foreign talent trained at the world's top business schools. The company must become global, not only in its strategy, but also in its culture and people. Lenovo, for example, has adopted English as its official language, which greatly facilitates company-wide learning, and contributes to fostering of a global corporate identity. But this human resource objective is not easy. In most successful global companies, executives from the home country prefer to prepare local managers who may accede to senior jobs at headquarters. Because national champions are still in essence tied to the state, their leaders must remain home-country nationals.

PROTON: DOING SO MANY THINGS WRONG

In 1983, then Prime Minister Dr. Mahathir Mohamad launched Proton, the Malaysian National Car Project, and a number of other industrial mega-projects to catapult Malaysia into the 21st century. When Proton launched its first model, the Saga, consumers dubbed it the *Potong Harga* meaning "cut-price." To keep prices artificially lower than imports, the state imposed heavy import duties on foreign-made cars while giving customers of a new Proton car a 50 percent rebate on the excise duty. Value-priced with a great deal of national pride behind it, Proton's Saga – essentially a retooled version of an aging Mitsubishi Lancer – overtook all other brands, securing 73 percent of the Malaysian passenger car market by 1988.

But the Malaysian market was simply not large enough to support the huge economies of scale needed for efficient production. Thus, Proton would need to export products for long-term viability. However, the lack of direct competition at Proton models' price points enabled Proton to continue selling very outdated designs of low quality with few of the "extras" such as life-saving technology (e.g., electronic stability control and anti-lock braking systems) that foreign brands had featured for many years. Consequently, Proton fared terribly in the brutal global car market. In 2010, Proton lost money on its exports of merely 20,000 cars, which accounted for 9.2 percent of total sales. Its outdated models drew unflattering attention. For example, the UK's massively popular automobile program *Top Gear* reviewed the new Proton Savvy (£7,830 to £8,530): "Truly awful, but we are grateful to Proton for reminding us of how good every other small car on sale in the UK is. We suggest you try buying one of those instead."[38] Not surprising, Proton sales in the UK dropped from a hardly whopping 2,700 in 2002 to a measly 767 in 2010.

Worse, Proton's artificially low price lost its domestic appeal as Malaysians became more prosperous. By 2011, its market share at home had dropped below 30 percent. But before we give up on national champions, let us end this chapter on a more positive note with the success story of Emirates.

EMIRATES AIRLINES: GLOBAL BRAND AND NATIONAL CHAMPION[39]

The largest airline in the Middle East is Emirates Airlines, a subsidiary of The Emirates Group, wholly owned by the government of Dubai. Operating over 2,400 passenger flights per week, Emirates serves 120 cities in 70 countries across all continents. Founded in 1985, Emirates became profitable within the first year and has steadily built its network. In the period 2000–12, its compound annual growth rate was 17.6 percent for passengers, 23.1 percent for sales revenues, and 12.3 percent for profits – remarkable for a brutally competitive industry.[40] Sir Richard Branson of Virgin Airlines famously said, "The fastest way to become a millionaire is to start out a billionaire and then go into the airline business." Moreover, Dubai is located in an area better known for threats to air travel than for a positive flight experience.

RATIONALE: NATIONAL SECURITY

In the mid-1980s, Bahrain's Gulf Air began to cut back services to Dubai. This made Dubai less accessible, dramatically reducing

Dubai's attractiveness for business and threatening the growth and prosperity of the home economy. As a result, the ruling Royal Family funded the founding of Emirates.

C3 FRAMEWORK

The leadership of Emirates made the right decisions and took the right actions in the three areas critical to a national champion's success.

Community

Even though Emirates received two used Boeing 727 and $10 million in start-up capital (repaid in a year), the government of Dubai required it to operate independently of government subsidies. The state did help Emirates by investing $4.5 billion to build a first-rate travel infrastructure and tourist draw, Dubai International Airport's Terminal 3, for the airline's exclusive use. Furthermore, there is the suspicion that the government financially supports Emirates, sponsoring activities in order to make Dubai a global hub and a tourism heaven. It is true that the state also profits from increased incoming traffic. After all, Dubai had limited resources. The oil is all in neighboring Abu Dhabi.

Competition

Emirates has a negligible home market (the population of the entire United Arab Emirates is only eight million), so it had to attract international passengers, who have many carrier options unless they plan to fly to, or through, Dubai. Thus, entering foreign markets early was not an option; it was a dire necessity.

Company

The state appointed Sir Maurice Flanagan as Emirates' founding CEO. Flanagan was an industry veteran: after serving in the Royal Air Force, he joined British Airways as a management trainee in 1953. Clearly not a government bureaucrat, but an industry buff, he has been largely responsible not only for Emirates' inaugural flight, but also for its ongoing success. Over his career, he has been repeatedly honored for his contributions to the industry, including *Flight International* magazine's Personality of the Year, membership of the British Travel Industry Hall of Fame, and the Aviation Legend award by the Centre for Asia Pacific Aviation. The current Chairman, Sheikh Ahmed bin Saeed Al Maktoum, is a senior member of the Royal Family, but four of nine members in the C-suite are non-nationals. Emirates employs those with business experience in general, and industry experience in particular, in its operations and governance.

"Open" is the watchword for Emirates. Its corporate philosophy emphasizes its openness to change, to new ideas, to diversity, and to opportunity. It views diversity as a defining strength of the company: it actively recruits the world's best and brightest, and its sizable workforce hails from 163 countries.

Given the intense competitive environment and limited state support, Emirates needed to orient its services to the market. Otherwise it would have gone bankrupt before the end of the 1980s. In sum, Emirates had most, if not all, the conditions in place to build a strong brand.

MARKETING STRATEGY TO CREATE A STRONG BRAND

In contrast to a *quasi-monopoly brand* that consumers buy because they lack any other option, the principles of developing a *strong national champion brand* do not differ from those used by any other company. The national champion must define its target segment, develop a brand promise or position, and determine a marketing mix (product/service, price, promotion, and place/distribution) to fulfill the brand promise.

Target segment

A senior executive at Emirates described its target consumer as "a person who is willing to pay a premium for additional services. Also for those customers who care about accessibility and availability as Emirates provides one of most extensive city pair connectivity with high capacity." The target segment is therefore international travelers who care about schedule convenience embodied in accessibility and availability, and who seek service rather than price. This target segment generally looks for a global brand. From the beginning, Emirates decided to operate outside the Middle East, as a global airline rather than a regional one. With connectivity and availability in mind, it employed the following slogans to reach this target: "Fly Emirates. To Over 100 Destinations" and "Fly Emirates, in Six Continents." Most recently, it has started to use "Fly Emirates. Keep Discovering."

Brand promise

Mike Simon, Senior Vice President, Corporate Communications, formulates Emirates' brand promise, "From day one, Emirates has set out to be an innovative, modern, and customer-oriented provider of high quality air travel services. Our brand positioning is that of a leading international and quality airline serving the global community." Anyone who has flown recently on US carriers knows how ambitious this brand promise is to fulfill. But Emirates has delivered consistently through world-class service and an integrated marketing mix, wherein the various elements mutually support each other.

Product/service

Among the first airlines to fly the path-breaking Airbus A380, Emirates has one of the world's most modern fleets, making for fewer breakdowns and delays. It is famous for its high-end in-flight cuisine and wine, its high level of service quality, and its service innovations such as individual entertainment centers and phones for passengers in *all* cabins.

Price

Emirates has a prestigious global brand image, but its price positioning uniquely places its services between the world's most expensive airlines and the low-cost, no-frills carriers. The Airbus A380 helps Emirates to service those routes where it has limited landing rights, thus ensuring a larger volume of passengers on a single trip at a lower cost per head. High total volume and occupancy rates combined with low operating costs give Emirates a distinct cost advantage; staff costs are about 20 percent of total versus an industry average of up to 35 percent. Consequently, it can offer luxury travel/brand experience as its peers, but at prices of up to 40 percent less. Thus, Emirates does not compete with price-based carriers, but it does offer better value than such established rivals as Air France or Lufthansa.

Promotion

The main component of Emirates promotion activities is its sponsorship of sports events. In 2004, Emirates and Arsenal Football Club signed the biggest club sponsorship in English soccer history to date. The deal included naming rights for a 15-year term to the new stadium, "Emirates Stadium," in Ashburton Grove, London, as well as an eight-year shirt sponsorship ("Fly Emirates") deal from the 2006/2007 season onward, worth some £100 million. By the end of 2012, Arsenal had signed a new £150 million deal with Emirates airline, extending its shirt sponsorship to 2019. The naming rights to the Emirates Stadium in north London were also extended to 2028 as part of the deal. Emirates also concluded sponsorship agreements with a number of other soccer clubs, the Asian Football Confederation, and Fédération Internationale de Football Associations (FIFA).

Soccer, the most popular sport worldwide, is the focus of its sponsorship activities. But Emirates has sponsored other sports with global popularity (e.g., the US Open and other tennis events, and the European Ryder Cup and other golf events) as well as sports with a local following (e.g., New Zealand yacht racing and Australian Rules football). Thus, Emirates strategically targets various sports events throughout different continents to reach the biggest audience possible, while allowing local variation. In 2011–12, it spent over $1 billion on these sales and marketing efforts.[41]

Distribution

Dubai's location, within eight hours of most cities around the world, enabled Emirates to build a global presence that now flies passengers from one continent to another. Dubai International Airport's Terminal 3 is one of the largest and most comfortable terminals in the world. Emirates' international network does not focus only on large cities. It was also one of the first airlines to cater to traditionally neglected destinations such as Birmingham, Newcastle, Manchester, and Hamburg within Europe, and Kochin, Calcutta, and Ahmedabad in India. Consider the British businessman who must change planes somewhere to fly from Birmingham to Bangkok. Only the most patriotic Englishman would choose Heathrow over Dubai!

THREATS

The elements of the marketing mix work together in fulfilling the Emirates brand promise. But the financial crisis hit Dubai hard, established airlines are struggling, and rising oil prices are continuing to beleaguer the Emirates. Furthermore, Emirates is certainly not without disgruntled passengers, complaining of delays, missed connections, and poor in-flight service.[42] While 100 percent satisfaction is impossible in service industries, many complaints indicated a lack of apparent effort to engage in service recovery.

Perhaps most worrisome is increased competition from Etihad Airways. Established by royal decree in 2003 and based in neighboring Abu Dhabi (the largest and wealthiest of the United Arab Emirates), Etihad has borrowed from Emirates' marketing strategy. It went on a buying spree, placing what was the largest aircraft order in commercial aviation history at the Farnborough Airshow in 2008, for up to 205 aircraft – 100 firm orders, 55 options and 50 purchase rights. Etihad received the title of "World's Leading Airline" four years in a row from 2009 through

2012 at the World Travel Awards – according to the *Wall Street Journal*, the travel industry's equivalent of the Oscars – as well as numerous other awards.[43]

Etihad's promotion strategy also focuses on sports sponsorships. It is the official sponsor of Manchester City Football Club, winner of the 2012 Premier League title, one of the most prestigious prizes in soccer. Manchester City's stadium is now called the Etihad Stadium. On the downside, its profitability is questionable. In 2011, it turned a profit for the first time in its history, a disappointing $14 million on record revenues of nearly US$4.1 billion.

Notwithstanding these threats, one lesson is clear for national champions. Emirates Airlines has networked together a global empire, earned consistently solid profits, and built a global brand that people love and respect without ongoing state protection and support.

MANAGERIAL TAKEAWAYS

From China to Russia, emerging markets are seduced by the siren call of national champions. Citing industrial policy, strategic trade, or national security concerns, states set up "go-out" policies that, according to one astute observer, let national champions "enjoy monopoly at home, allowing them to accrue abnormal profits, and subsidize them with generous bank credits so they can flex superior monetary muscle" against foreign competitors.[20] And although there are many successes, the performance of national champions in hypercompetitive B2C industries has been clearly lagging behind performance in business to business industries, where brands play much less of a role, up-front capital investments may be huge, and the government is often an important customer. To increase the chances of successful branding in B2C markets, we argue that public policy-makers and company executives must work together in these three areas.

1. *Community*: Public policy-makers should do their best to:
   - root out incompetence, corruption, and cronyism;
   - support rather than direct business activities;
   - have the state take a minority stake in the company;
   - provide temporary and conditional protection, setting market-based performance measures.

2. *Competition*: Executives of national champions should welcome the state's effort to:
   - foster home market rivalry;
   - stimulate foreign market entry so that the champions can improve their skills and capabilities.

3. *Company*: Public policy-makers should empower every national champion to:
   - orient its efforts to market needs, not political ambitions;
   - populate the C-suite based on business competence;
   - hire world-class global talent;
   - cultivate global organizational learning processes.

CONCLUSION

LOOKING AHEAD

Perceptions, even of astute observers, are driven by what currently exists and straight-line projections of this. This is often sold by the business consulting industry as best practice. It is much harder to see turning points, especially those that differ radically from the trajectory in place. While China has been manufacturing for the world over the past three decades, the world will manufacture for China over the next three. Over this time, Chinese firms will have moved on to multinational operations and global brands. In other words, despite the many obstacles to building global brands from emerging markets, we have tried to demonstrate that by, using the eight routes in this book, some Chinese and other emerging market firms will find ways to overcome them.

We hope that we have taken the reader on a journey similar to ours in writing this book: the discovery of the many emerging market brands that are yearning to go global. However, we realize that this is a work in progress. The story of the emerging markets is a relatively young one and could still be derailed. Globalization has on previous occasions gone in reverse – for example, following the fall of the Roman and Han Empires, as well as after World War I.

Despite China's somewhat earlier start on economic reforms, most of the Chinese companies profiled in this book are less than

20 years old into their development as modern corporations. While some other emerging market brands may be older, the economic clout of emerging markets is recent and still unfolding. As such, it is unrealistic to expect that we should already be observing emerging market brands that are as famous as Chanel, Coca-Cola, Samsung, or Toyota.

Emerging market entrepreneurs, managers, and policy-makers are not blind to the obstacles facing them. This is illustrated by a recent statement from Wang Yong, head of the powerful State-owned Assets Supervision and Administration Commission, which controls 117 Chinese national champions, collectively holding assets worth $4.4 trillion. He called upon state-owned enterprises to learn from private and foreign companies as well as shift their business model to a more market-oriented one. Yet he sees this as a gradual process, one which will take time to implement given the wide-ranging responsibilities these companies have to local people, communities, and the economy.

It is important to remember that, despite the large number of brands we have profiled in the book, many more companies are not yet global brands but have the potential to build global brands. For example, we visited the Huiyuan Juice company headquarters outside Beijing that was co-located with a huge, state of the art, juice-processing facility. Huiyuan is an integrated company that owns 42 juice factories, and 18 pulp-processing factories that produce 500,000 tons of pulp and 200,000 tons of concentrate; as well as more than 10 million acres of farm land worked by millions of farmers. It exports concentrate and purée to over 30 countries across five continents. Huiyuan, with its various brands, has more than a 50 percent share of the branded 100 percent juice market in China. No wonder Coca-Cola attempted to buy the downstream business. While Coca-Cola failed to get regulatory approval from the Chinese government for its acquisition, Huiyuan seems to be the type of firm that has the potential to attempt to become a global brand at some future date.

What was so energizing about our visits to emerging market firms in China, India, Brazil, and elsewhere was the sheer ambition that they displayed. The best of them are both strategic and entrepreneurial. They are constantly seeking new business opportunities and have the guts to place big bets behind them. We were often astonished at the uncanny ability of successful entrepreneurs from emerging markets to spot the next markets and industries that they could enter, often unrelated to their current enterprises. The usual business advice of sticking close to one's core competencies does not deter them. They assured us that with determination they would acquire the needed capabilities. When we asked the executives of Midea, a Chinese home appliances firm, to describe the core of their corporate culture, the answer was "Never give up, no matter what."

The Huiyuan and Midea stories may seem unusual, and in some sense, they are. But from another perspective, they may be simply ordinary. Consider a small thought experiment. Suppose that there are more than a thousand companies in China who have mastered the art of making world-class products. Probably, this is a conservative estimate. Now, what if a hundred of them decide to slowly abandon their traditional, contract manufacturing, private label model, and instead aspire to become global brands. Is it then really that difficult to imagine 10, or perhaps even 20, global brands emerging from China alone within the next decade? And this is just China ...

As emerging markets grow in economic power, their companies will become richer and more multinational, some of them will invest in building global brands, and of these, a few will eventually succeed. We do not doubt the enormity of this task, but nor do we doubt global brand breakout from these countries.

HURDLES TO OVERCOME ON THE ROAD TO GLOBAL BRANDS

While we are optimistic about the potential of emerging market companies to build global consumer brands, we are not oblivious to four hurdles that these companies need to overcome to transform potential into reality. While these four obstacles can be observed in many emerging markets, Chinese firms in particular need to confront them.

HURDLE 1: IMPROVE TRANSPARENCY

Many Chinese firms lack transparency, particularly with respect to ownership structures and governance standards. Despite our best efforts, it was often impossible to penetrate the opaque ownership structures that went through a mother company (parent) and several daughter companies (subsidiaries), some of which might be listed. At one listed company, we learnt that the listed portion referred to only one factory for one product category. Most of these related companies transact significant business with each other. Sometimes, the entire raw materials or key inputs for a listed firm may come from another nonlisted firm in the network. In such a case, unless the transfer price mechanism is known and market-compliant, the profits in the listed firm are subject to a degree of arbitrariness. Indian firms used to have such complex shareholding patterns before the reforms of 1991, but in the last decade they have made considerable strides in unraveling them.

The composition and profiles of the members of the board of directors is sketchy. As a result, we were unable to gain a full grasp of the ownership and governance structures of Chinese firms. In fact, we were often advised not to raise the ownership issue in our interviews as it would jeopardize the entire interview. Even when brought up with senior Western managers of Chinese firms, it was clear they were uneasy discussing this issue. Greater probing led us to believe that it was not that these executives did not wish to reveal the ownership, but that they were ignorant of it. The State and the Communist Party not only control many of the state-owned firms and their top leadership (which are typically appointments approved by the Party), but, one suspects, also exert significant influence on the behavior of private companies. Illustrative of this is a front-page article in the leading newspaper *China Daily* with the headline "Party continues to expand," celebrating that, to date, close to one million companies (including 47,000 foreign firms) have established Party organizations in their companies. This, according to Wang Jingqing, Vice-Minister of the Organization Department of the Communist Party of China Central Committee, has "helped companies learn about the latest national policies and [has] improved relations between employers and employees."[1] Perhaps. But a less benign explanation is that the hand of the Party is never far away. Russia is the other significant emerging market where one also gets this feeling of the hand of the State. Yet Russia is more privatized than China.

The lack of transparency is endemic to China as its political system attempts to control the flow of information in society. In Beijing, we were unable to access Facebook and Twitter as well as many other websites. How do you build a global brand in today's world without social media? The desire to release limited information spills over into the corporate sector. Most of the corporate websites are of poor quality, providing minimal information, and some have not updated their English-language websites in years despite having annual revenues running into billions of dollars.

Many companies are supposedly owned by the employees. For example, the two listed companies that comprise Haier claim to be a collective that is employee owned, yet it appears that the employees do not know exactly what they own, nor do they receive dividends. We believe that it is more difficult for state-run and state-employee-managed firms to build global consumer brands. The investment in the marketing efforts required to build brands, where the returns cannot be demonstrated as easily as say in building a factory, is always suspect. Who owns the cash flows being generated by the firm and who can make the decisions on whether to pay them as dividends or invest in the softer aspects of building a global brand is unclear.

An important item on the Chinese corporate manifesto for the future must be to open the ownership structure up to scrutiny. We are hopeful that this will happen. Our field research revealed that Chinese companies are increasingly becoming aware that improving transparency will be beneficial to them. External forces are also encouraging Chinese firms to change in this respect in order to succeed in their quest to become more global. For example, in 2013, the *Financial Times* reported that "Huawei has pledged to start disclosing more detailed financial information and shareholding information as the Chinese telecom equipment maker tries to dispel fears about suspected ties to China's military that are hampering its global expansion."[2] All that was known until then was that the founder owned 1.4 percent, with the rest in the hands of a "body representing 65,000 Huawei staff."

HURDLE 2: ENHANCE PROFITABILITY AND INTEGRITY OF FINANCIAL STATEMENTS

Many large Chinese firms seem to operate on low profit margins. For example, despite having about similar levels of market share in the PC business, Lenovo's operating margins in 2012 were a quarter of Hewlett-Packard's. This led *The Economist* to observe that the Asian model of capitalism "prizes market share over profits."[3] But profits are necessary too if one is to invest into building global brands.

The low profit margins lead one to question the returns to capital at many Chinese firms, especially in light of the preferential land and capital they receive by being "favored firms" in China. The same article in *The Economist* went on to state: "the state draws up long term plans, funnels cash to industries it deems strategic and works hand-in-glove with national champions, like Huawei and Haier."[3] If these subsidies were to disappear, and this were combined with increasing Chinese labor costs, one has to wonder whether the Chinese business model would be sustainable. At a minimum, we believe that this model will have to evolve and we are skeptical of a unique "Asian business model."

Beyond the low profit margins, there is the question of integrity of financial statements. Results for firms are often released far after the end of the financial year. Numbers, often round numbers, projected by leaders of these firms during the year have an uncanny way of being met. While many of the firms are audited by international firms, the problems at India's Satyam demonstrate that this does not always guard against errors and fraud. We want to emphasize here that the integrity of financial statements is not merely a problem in China, or even an emerging market problem. Scandals such as those of Enron, WorldCom, and Lehman Brothers have highlighted that the integrity of financial statements is a worldwide concern. Yet, relatively, emerging market firms need to make greater strides on this front. Brands are about trust; and everything that a firm does, enhances or detracts from the brand.

HURDLE 3: MOVE FROM IMITATION TO INNOVATION

For years, brands from emerging markets focused on the domestic market. In a relatively closed economy, they usually mimicked the products of Western or Japanese firms. The term "reverse-engineering" was common in India to describe the process of figuring out how to manufacture innovative products from the West. Like the Japanese and Koreans before them, Chinese firms are masters at this. In the early stages of a company, it can grow by merely imitating Western products and brands. But as emerging market companies grow and rise to prominence, they must make the transition from imitation to innovation. They have to offer a differentiated product and proposition to Western consumers. This requires building and acquiring both research and development (R&D) and marketing capabilities, as well as an organizational culture that encourages bottom-up ideas.

The highly hierarchical and family-controlled culture that dominates many emerging market firms is not always conducive to innovation and branding. Some state planners in China and family business owners in India love to think that this is the route to world-beating innovation and brands. But apart from a few high-profile exceptions, this thinking is mostly delusional. Innovation and branding as sustained capabilities are best nurtured in professionally managed firms rather than left to the vagaries of state bureaucrats or the offspring of exceptional entrepreneurs.

Investments in innovation and brands are rational only if intellectual property (IP) is protected and the protections are enforced. In our work, we have noticed numerous examples of the blatant copying of Western products, brand names, and brand logos. If emerging market firms would take these global, they would open their companies up to expensive lawsuits before international tribunals. Hopefully, this situation will improve as emerging market companies mature and realize that it is in their own interest to support IP protection and enforcement.

On this front, one sees great leaps forward in China. Companies such as Huawei, Galanz, Haier, and ZTE have global R&D operations with centers in the Americas, Europe, and Japan. The push to register patents abroad is starting to increase among Chinese firms, and has made some of these firms into large filers in the US patent regime. While foreign patent applications by Chinese firms still lag behind applications by Western firms, the writing is on the wall. *The Economist* cautions "Geeks in the West should not relax."[4] The R&D facilities of companies such as Lenovo that we visited were impressive. Lenovo's Shanghai R&D facility is one of four in China and works closely with the firm's R&D centers in Yokohama (Japan) and Raleigh (NC, USA). They actively rotate people across these centers and encourage diversity.

HURDLE 4: ACCEPT MANAGEMENT DIVERSITY AND A GLOBAL MINDSET

Building a global brand in today's world with distributed economic power requires managing across many countries. The consumer insights needed from the different parts of the world require a global mindset in the top management teams of the firm. This is of course not a problem unique to emerging market firms as French, Japanese, and even British firms struggle to incorporate emerging market talent into their top management teams. Emerging market firms desiring to build global brands in Western countries face the opposite problem of how to get Westerners integrated into their top management. There is little history in many of these countries of multicultural management teams.

Given the structure of their societies, companies from Brazil, India, and South Africa have some advantage on this front. Firms from these countries are already used to dealing with a top management team that look different from each other despite sharing a common nationality. Indian and South African companies are also used to doing business in English, even if their mother tongue may be Hindi, Bengali, Afrikaans, or Xhosa. We do recognize that the top management of firms from these countries is still overwhelmingly from the home country. But at least they can potentially work with a more multinational top management team.

China, on the other hand, is culturally and linguistically more homogenous. The language barrier also makes it harder to incorporate foreigners. Chinese firms aspiring to build global brands will have to follow German multinationals such as Allianz, Daimler, and Siemens, where all documents are written in English, which is the company's working language. Even French firms like Alcatel-Lucent have now adopted English as their working language. Like it or not, the global business language does not seem destined to change even if this turns out to be the Chinese century. It is Chinese firms that will have to change. There are encouraging signs, however, as Lenovo has adopted English as its official internal language.

In sum, merging market companies have to overcome some significant hurdles before they can reach their full branding potential. But lest managers of Western multinationals sit back and relax, we caution that, if history is any guide, they will be able to do so. After all, 19th-century US firms and 20th-century Japanese and Korean firms faced and overcame essentially the same challenges and in the process became household names around the globe.

NOTES

INTRODUCTION

1 All numbers are from *The Economist*, August 4, 2011: http://www.economist.com/blogs/dailychart/2011/08/emerging-vs-developed-economies (accessed January 21, 2013).

2 Sara Bongiorni (2005), "A Year Without Made in China," *Christian Science Monitor*, December 20.

3 http://en.wikipedia.org/wiki/Historical_GDP_of_the_People's_Republic_of_China (accessed January 21, 2013).

4 Brand China, "Show People What You're Really Made Of", Calling Brands report, November 2011.

5 http://plasticsnews.com/china/english/design/headlines2.html?id=1309204644 (accessed January 21, 2013).

6 http://www.interbrand.com/en/best-global-brands/2012/Best-Global-Brands-2012.aspx (accessed January 21, 2013).

7 Quoted in Ying Fan (2006), "The Globalisation of Chinese Brands," *Marketing Intelligence & Planning*, 24 (4), 365–79.

8 http://www.bloomberg.com/news/2011-09-07/china-won-t-lose-competitiveness-for-3-5-years-welch-says.html (accessed January 21, 2013).

9 *Bloomberg News* (2011), "China Must Create '10,000 Apples,' Welch Says," September 7.

10 Enid Tsui (2011), "Made in China Does Not Always Translate Well," *Financial Times,* December 29.

11 http://en.wikipedia.org/wiki/Porcelain (accessed January 21, 2013).

12 Maggie Chao, Elaine Chow, Gil Kerbs, and Kate Long (2012), "Thanks, But No Thanks to Made in China," Knowledge@Wharton, January 3.

13 Indeed, not only foreign consumers, but also the Chinese disfavor the "Made in China" label. Surveys in US and Chinese universities have demonstrated a preference for foreign brands over Chinese brands.

14 Personal interview at Shanghai headquarters of Bright Foods, November 1, 2012.

15 Wang Jian (2007), "Brand Perception the Key for Chinese Companies," *China Daily*, March 15, http://english.peopledaily.com.cn/200703/15/eng20070315_357795.html (accessed January 21, 2013).

16 Barry Naughton (2007), *The Chinese Economy: Transitions and Growth*, Cambridge, MA: MIT Press.

17 Martin Lindstrom (2011), "How the Chinese Became Global Branding Geniuses," Fast Company.com, 20 April, http://www.fastcompany.com/1748843/how-the-chinese-once-tone-deaf-to-brands-became-global-branding-geniuses (accessed January 21, 2013).

18 http://plasticsnews.com/china/english/design/headlines2.html?id=1309204644 (accessed January 21, 2013).

19 Gordon Orr and Erik Roth (2012), "A CEO's Guide to Innovation in China," *McKinsey Quarterly*, (February), 1–10.

20 Ying Fan (2006), "The Globalisation of Chinese Brands," *Marketing Intelligence & Planning*, 24 (4), 365–79.

21 Benjamin A. Shobert (2011), "China's Brands in the Shadows," www.atimes.com, December 2.

22 Steve Toloken (2012), "China Injection Moulder Fu Hong Finding Success with Own Brand," Plastic News.com, January 27.

23 http://www.chinaipmagazine.com/en/news-show.asp?id=3825 (accessed January 21, 2013).

24 Kathrin Hille (2011), "Chinese Brands Star in Hollywood Movie," *Financial Times*, July 20, p. 17.

25 Michael Kan (2012), "Lenovo Looks to Build Brand as it Reaches for the Top PC Vendor Spot," *PC World*, February 27, http://www.pcworld.idg.com.au/article/416619/lenovo_looks_build_brand_it_reaches_top_pc_vendor_spot (accessed January 21, 2013)

26 http://www.digitaltrends.com/ces/gauging-the-rise-of-the-chinese-tech-brands (accessed January 23, 2013).

27 *Fortune* (2012), "Those Logos Look Awfully Familiar," October 29, p. 14.

28 Patti Waldmeir (2011), "Silver Lining Sought Overseas as Domestic Demand Declines," *Financial Times*, October 31, p. 25.

29 Recorder report, "Vietnam's Coffee King Plans Next Prestige Global Brand," November 11, 2012.

CHAPTER 1

1 http://factsanddetails.com/japan.php?itemid=524&catid=16&subcatid=110 (accessed January 21, 2013).

2 http://www.country-data.com/cgi-bin/query/r-7176.html (accessed January 21, 2013).

3 http://www.fairimage.org/tradewithjapan.htm (accessed January 21, 2013).

4 http://www.anythingaboutcars.com/1960s-foreign-cars.html (accessed January 21, 2013).

5 http://www.country-data.com/cgi-bin/query/r-7176.html (accessed January 21, 2013).

6 http://factsanddetails.com/japan.php?itemid=524&catid=16&subcatid=110 (accessed January 21, 2013).

7 Richard S. Chang (2012), "Revenge of the Econobox: Early Japanese Imports Find Admirers," *New York Times*, February 3.

8 http://www.anythingaboutcars.com/1960s-foreign-cars.html (accessed January 21, 2013).

9 See Geert Hofstede (2001), *Culture's Consequences* (2nd edn), Thousand Oaks, CA: Sage, for an in-depth discussion of the role of long- versus short-term orientation on company behavior.

10 http://en.wikipedia.org/wiki/Pearl_River_Piano_Group (accessed January 21, 2013).

11 Bo Li (2006), "Pearl River Piano Group: the Unique International Way," *Global Entrepreneur*, (6). (李波, 珠江钢琴集团: 独特的国际化路径,《环球企业家》, 2006年第6期)

12 Xuhui Yu (2006), "Pearl River Piano: The Evolution to a Global Challenger," *21st Century Business Review*, (9), 70–3. (余旭辉, 珠江钢琴: 向全球挑战者的"进化",《21世纪商业评论, 2006年第9期, pp. 70–3).

13 http://www.plumb-acoustic-digital-pianos.com/Pearl-River-Piano.html (accessed January 21, 2013).

14 For an in-depth treatment of how brand reputation can affect perceived product quality, see Jan-Benedict E.M. Steenkamp (1989), *Product Quality*, Assen, The Netherlands: Van Gorcum; Valarie A. Zeithaml (1988), "Consumer Perceptions of Price, Quality, and Value: A Means-End Model and Synthesis of Evidence," *Journal of Marketing*, 52 (July), 2–22.

15 Ron Gluckman (2012), "Every Customer Is Always Right," *Forbes*, May 21, pp. 38–40.

16 Haier is listed as two different legal firms, but to make the section easier to digest, we will consider them a single firm as one is a subsidiary of the other.

17 http://en.wikipedia.org/wiki/Haier (accessed May 20, 2012).

18 Lynn Sharp Paine (2001), "The Haier Group," Harvard Business School Case No. 398-101.

19 Jin Zhanming (2009), "Corporate Strategies of Chinese Multinationals," in Jean-Paul Larcon (ed.), *Chinese Multinationals*, Singapore: World Scientific Publishing, p. 13.

20 For a discussion of the "Hard Way First" and "Easy Way First" approaches, see Jin Zhanming (2009), "Corporate Strategies of Chinese Multinationals," in Jean-Paul Larcon (ed.), *Chinese Multinationals*, Singapore: World Scientific Publishing, pp. 25–7.

21 Hu Zuohao and Wang Gao (2009), "International Marketing Strategies of Chinese multinationals," in Jean-Paul Larcon (ed.), *Chinese Multinationals*, Singapore: World Scientific Publishing, p. 107.

22 Pete Engardio and Michael Arndt (2006), "Haier: Taking a Brand Name Higher," *Business Week*, July 31, http://www.businessweek.com/magazine/content/06_31/b3995009.htm

23 Hu Zuohao and Wang Gao (2009), "International Marketing Strategies of Chinese Multinationals," in Jean-Paul Larcon (ed.), *Chinese Multinationals*, Singapore: World Scientific Publishing, p. 116–17.

24 *Business Weekly* (2011) "Haier Refrigerator: Brand Potential in the Foreign Market," (11), pp. 58–60.

25 Yibing Wu (2003), "China's Refrigerator Magnate," *McKinsey Quarterly*, https://www.mckinseyquarterly.com/Chinas_refrigerator_magnate_1323 (accessed January 21, 2013).

26 Guang Chen (2009), "Haier Refrigerator Becoming World No.1," *Consumption Daily*, December 15.

27 Chuanxiu Jiang (2011), "Haier's Global Strategy: Competing in the European Market," *Household Appliance*, (3), 57.

28 Patti Waldmeir (2012), "Chinese Wares Face Struggle for Acceptance," *Financial Times*, May 22, p. 4.

29 *The Economist* (2012), "Chinese Carmakers: Still in Second Gear," http://www.economist.com/node/21554192 accessed 23/01/13 (accessed January 21, 2013).

30 http://www.autoguide.com/auto-news/2011/12/chinese-cars-improving-says-latest-jd-power-survey.html (accessed January 21, 2013).

31 Keith Bradsher (2012), "Chinese Cars Make Valuable Gains in Emerging Markets," *New York Times*, July 5.

32 Ratan Tata, Tata Motors' annual report for 2011–12.

CHAPTER 2

1 See Nirmalya Kumar and Jan-Benedict E.M. Steenkamp (2007), *Private Label Strategy*, Cambridge, MA: Harvard Business School Press, for the pros and cons of private label manufacturing.

2 Nirmalya Kumar (2004), *Marketing as Strategy*, Cambridge, MA: Harvard Business School Press.

3 Hon Hai is registered in Taiwan and Foxconn is the subsidiary. It appears that the vast majority of Hon Hai's revenues come from Foxconn, and we will refer to this firm as Foxconn, following the popular press.

4 James Rupert (2010), "Soccer Ball Makers in Poverty," *The Sydney Morning Herald*, June 11, http://www.smh.com.au (accessed January 23, 2013).

5 Chris Nuttall, Kathrin Hille and Robin Kwong (2012), "Apple Moves to Share the Burden in China," *Financial Times*, March 31, p. 15.

6 http://www.chinadaily.com.cn/bizchina/2011-06/01/content_12622858.htm (accessed January 23, 2013).

7 Wikipedia. http://en.wikipedia.org/wiki/Galanz (accessed January 23, 2013).

8 Don Sull (2005), "Dynamic Partners," *Business Strategy Review*, (Summer), 5–10.

9 http://www.galanz.com/ProductShow.aspx?ColId=141&SecId=143&Seclds=49&id=353 (accessed January 21, 2013).

10 http://www.galanz.com/About.aspx?ColId=94&SecId=99 (accessed January 21, 2013).

11 Parts of the HTC story are based on a telephone interview between the authors and Matthew Costello, Chief Operating Office, HTC, March 7, 2012.

12 http://www.htc.com/us/press/htc-launches-3-new-4g-smartphones/23 (accessed January 21, 2013).

13 Lowell D'Souza (2011), "Why B2B Firms Should Target B2C Markets," *Marketing Bones*, October 6.

14 *The Economist* (2012), "The Company that Spooked the World," August 4.

15 Huawei Annual Report 2011.

16 Zhengfei Ren's talk: Make Ourselves Wolf-like, August 10, 2011, http://www.iceo.com.cn/renwu/35/2011/1008/231520.shtml (accessed January 21, 2013).

17 According to Victor Xu, chief strategy and marketing officer for Huawei Devices.

18 http://www.huaweidevice.com/worldwide/newsIndex.do?method=view&newsId=158&directoryId=5024 (accessed January 23, 2013).

19 Lee Chyen Yee (2012), "Huawei Sees Smartphones Leading Growth in Consumer Devices," Reuters, September 24.

20 Company information.

21 Peter Burrows, "The New Smartphone Powerhouse: Huawei," *Bloomberg Businessweek*, July 19, 2012.
22 http://www.economist.com/node/21559922 (accessed January 23, 2013).
23 Mike Bastin (2011), "Companies Still Struggle to Build Brands," *China Daily*, August 25, p. C3.

CHAPTER 3

1 http://www.merriam-webster.com/dictionary/diaspora (accessed September 25, 2012).
2 Tarun Khanna and Paula Campbell (2008), "Diasporas: Causes and Effects," Harvard Business School Note.
3 Data refer to 2010, and are from the US Census Bureau.
4 For acculturation processes, see: Judit V. Arends-Tóth (2003), *Psychological Acculturation of Turkish Migrants in the Netherlands: Issues in Theory and Assessment*, Amsterdam: Dutch University Press; Peter Flannery, Steven P. Reise, and Jiajuan Yu (2001), "An Empirical Comparison of Acculturation Models," *Personality and Social Psychology Bulletin*, 27(August), 1035–45; Teresa LaFromboise, Hardin L.K. Coleman, and Jennifer Gerton (1993), "Psychological Impact of Biculturalism: Evidence and Theory," *Psychological Bulletin*, 114 (3), 395–412; Andrew Ryder, Lynn E. Alden, and Delroy L. Paulhus (2000), "Is Acculturation Unidimensional or Bidimensional? A Head-to-Head Comparison in the Prediction of Personality, Self-Identity, and Adjustment," *Journal of Personality and Social Psychology*, 79 (1), 4–65; Jeanne L. Tsai, Yu-Wen Ying and Peter A. Lee (2000), "The Meaning of 'Being Chinese' and 'Being American'," *Journal of Cross-Cultural Psychology*, 31 (3), 302–32.
5 Dana L. Alden, Jan-Benedict E.M. Steenkamp, and Rajeev Batra (2006), "Consumer Attitudes toward Marketplace Globalization: Structure, Antecedents, and Consequences," *International Journal of Research in Marketing*, 23 (September), 227–39; Güliz Ger (1999), "Localizing in the Global Village: Local Firms Competing in Global Markets," *California Management Review*, 41 (Summer), 64–83; Robert Holton (2000), "Globalization's Cultural Consequences," *AAPS*, 570 (July), 140–52.
6 Titus Munson Coan (1875), "A New Country," *The Galaxy*, 19 (April), 463.
7 John W. Berry (1990), "Psychology of Acculturation," in John J. Berman (ed.), *Cross-Cultural Perspectives: Proceedings of the Nebraska Symposium on Motivation*, Lincoln, NE: University of

Nebraska Press, pp. 201–34; J.W. Berry, U. Kim, S. Power, M. Young, and M. Bujaki (1989), "Acculturation Attitudes in Plural Societies," *Applied Psychology*, 38 (2), 185–206; John W. Berry and D.L. Sam (1997), "Acculturation and Adaptation," in John W. Berry, Marshall H. Segall, and Cigdem Kagitcibasi (eds), *Handbook of Cross-Cultural Psychology*, Volume 3: *Social Behavior and Applications* (2nd edn), Boston, MA: Allyn & Bacon, pp. 291–326. The acculturation literature also describes other outcomes, such as changes in the host culture due to home-country cultural forces as well as the fusion of the home- and host-country cultures into a new culture. Appadurai (1990, p. 295) believes that "as rapidly as forces from various metropolises are brought into new societies, they tend to become indigenized in one way or another." See Arjun Appadurai (1990), "Disjuncture and Difference in the Global Cultural Economy," *Theory, Culture & Society*, 7 (2/3), 295–31; Hubert J.M. Hermans and Harry J.G. Kempen (1998), "Moving Cultures," *American Psychologist*, 53 (10), 1111–20. While interesting, this is outside the scope of this book.

8 For a marketing application of this framework, see Dana L. Alden, Jan-Benedict E.M. Steenkamp, and Rajeev Batra (2006), "Consumer Attitudes toward Marketplace Globalization: Structure, Antecedents, and Consequences," *International Journal of Research in Marketing*, 23 (September), 227–39.

9 James W. Gentry, Sunkyu Jun, and Patriya Tansuhaj (1995), "Consumer Acculturation Processes and Cultural Conflict: How Generalizable Is a North American Model for Marketing Globally?" *Journal of Business Research*, 32, 129–39.

10 Obviously, there are exceptions. For example, the spread of kebab in Europe followed the Turkish diaspora, many of whom would fall into the category of ethnic affirmers. The relative success of the Turkish cuisine may have less to do with social demonstrance and more with the desire of the mainstream population to try something new and different, and clearly many host-country nationals liked what they saw.

11 The description of Reliance's strategy in the US is based on Ram NaReddy, Prasad Sivakumar, Naveen Gangwar, and Nitin Kachhwaha (2012), "Reliance BIG Cinemas," University of North Carolina.

12 Out of the total 200 screens in the US, 55 are India-focused screens, while the others are primarily Hollywood screens.

13 The story of Islamic banking is based on *Fortune* (2011), "Islamic Finance Connects Global Opportunities," July 25; Robin Wigglesworth (2011), "Niche Market Defies its Critics, Gaining in Depth and Sophistication," *Financial Times*, September 22, p. 3.

14 It is easy to forget that, for a long time, charging interest was (at least officially) forbidden in the Western world as well. This was based on Old Testament texts such as "Do not take interest or any profit from them, but fear your God, so that they may continue to live among you. You must not lend them money at interest or sell them food at a profit" (Leviticus 25: 36–7). Ingenious casuistry gradually softened the ecclesiastical reprobation of usury, but only when Christian principles ceased to have a full binding force in the community did banking – a profession openly based upon usury – become possible. See William H. McNeill's magisterial *Rise of the West: A History of the Human Community*, Chicago: University of Chicago Press, 1991, p. 584.

15 Teresa LaFromboise, Hardin L.K. Coleman, and Jennifer Gerton (1993), "Psychological Impact of Biculturalism: Evidence and Theory," *Psychological Bulletin*, 114 (3), 395–412.

16 The ICICI example draws heavily on Chapter 8 of Tarun Khanna (2008), *Billions of Entrepreneurs: How China and India Are Reshaping their Futures – and Yours*, Boston, MA: Harvard Business School Press.

17 Tarun Khanna (2008), *Billions of Entrepreneurs: How China and India Are Reshaping their Futures – and Yours*, Boston, MA: Harvard Business School Press.

18 Financial data were obtained from ICICI's 18th Annual Report and Accounts 2011–2012, http://www.icicibank.com/aboutus/investor.html (accessed October 27, 2012).

19 http://www.millwardbrown.com/BrandZ/Top_100_Global_Brands.aspx (accessed October 27, 2012).

20 *Wingspan* (2012), "Spanning the World," October, p. 51.

21 Adam Thomson, "North of the Border," *Financial Times*, August 22, 2012, p. 5.

22 Unless footnoted otherwise, information and quotations regarding Corona were extracted from Chapter 2 of Douglas B. Holt's book *How Is Cultural Branding Different?*, Boston, MA: Harvard Business Press, 2008.

23 Rohit Deshpande (2001), "Corona Beer," Harvard Business School, Case 9-502-023.

24 Devin Leonard (2112), "The Plot to Destroy America's Beer," *Bloomberg Businessweek*, October 29, pp. 64–71.

25 http://en.wikipedia.org/wiki/Bollywood (accessed September 26, 2012).

26 Chee Wan Ng (2011), "Weaving the World Together," *The Economist*, November 19, pp. 68–70.

27 Information on restaurant locations was obtained from http://www.campero.com (accessed October 3, 2012). Posted reviews indicate

that Pollo Campero is frequented not only by Hispanics, but also by non-Hispanic Americans.

28 Luke McLeod-Roberts (2012), "Brazilian Guarana Drink Sales Take Off in Japan," *Financial Times* Special Report on Latin American Brands, June 21, p. 3.

29 Manish Khandelwal and John H. Roberts (2011), "Dabur India," Stanford Graduate School of Business, Case IB-9, p. 5.

30 http://www.dabur.com/About%20Dabur-Dabur%20At-a-Glance (accessed April 18, 2012).

31 J.R. McNeill and William H. McNeill (2003), *The Human Web: A Bird's Eye View of World History,* New York: Norton.

32 Source: Dabur Annual Report 2011–2012, http://www.dabur.com/Root-Annual-Reports-2011–12. For example, Dabur Amla Hair Oil is the largest brand in the hair oils category in Saudi Arabia, with a market share of 41.6 percent.

33 Dabur India Limited (2012), presentation at the UBS India CEO/CFO Forum, Mumbai; Dabur Annual Report 2011–2012.

34 Sunil Duggal, personal communication to the authors, November 16, 2012.

35 In the fiscal year 2011–12, international business grew by 78.3 percent. However, this was partially due to the fact that it was the first full year of the two overseas acquisitions – Turkey-based Hobi Group and US-based Namaste Laboratories in the Dabur fold. During the year, these acquisitions were assimilated and integrated with the existing organic overseas business. If we look at the growth in sales of the organic business excluding acquisitions, the international business grew by a still very impressive 27.1 percent. Dabur International accounted for 58 percent of Dabur's international sales, Hobi for 8.5 percent, and Namaste Labs for the remaining 33.5 percent.

36 Source: Dabur Annual Report 2011–2012; http://www.dabur.com/Root-Annual-Reports-2011–12 (accessed January 21, 2012).

CHAPTER 4

1 http://animals.nationalgeographic.com/animals/mammals/jaguar/ (accessed January 26, 2013).

2 http://www.atkearney.com/paper/-/asset_publisher/dVxv4Hz2h8bS/content/emerging-and-established-markets-converge/10192 (accessed January 26, 2013).

3 *The Economist* (2011), "Role Reversal: Emerging-Market Firms Are Increasingly Buying Up Rich-World Ones," September 24.

4 Winter Nie (2012), "Expect China's Private Sector Entrepreneurs to Take the Lead," IMD paper, June.

5 Simon Rabinovitch and Patrick Jenkins (2012), "Chinese Banker Eyes Bargain Abroad," *Financial Times*, September 17, p. 16.

6 Rebecca McReynolds (2012), "China, the Game Changer," Chazen Global Insight, Columbia Business School, http://www4.gsb.columbia.edu/chazen/globalinsights/article/7325438/China,+the+Game-Changer (accessed October 3, 2012).

7 Anousha Sakoui (2012), "Reaching Out in the Search for Growth, Deal & Dealmakers," *Financial Times*, September 19, p. 3 (special insert).

8 http://www.economist.com/node/21528982 (accessed January 26, 2013).

9 The next three paragraphs borrow heavily from Nirmalya Kumar (2009), "How Emerging Giants Are Rewriting the Rules of M&A," *Harvard Business Review*, May, 115–21.

10 Patti Waldmeir and Shirley Chen (2012), "Bright Future for Breakfast," *Financial Times*, June 26, p. 23.

11 For a detailed discussion of the principles and process related to brand consolidation, see Nirmalya Kumar (2003), "Kill a Brand, Keep a Customer," *Harvard Business Review*, (December), 86–95.

12 http://www.eetimes.com/electronics-news/4395447/Lenovo-to-acquire-Brazil-s-biggest-PC-maker (accessed October 1, 2012).

13 John Ackerly and Måns Larsson (2005), *The Emergence of a Chinese Global PC Giant: Lenovo's Acquisition of IBM's PC Division*, Cambridge, MA: Harvard Business Press, 2005.

14 The 2011 revenue and volume sales numbers come from Norihiko Shirouza (2012), "Geely, Volvo Near Pact on Technology Sharing," *Wall Street Journal Europe*, March 9–11, p. 22.

15 We realize, of course, that a car company also generates revenue through selling components and other activities, but this comparison based on overall revenues makes the key point – that they are reaching very different segments of car-buyers.

16 Li Fangfang (2011), "Auto Firms Set New Course Abroad," *China Daily*, August 25, p. C4.

17 Norihiko Shirouza (2012), "Geely, Volvo Near Pact on Technology Sharing," *Wall Street Journal Europe*, March 9–11, p. 22.

18 Mike Rutherford ponders Tata's takeover of Land Rover and Jaguar, 28 March 2008, http://www.telegraph.co.uk/motoring/columnists/mike-rutherford/2751431/Car-finance-with-Mr-Money.html (accessed January 26, 2013).

19 Vikas Bajaj (2012), "Jaguar Turns the Corner with Tata," *The Hindu*, September 3.

20   John Reed (2012), "The Car that Saved JLR," *Financial Times/FT.com magazine*, September 29/30, pp. 28–33.

21   M. Anand (2008), "The Price of Owning the Cat," *Outlook Business*, April 19, pp. 38–46.

22   *The Economist* (2010), "Being Eaten by the Dragon," November 11.

23   "From Guard Shack to Global Giant," *The Economist*, January 12, 2013.

24   Lei Bi (2008), "Interview Record: Li Dongsheng Suggests Supportive Government Policy in the Flat Screen TV Industry"(毕蕾, 访谈实录: 李东生建议立法引导平板电视健康发展), http://www.tcl.com/index.php/news/463.html, March 8 (accessed January 26, 2013).

25   Qingchun Chen (2010), "TCL Tackling Globalization," *CEO/CIO*, (21), p. 168.

26   John Reed (2012), "The Car that Saved JLR," *Financial Times/FT.com magazine*, September 29/30, p. 32.

CHAPTER 5

1   For a quantitative analysis of previous research, see Peeter W.J. Verlegh and Jan-Benedict E. M. Steenkamp (1999), "A Review and Meta-Analysis of Country-of-Origin Research," *Journal of Economic Psychology,* 20 (5), 521–46; see also Julie M. Pharr (2005), "Synthesizing Country-of-Origin Research from the Last Decade: Is the Concept Still Salient in an Era of Global Brands?" *Journal of Marketing Theory and Practice*, 13 (Fall), 34–45.

2   Hakuhodo (2008), Hakuhodo Global HABIT 2007. http://www.hakuhodo.jp/pdf/2008/20080318.pdf (accessed May 26, 2012).

3   Jan-Benedict E.M. Steenkamp (1989), *Product Quality*, Assen, The Netherlands: Van Gorcum.

4   This is not to say that country of manufacture may not matter as well. It denotes the location of manufacture or assembly of a product. In today's global branding world, companies source components around the globe, and the role of the country of manufacture in consumer decision-making has lost much of its importance. For example, on the back of the iPad, one can find: "Designed by Apple in California. Assembled in China." From the consumer's point of view, the relevant country image is the US, not China (unless there are specific problems such as child labor, sweatshops, etc.).

5   See, for example, Martin S. Roth and Jean B. Romeo (1992), "Matching Product Category and Country Image Perceptions: A Framework for Managing Country-of-Origin Effects," *Journal of International Business Studies*, 23 (3), 477–97. We added social

responsibility to this set, based on our academic and consulting experience.

6   Larry L. Carter (2009), "Consumer Receptivity of Foreign Products: The Roles of Country-of-Origin Image, Consumer Ethnocentrism, and Animosity," Unpublished doctoral dissertation, Old Dominion University, Norfolk, VA, USA.

7   Calling Brands (2011), "Brand China, Show People What You Are Made Of," November, p. 10, with slight adaptation to broaden the scope from Europe to Europe and the US.

8   Discussion of these four factors is based on: FutureBrand (2012), *2011–2012 Country Brand Index*; documentation for the 2012 Anhalt-GfK Roper Nation Brands Index; Marc Fetscherin (2010), "The Determinants and Measurement of a Country Brand: The Country Brand Strength Index," *International Marketing Review*, 27 (4), 466–79.

9   FutureBrand (2012), *2011–2012 Country Brand Index*, p. 29.

10   Patti Waldmeir (2012), "China Outcry at New Tainted Milk Scandal," *Financial Times*, June 16/17, p. 9.

11   FutureBrand (2012), *2011–2012 Country Brand Index*, p. 67.

12   Patti Waldmeir (2012), "Chinese Wares Face Struggle for Acceptance," *Financial Times*, May 22, p. 3.

13   For an in-depth discussion of stereotypes and their role in social categories and schemas, see Susan T. Fiske (1998), "Stereotyping, Prejudice, and Discrimination," in Daniel T. Gilbert, Susan T. Fiske, and Gardner Lindzey (eds), *Handbook of Social Psychology*, Vol. 2 (4th edn), Boston, MA: McGraw-Hill, pp. 357–411; Susan T. Fiske and Shelley E. Taylor (1991), *Social Cognition* (2nd edn), New York: McGraw-Hill.

14   Durairaj Maheswaran (1994), "Country of Origin as Stereotype: Effects of Consumer Expertise and Attribute Strength on Product Evaluations," *Journal of Consumer Research*, 21 (September), 354–65; Sung-Tai Hong and Robert S. Wyer (1989), "Effects of Country-of-Origin and Product-Attribute Information on Product Evaluation: An Information Processing Perspective," *Journal of Consumer Research*, 16 (September), 175–87; Peeter W.J. Verlegh, Jan-Benedict E.M. Steenkamp, and Matthew T.G. Meulenberg (2005), "Country of Origin Effects in Consumer Processing of Advertising Claims," *International Journal of Research in Marketing*, 22 (June), 127–39; Alexander Josiassen, Bryan Lukas, and Gregory Whitwell (2008), "Country-of-Origin Contingencies: Competing Perspectives on Product

Familiarity and Product Involvement," *International Marketing Review*, 25 (4), 423–40.

15 As found, for example, in an advertisement that appeared in *USA Today*, November 13, 2012, p. 3B.

16 Jill G. Klein (2002), "Us Versus Them, Or Us Versus Everyone? Delineating Consumer Aversion to Foreign Goods," *Journal of International Business Studies*, 33 (2), 345–63.

17 Jill G. Klein, Richard Ettenson, and Marlene D. Morris (1998), "The Animosity Model of Foreign Product Purchase: An Empirical Test in the People's Republic of China," *Journal of Marketing*, 62 (January), 89–100.

18 *Wall Street Journal* (2012) "Japanese Auto Sales Plunge Amid China Rage," September 10, pp. B1–B2.

19 *Wall Street Journal* (2012) "Dispute Tests Japanese Brands," September 27, p. A11.

20 Junhong Chu (2013), "Quantifying Nation Equity with Sales Data: A Structural Approach," *International Journal of Research in Marketing*, 30 (1), 19–35.

21 Tommaso Ebhart and Craig Trudell (2012), "Fiat in America: If at First You Don't Succeed ...," *Bloomberg Businessweek*, March 18, pp. 23–4.

22 *Wall Street Journal* (2012) "Car Quality Slips at Ford, Chrysler," June 21, p. B3.

23 This figure was inspired by Martin S. Roth and Jean B. Romeo (1992), "Matching Product Category and Country Image Perceptions: A Framework for Managing Country-of-Origin Effects," *Journal of International Business Studies*, 23 (3), 477–97.

24 See, for example, http://www.shiseido.com/Future-Solution-LX/futuresolutionlx,en_US,sc.html&fromTopNav (accessed November 14, 2012); Christopher A. Bartlett (2004), "P&G Japan: The SK-II Globalization Project," Harvard Business School Case 9-303-003.

25 Victor V. Cordell (1992), "Effects of Consumer Preferences for Foreign Sourced Products," *Journal of International Business Studies*, 23 (2), 251–69.

26 http://going-global.economist.com/blog/2011/08/04/the-country-of-origin-effect (accessed September 26, 2012).

27 This was confirmed in an interview we had with a representative of Lasante in Seoul on August 28, 2011.

28 See France Leclerc, Bernd H. Schmitt, and Laurette Dube (1994), "Foreign Branding and its Effects on Product Perceptions and Attitudes," *Journal of Marketing Research*, 31 (May), 263–70.

29 Calling Brands (2011), *Brand China, Show People What You Are Made Of*, November, p. 15.

30 http://hyundaiusa.com/assurance/america-best-warranty.aspx (accessed June 5, 2012).

31 http://www.euroncap.com/Content-Web-Article/91fea4d4-30b5-484d-9dc5-140e0181278c/chinese-manufacturers-investing-in-safety.aspx (accessed January 23, 2013).

32 John Reed (2012), "Hyundai Reaps the Rewards of Drive for Quality Design and Technology," *Financial Times*, May 8, p. 18.

33 *Bloomberg Businessweek* (2012), "China's Plans for its Own Car Brands Stall," September 9, pp. 21–22.

34 Rover, Britain's former state car-maker, was acquired by Nanjing Automobile Group in 2005, which in 2007 merged with SAIC. It was unable to purchase the rights to the Rover brand name (as this is owned by Tata Motors) and created the Roewe marque as a replacement. Its models are sold under the MG marque in most markets outside China.

35 Andrew Roberts and Stephanie Wong (2012), "From Mao Jackets to Silk Suits," *Bloomberg Businessweek*, February 19, 26–7.

36 Rachel Sanderson, Kathrin Hille, and Vanessa Friedman (2012), "Style Rises in the East," *Financial Times*, April 9, p. 7.

37 http://business.asiaone.com/Business/News/Story/A1Story20101128-249636.html (accessed November 17, 2012).

38 http://businessreportthailand.com/barcelona-and-real-madrid-seal-chang-beer-sponsorship-deal-122342 (accessed November 17, 2012).

39 Thailand Beverage Annual Report 2011; http://thaibev.listedcompany.com/misc/AR/20120413-THAIBEV-AR2011-EN.pdf (accessed January 23, 2013)

40 *AdAge* (2012), "Eastern Influence," September 15, p. 13 (accessed January 23, 2013).

41 *AdAge* (2012), "Eastern Influence," September 15, p. 11 (accessed January 23, 2013).

42 Keith Dinnie et al. (2010), Nation Branding and Integrated Marketing Communications: An ASEAN Perspective," *International Marketing Review*, 27 (4), 388–403.

43 See also the FT Special Report "Doing Business in Wallonia," which appeared in the *Financial Times*, November 13, 2012.

44 This example is taken from http:/nation-branding.info/2009/05/06branding-bangladesh/ (accessed December 6, 2011).

45 One of the authors participated in one of its activities, which involved the Korean Prime Minister, other ministers, and captains of industry.

46 See http://nation-branding.info/2011/07/13/south-korea-entering-the-top-ten-most-valuable-country-brands (accessed September 27, 2012).

47 Sarah Mishkin (2012), "The Quest to Craft a Brand Image," *Financial Times,* September 13, p. 12.

48 http://www.icimarcom.com/MIT.html (accessed January 23, 2013).

49 http://www.brandingtaiwan.org/AboutUsEN (accessed October 2, 2012).

CHAPTER 6

1 J. Paul Peter and Jerry C. Olson (1993), *Consumer Behavior* (3rd edn), Boston, MA: Irwin, p. 413.

2 Chris T. Allen, Susan Fournier, and Felicia Miller (2008), "Brands and their Meaning Makers," in Curtis P. Haugtvedt et al. (eds.), *Handbook of Consumer Psychology*, New York: Erlbaum, pp. 781–822.

3 http://en.wikipedia.org/wiki/Harley_Owners_Group (accessed June 11, 2012).

4 Douglas B. Holt (2004), *How Brands Become Icons: The Principles of Cultural Branding*, Boston, MA: Harvard Business School Press, p. 35.

5 We give some examples just to illustrate that cultural symbols can have multiple and contrasting meanings in different countries. We do not claim to be exhaustive or that a particular cultural interpretation is restricted to the country mentioned in the text. See David A. Ricks (2006), *Blunders in International Business,* Malden, MA: Blackwell Publishing, for a highly readable collection of examples.

6 http://history1900s.about.com/cs/swastika/a/swastikahistory.htm (accessed September 27, 2012).

7 The basic structure of this process was developed by Grant McCracken (1986), "Culture and Consumption: A Theoretical Account of the Structure and Movement of the Cultural Meaning of Consumer Goods," *Journal of Consumer Research*, 13 (June), 71–84; see also Wayne D. Hoyer, and Deborah J. MacInnis (2001), *Consumer Behavior* (2nd edn), Boston, MA: Houghton Mifflin; Chris T. Allen, Susan Fournier, and Felicia Miller (2008), "Brands and Their Meaning Makers," in Curtis P. Haugtvedt et al. (eds.), *Handbook of Consumer Psychology*, New York: Erlbaum, pp. 781–822; Douglas B. Holt (2004), *How Brands Become Icons: The Principles of Cultural Branding*, Boston, MA: Harvard Business School Press.

8 The expression "Egypt: Gift of the Nile," was first used 2,500 years ago by the famous Greek historian Herodotus in his *Account of Egypt*. He writes: "it [Egypt] is a gift of the river [Nile]." Certainly, Egypt

should be able to leverage this cultural heritage, which is etched in the collective psyche of mankind beyond attracting tourists.

9 http://www.shanghaitang.com/world-of-shanghai-tang/mandarin-collar-society1/mcs-mission/untitled-object7.html (accessed October 4, 2012).

10 The logo can be found at http://en.wikipedia.org/wiki/Shanghai_Tang (accessed January 23, 2012).

11 Douglas B. Holt (2004), *How Brands Become Icons: The Principles of Cultural Branding*, Boston, MA: Harvard Business School Press, p. 36.

12 Inga Katharina Radziejewski (2011), "The Luxury Brand Formula for China," ESB Business School, p. 96.

13 Interestingly, Nicki Minaj (real name Onika Tanya Maraj; born December 8, 1982) was actually born in Saint James, Trinidad and Tobago. When she was five years of age she moved to the New York City borough of Queens, where she grew up. Although that is not something in her imagery that is emphasized, it does illustrate one of the strongest and globally most appealing aspects of the American culture – its openness to foreigners and the limitless opportunities it offers to immigrants, provided they work hard. The story of success through one's own effort, rather than through connections and birth (which supposedly is characteristic of Europe and Asia) – the so-called "from newsboy to millionaire" – is another powerful resource of the US culture.

14 Our analysis of Herborist draws heavily on insights provided to us by Zhuo (Joe) Wang, CEO of Shanghai Jawha and on a speech delivered by him at the 2012 WWD Beauty CEO Summit, Palm Beach, FL, US.

15 Zhao Xu (2012), "Tough on the Outside," *China Daily*, November 4, p. 4.

16 Zuczug story based on Laurie Burkitt (2012), "What China's Trendsetters Are Wearing," *Wall Street Journal*, November 15, pp. D1, D4.

17 The Haiavanas case is based on a report written by Niraj Khalpada, Rajesh Lakhanpal, Luiz Moreira, Jitendra Singh, and Yogesh Sontakke (2012), "Havaianas – International Expansion," London Business School.

18 Alpargatas' other major brands are Rainha, Sete Leguas, Topper, Timberland, Mizuno, Megashopp, and Dupe. Rainha and Sete Leguas are sold in domestic markets. The former is a traditional sports apparel brand in Brazil, and the latter the market leader in professional rubber wellington boots. Timberland and Mizuno are the international brands licensed for Alpargatas in Brazil, whereas Megashopp is the outlet store chain for all of Alpargatas' brands in Brazil and Argentina.

Topper, Dupe, and Havaianas are the brands responsible for Alpargatas' international success. Topper is the market leader in Brazil and Argentina for sports shoes (predominantly soccer shoes), whereas Dupe is the low-end brand for sandals and children's shoes.

19 In Brazil, flip-flops are called *sandálias havaianas*, or more commonly, just havaianas. Ironically, *sandálias havaianas* translates as "Hawaiian slippers" (or flip-flops). Thus, this exemplar of the Brazilian culture actually is Portuguese for Hawaii! Based on http://en.wikipedia.org/wiki/Flip-flops (accessed June 19, 2012).

20 http://adage.com/article/global-news/watch-world-cup-havaianas-flip-flops/143741 (accessed June 19, 2012).

CHAPTER 7

1 Lees is "the sediment from fermentation of an alcoholic beverage," http://www.merriam-webster.com/dictionary/lees (accessed October 28, 2012).

2 http://www.mysupermarket.co.uk/#/shelves/champagne_and_sparkling_wines_in_tesco.html (accessed July 18, 2012).

3 *Global Sparkling Wine Production*, http://www.wine-business-international.com/.../mwbi_408_s44-50_ra_spar (accessed July 19, 2012).

4 http://www.evian.com/files/Evian%20AWQR%202012%20ENG%20California.pdf (accessed November 14, 2012).

5 See http://www.perrier.com/en (accessed November 14, 2012) for a great example of how to brand mineral water. It is described as a love story (nicely tying in with France's reputation as country of "timeless romance;" see Chapter 5) between water and gas that began 120 million years ago.

6 Its first mention is Genesis 14: 1–3 (New International Version; emphasis added): "At the time when Amraphel was king of Shinar, ... Arioch king of Ellasar, Kedorlaomer king of Elam and Tidal king of Goyim, ... these kings went to war against Bera king of Sodom, Birsha king of Gomorrah, Shinab king of Admah, Shemeber king of Zeboyim, and the king of Bela (that is, Zoar). ... All these latter kings joined forces in the Valley of Siddim (that is, the *Dead Sea Valley*)."

7 http://www.cleopatraschoice.com/dead-sea-products.html, http://www.premier-deadsea.co.il (both accessed July 19, 2012).

8 http://www.beautypremier.co.uk/?page=deadsea (accessed September 24, 2012).

9 http://www.unglobalcompact.org/docs/news_events/8.1/ttw_fin.pdf (accessed September 24, 2012).

10 Syl Tang (2012), "Even the Wealthy Buy Gems That Are Not the Real Thing," *Financial Times*, September 8, p. 14.
11 Quoted in: Syl Tang (2012), "Even the Wealthy Buy Gems That Are Not the Real Thing," *Financial Times*, September 8, p. 14.
12 http://www.forevermark.com/en/A-Forevermark-Diamond/Responsible-Sourcing-/Mining-Sources (accessed September 24, 2012).
13 http://www.debeersgroup.com/Operations/Diamond-Brands/Forevermark (accessed July 20, 2012).
14 http://en.wikipedia.org/wiki/Darjeeling_tea (accessed October 3, 2012).
15 http://www.cheese-france.com/cheese/roquefort.htm (accessed September 24, 2012).
16 http://www.wipo.int/geo_indications/en/about.html, http://www.wipo.int/treaties/en/general (both accessed November 5, 2012).
17 http://www.wipo.int/treaties/en/ip/paris/summary_paris.html (accessed November 5, 2012).
18 Elizabeth Barham (2003), "Translating Terroir: The Global Challenge of French AOC labeling," *Journal of Rural Studies*, 19, 127–38.
19 http://www.wipo.int/geo_indications/en/about.html, http://www.wipo.int/treaties/en/general (both accessed November 5, 2012).
20 http://en.wikipedia.org/wiki/Appellation_d'origine_contr%C3%B4l%C3%A9e (accessed July 20, 2012).
21 http://www.wine-searcher.com/m/2012/09/south-african-winemakers-call-for-regional-shake-up (accessed October 4, 2012).
22 http://www.habanos.com/article.aspx?aid=13&lang=en (accessed January 24, 2013).
23 Nadja El Benni and Sophie Reviron (2009), "Geographical Indications: Review of Seven Case Studies Worldwide," NCCR Trade working paper. The description of the production process is taken from this fascinating paper.
24 http://en.wikipedia.org/wiki/Geographical_indication (accessed July 27, 2012).
25 http://www.wipo.int/geo_indications/en (accessed October 4, 2012).
26 http://en.wikipedia.org/wiki/Cinnamon (accessed September 24, 2012).
27 http://www.island.lk/index.php?page_cat=article-details&page=article-details&code_title=57279 (accessed July 24, 2012).
28 http://pureceyloncinnamon.com/ (accessed July 24, 2012).
29 http://www.fronterawines.com/en/ (accessed July 31, 2012).
30 Cf. Johan Bruwer and Ray Johnson (2010), "Place-based Marketing and the Regional Branding Perspective in the California Wine Industry," *Journal of Consumer Marketing*, 27 (1), 5–16.
31 http://www.conchaytoro.com/web/wine-ratings (accessed September 25, 2012).

32 Cf. Larry Lockshin et al. (2006), "Using Simulations From Discrete Choice Experiments To Measure Consumer Sensitivity to Brand, Region, Price, and Awards in Wine Choice," *Food Quality and Preference*, 17 (2–3), 166–78.

33 http://www.wine.com/V6/Almaviva-2008/wine/111183/detail.aspx (accessed November 14, 2012). At wine.com, the 2008 vintage retailed at $109 but was sold out. The 2009 vintage was available for $129.

34 http://www.interbrand.com/en/best-global-brands/2012/Best-Global-Brands-2012.aspx (accessed January 24, 2013).

35 The Café de Colombia story is based on the following sources: Rohit Deshpandé (2004), "Café de Colombia," Harvard Business School Case 9-502-024; Luis Fernando Samper, Café de Colombia: Protecting and Promoting a Well-Known Origin, presentation given in Beijing, June 2007.

36 The application documents can be found at http://cafedecolombia. cz/en/PGI/CafeDeColombiaApplicationEN.pdf (accessed October 3, 2012).

37 Based on Luis Fernando Samper, "Café de Colombia: Protecting and Promoting a Well-Known Origin," presentation given in Beijing, June 2007. For the importance of knowledge about the supply chains for agricultural products, see Jan-Benedict E.M. Steenkamp (1997), "Dynamics in Consumer Behavior With Respect to Agricultural and Food Products," in Berend Wierenga, Aad van Tilburg, Klaus Grunert, Jan-Benedict E.M. Steenkamp and Michel Wedel (eds.), *Agricultural Marketing and Consumer Behaviour in a Changing World*, Norwell, MA: Kluwer Academic Publishers, pp. 143–88.

38 "Other Mild Arabicas" refers to arabicas from Costa Rica, Guatemala, Honduras, and Mexico. International Coffee Organization (2011), "Rules on Statistics Indictor Prices," London (UK). The three year-moving average was calculated by averaging the average yearly price as reported by the International Coffee Organization for the current year and the previous two years.

39 In an econometric analysis, it was found that at least half the premium can indeed be explained by the branding strategy. Among the other factors upholding the premium price were arbitrage and the relative scarcity of Colombian Coffee with respect to other substitute qualities. See Daniele Giovannucci (2002), "Colombia Coffee Sector Study," World Bank Report.

CHAPTER 8

1 http://www.chinamobileltd.com/ir.php?menu=11&year=2012& month=09 (accessed January 21, 2013)

2   *The Economist* (2012), "Special Report: State Capitalism," January
    21, p. 4.

3   Colbertism and mercantilism are often used interchangeably. Colbert's
    central principle was that the economy of France should serve the state.
    He believed that state intervention was needed to secure the largest
    part of limited resources. At the time, when paper money did not exist,
    a strong state needed to accumulate gold, and this required a trade
    surplus. By developing national champions, Colbert sought to build a
    French economy that sold abroad and bought domestically. It is clear
    why this philosophy appeals to governments, even in the 21st century.

4   Andrew Shonfield (1965) *Modern Capitalism: The Changing Balance
    of Public and Private Power*, New York: Oxford University Press;
    Stephen S. Cohen (1969) *Modern Capitalist Planning: The French
    Model*, Berkeley, CA: University of California Press; John Zysman
    (1977) *Political Strategies for Industrial Order: State, Market, and
    Industry in France*, Berkeley, CA: University of California Press.

5   Michel Crozier (1964), *The Bureaucratic Phenomenon*, Chicago:
    University of Chicago Press.

6   State capitalism is defined as "the government attempts to ensure
    that company-level behavior results in country-level maximization
    of economic, social, and political benefits" [Li-Wen Lin and Curtis J.
    Milhaupt (2011), "We Are the (National) Champions: Understanding
    the Mechanisms of State Capitalism in China," Columbia Law and
    Economics Working Paper No. 409, pp. 46–7]. While this sounds
    good, possibly even disinterested, the big question is what the country's
    desired benefits are. These are typically determined by the political and
    managerial elites.

7   See Paul A. Geroski (2005), "Competition Policy and National
    Champions," speech to WIFO (Austrian Institute of Economic
    Research) in Vienna, March 8. Text available at http://www.
    competition-commission.org.uk/assets/competitioncommission/docs/
    pdf/non-inquiry/our_peop/members/chair_speeches/pdf/geroski_wifo_
    vienna_080305 (accessed June 25, 2012). This section draws on
    Geroski's paper as well as on the OECD (2009) Policy Roundtables
    report *Competition Policy, Industrial Policy and National Champions*,
    and Theodore H. Moran (2008), "What Policies Should Developing
    Country Governments Adopt Toward Outward FDI: Lessons from
    the Experience of Developed Countries," in Karl P. Sauvant (ed.), *The
    Rise of Transnational Corporations from Emerging Markets: Threat or
    Opportunity?*, Northampton, MA: Elgar, pp. 272–98.

8 This argument is based on Li-Wen Lin and Curtis J. Milhaupt (2011), "We Are the (National) Champions: Understanding the Mechanisms of State Capitalism in China," Columbia Law and Economics Working Paper No. 409.

9 Quotes by Harvard Business School Professor Josh Lerner (2012), *Boulevard of Broken Dreams*, Princeton, NJ: Princeton University Press; and former Chairman of the Council of Economic Advisers Michael J. Boskin (2012), "Washington's Knack for Picking Losers," *Wall Street Journal*, February 15, p. A13, respectively. Quotes by Neelie Kroes and Deborah Majoras are taken from Deborah P. Majoras (2007), "National Champions: I Don't Even Think it Sounds Good," speech at the ICC/EU Competition Day, March 26.

10 http://en.wikipedia.org/wiki/Air_France, http://en.wikipedia.org/wiki/Lufthansa (both accessed March 18, 2012).

11 Embraer press release, January 11, 2012, http://www.embraer.com/pt-BR/ImprensaEventos/Press-releases/noticias/Documents/001-Embraer%20Deliveries%204Q11-Ins-VPF-I-12.pdf (accessed January 28, 2013).

12 *USA Today* (2012), Brazil's Embraer Jets are Sized Just Right," July 6, p. 1B.

13 Joanna Chiu (2012), "Initial Jet Made in China Lures More Orders," *Wall Street Journal*, November 14, p. B6.

14 Clyde Prestowitz (2012), "The World Can't Referee Two Different Trade Games," *Financial Times* March 21, p. 9.

15 Both quotes in this paragraph are taken from Andrew Parker (2012), "A Dogfight for the Duopoly," *Financial Times* August 7, p. 7.

16 Theodore H. Moran (2008), "What Policies Should Developing Country Governments Adopt Toward Outward FDI: Lessons from the Experience of Developed Countries," in Karl P. Sauvant (ed.), *The Rise of Transnational Corporations from Emerging Markets: Threat or Opportunity?*, Northampton, MA: Elgar, pp. 272–98.

17 Paul Betts (2011), "France Loses Out with its National Champions," *Financial Times*, December 23, p. 14.

18 Theodore H. Moran (2008), "What Policies Should Developing Country Governments Adopt Toward Outward FDI: Lessons from the Experience of Developed Countries," in Karl P. Sauvant (ed.), *The Rise of Transnational Corporations from Emerging Markets: Threat or Opportunity?*, Northampton, MA: Elgar, pp. 272–98.

19 *Telegraph* (2011), "UK Car Manufacturing and Exports Head for Records," December 28, http://www.telegraph.co.uk/finance/

newsbysector/industry/engineering/8976103/UK-car-manufacturing-and-exports-head-for-records.html (accessed April 7, 2012).

20 Shujie Yao (2011), "Going Global – and the Future – Depend on Innovation," *China Daily*, distributed in *Daily Telegraph*, September 7.

21 Unirule Institute of Economics (2011), "The Nature, Performance, and Reform of the State-owned Enterprises," Beijing, p. 5. Report available at http://www.unirule.org.cn/xiazai/2011/20110617.pdf (accessed August 24, 2012).

22 *The Economist* (2012), "Special Report: State Capitalism," January 21.

23 *Financial Times* (2012), "TCI's Coal India Revolt Rattles Cosy State-Run Boards," March 16, p. 17.

24 Figures refer to the fiscal year 2011–2012. See http://www.coalindia.in/Documents/Coal_India_AR_2011_-_2012_17082012.pdf (accessed January 28, 2013).

25 Alberto Aldes and Rafael Di Tella (1997), "National Champions and Corruption: Some Unpleasant Interventionist Arithmetic," *Economic Journal*, 107 (443), 1023–42.

26 Richard Beason and David E. Weinstein (1996), "Growth, Economies of Scale, and Targeting in Japan (1955–1990)," *Review of Economics and Statistics*, 78 (2), 286–95.

27 Michael J. Boskin (2012), "Washington's Knack for Picking Losers," *Wall Street Journal*, February 15, p. A13.

28 Bruce Einhorn (2012), "China Mobile Pays A Price for Being First," *Bloomberg Businessweek*, January 9, pp. 40–1.

29 *The Economist* (2012), "Special Report: State Capitalism," January 21, p. 12.

30 The corporate governance literature highlights that the separation of cash flow rights from control rights is a central problem in controlling-shareholder regimes. If one shareholder owns all the shares, there is no problem as all the cash flows generated by the company can rightfully be claimed. But where a shareholder's *control* rights exceed its rights to *cash flows*, the well-known agency problem between the controller (majority shareholder) and minority shareholders is magnified, with the magnitude of the problem growing as the discrepancy increases. In the extreme case, the controller has only 50.1 percent of the shares, but can still appropriate most (all) of the cash flows (as well as other benefits such as patronage and corruption). This is a key reason why a minority shareholder position is so important. See Li-Wen Lin and Curtis J. Milhaupt (2011), "We Are the (National) Champions: Understanding the Mechanisms of State Capitalism in China," Columbia Law and Economics Working Paper No. 409.

31 Unirule Institute of Economics (2011), "The Nature, Performance, and Reform of the State-owned Enterprises," Beijing.

32 Sunil Gupta and Valarie A. Zeithaml (2006), "Customer Metrics and their Impact on Financial Performance," *Marketing Science*, 25 (6), 718–39.

33 *The Economist* (2011), "Privatisation in China," September 3. We note that China (through the powerful State-Owned Assets Supervision and Administration Commission (SASAC) pursues a policy of building several large enterprises in each key industry. This practice is obviously inconsistent with the opinion of *The Economist*. However, the apparent competition between firms within the same industry is undercut by SASAC's practice of rotating senior managers across national champions within the same industry. Such rotations obviously ignore the allegedly separate identity of the national champions and flout standard corporate law concepts. However, it is consistent with the notion that SASAC's primary concern is to build up capabilities for an entire sector, rather than for individual companies. See Li-Wen Lin and Curtis J. Milhaupt (2011), "We Are the (National) Champions: Understanding the Mechanisms of State Capitalism in China," Columbia Law and Economics Working Paper No. 409, for a compelling discussion.

34 *Business World* (2012), "Ajit Singh in Conversation with Anjuli Bhargava," July 9, p. 58.

35 *The Economist* (2011), "Privatisation in China," September 3.

36 Paul Betts (2011), "France Loses Out with its National Champions," *Financial Times*, December 23, p. 14.

37 *The Economist* (2012), "Special Report: State Capitalism," January 21, p. 14.

38 http://www.topgear.com/uk/proton (accessed January 8, 2013).

39 This section draws heavily on Adnan Sheikh, Ahmet Calik, Terrel Chang, and Stephanie Johnson (2012), "The Emergence of Emirates Airlines as a Global Brand," London Business School. All quotes are from this report.

40 Figures calculated by the authors, based on data obtained from annual reports which can be found at http://www.emirates.com/english/about/investor_relations/investor_relations.aspx (accessed September 28, 2012).

41 Annual report 2011–12; http://www.theemiratesgroup.com/english/facts-figures/annual-report.aspx (accessed September 28, 2012).

42 http://www.consumeraffairs.com/travel/emirates.html; http://emirates-airlines.pissedconsumer.com/emirates-disgusting-service-poor-security-delays-20120208295554.html (accessed September 28, 2012).

43 http://www.worldtravelawards.com/award-worlds-leading-airline-2012 (accessed January 28, 2013).

APPENDIX

1 "Party Continues To Expand," http://bbs.chinadaily.com.cn/thread-805346-1-1.html (accessed January 30, 2013).

2 Kathrin Hille, "Huawei Pledges More Disclosure To Dispel Fears and Fuel Expansion," *Financial Times*, January 22, 2013.

3 "Samsung and its Attractions: Asia's New Model Company," *The Economist*, October 1, 2011, p. 17.

4 "How Innovative Is China?," *The Economist*, January 5, 2013, p. 52.

INDEX

Printed and bound in Great Britain by
CPI Antony Rowe, Chippenham and Eastbourne